TUMULTUOUS MERRIMENT

TUMULTUOUS MERRIMENT

HEYWOOD HALE BROUN

RICHARD MAREK PUBLISHERS
NEW YORK

Library of Congress Cataloging in Publication Data

Broun, Heywood Hale, date.
    Tumultuous merriment.

    Includes index.
    1. Sports—United States. I. Title.
GV583.B68   796'.0973   79-1050
ISBN 0-399-90047-0

CONTENTS

FOR BUD LAMOREAUX
WHO TAUGHT ME
HOW TO DO THE JOB

FOR PAUL GREENBERG
WHO CODDLED AND PROTECTED
ME WHILE I LEARNED THE JOB

FOR GORDON MANNING
WHO GOT ME THE JOB
IN THE FIRST PLACE

FOR JANE BROUN
INSPIRER OF MY POLYCHROME
WARDROBE AND ZESTFUL COMPANION
ON A HUNDRED TV NEWS TRIPS

FOR THE SHADE OF SAMUEL JOHNSON
WHO SUPPLIED THE TITLE AND
CHAPTER HEADINGS FOR THIS BOOK

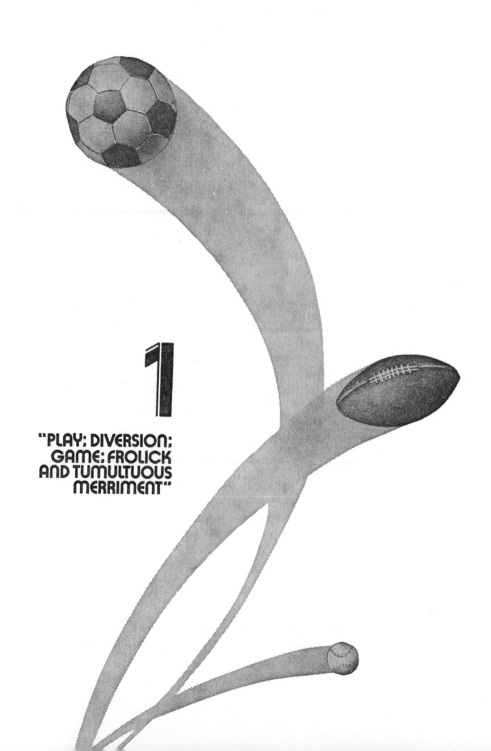

1

"PLAY; DIVERSION; GAME; FROLICK AND TUMULTUOUS MERRIMENT"

In his famous eighteenth-century dictionary, Samuel Johnson made a majestic trip through the English language, and somewhere between *abacke* and *zootomy*, got to *sport.*

Sport, he said, is "Play; diversion; game; frolick and tumultuous merriment."

The philosophical distance between Johnson's time and our own yawns fearfully in that definition. Who now, save an occasional small child, regards sport as diversion or as tumultuous merriment? How much frolick is there in the Ohio State-Michigan game, the modern Olympics, the Little League championship of a crossroads country town?

In the saner air of the eighteenth century, Dr. Johnson, on a walking tour, arrived at a smoothly inviting grassy hill. He at once saw its possibilities, emptied the pockets of his dun-colored suit into the hands of biographer Boswell, and rolled down the hill like a great laughing brown ball. There aren't too many athletic uses one can make of a battered, overweight body, but having discovered one, the great man made up the game on the spot, played it to the full, and arose hay-streaked and refreshed.

He had not performed this feat of horizontal dervishry in order to set a rolling record in the seniors, fat men's, or open divisions, and he certainly had not done it in order to clear his eyes, harden his muscles, or improve his physical tone. His idea of improving his physical tone was to ingest as much bread, meat, and beer as he could get past his teeth. His impulse had been simply, in the first word of his definition, to play.

Gloomy scientists assure us that play is serious business, part of nature's training, and that the cat we see playing with a ball of wool is actually getting ready to torture mice, while the puppy pursuing a ball is really hunting a terrified rabbit or a weary fox.

Next to big-time college coaches, scientists are the dourest people I know, and they hunt the pleasure principle more fiercely than the dog in their example chases the fox.

There are other scientific reasons that endeavor to explain play in utilitarian terms, explanations such as outlet-for-excess-energy, chance-to-work-off-hostility, means-of-serving-wish-fulfillment, etc. So also, coaches will tell you that sport builds character, creates a healthy moral climate, builds bonds of fellowship, and gives a chance to earn big money with the pros.

The motives for all this somber tosh are clear enough. Scientists abhor the inexplicable as nature abhors a vacuum. Since most pleasures are by their nature irrational, scientists like to find the grit of onward and upward under the foam of gaiety.

Coaches are aware that if they are simply teaching a diversion they will be paid, like dancing teachers and English professors, in a meager manner. It is obviously to their financial advantage to pose as saviors of youth, muscular alchemists who can take the base metal of bad boys and produce golden lads, saints who can block and shoot baskets.

It is to our discredit that we swallow all this stuff. I suppose the first dose of this sort of nonsense was administered by the duke of Wellington when he remarked that the Battle of Waterloo had been won on the playing fields of Eton. This piece of piety was produced long after Bonaparte had been safely immured on an inaccessible rock. It might be instructive for us to recall what he said on the morning of the battle, while the issue was still in doubt. Looking out at his regulars, "scum of the earth enlisted for drink" he had called them, he considered his line officers, schoolboys holding commissions purchased by their fathers. A large number of them were struggling to get umbrellas open against a June shower, and looking at these youthful athletes prepared for war by rugby and cricket, the man who was later to speak well of Eton turned to an aide and barked, "I don't know if they frighten Napoleon, but by God, they frighten me!"

Only the more respectable Wellington quotation remains in our guidebook of maxims, and was later reinforced by General Douglas MacArthur, whose flight beginning "On the fields of friendly strife" seemed to suggest that every time Army won a football game, Tyranny snarled and went back into its lair.

But if sport and play are primarily a part of our educational process, teaching us everything from rabbit-catching through moral standards to battle tactics, obviously pleasure has a small part in the process. None of the antic joy of Johnson's Roll would be a suitable part of a practice session where not only the outcome of the State game but also the fate of democracy might hang on proper execution of the pass patterns. If we listen to the coaches, the scientists, and the generals, play is too important to be left unstructured. Even the baby idly touching things hanging from the bars of his crib can be taken through a graded series of tactile sensations which may be useful later when his fingers brush the knurled red knob that may mean the end of half the world.

In the Middle Ages, ideas of right and wrong, philosophical principles, as well as debates about almost everything, joined the simple quarrels of the aristocracy in the tournament lists, where the lances of champions were presumably guided to the target by a deity interested in an orderly world.

It is sometimes hard to believe that a deity has time to judge among the mimeograph-paper lances of sociologists and anthropologists in our modern jousts, but let me bring in a champion to throw down a gage to the hosts of determinism, behaviorism, and puritan athleticism.

My man is Dr. Johan Huizinga, the Dutch historian and scholar, and he sweeps away all the play-as-a-learning-tool cant in a few cheerful and sensible sentences.

"Nature, so our reasoning mind tells us, could just as easily have given her children all those useful functions of discharging superabundant energy, of relaxing after exertion, of training for the demands of life, of compensating for unfulfilled longings, etc., in the form of purely mechanical exercises and reactions. But no, she gave us play, with its tensions, its mirth, and its fun.

"Now this last-named element, the *fun* of playing, resists all analysis, all logical interpretation. As a concept, it cannot be reduced to any other mental category."

13

There it is—the thing we seem to be so ruthlessly rooting out of our games lest it soften our fiber. Fun. Mirth. The joy of an old man finding anew the principle of the wheel in the outline of his bulging waistcoat. The pleasure of a couple of bad tennis players pooping parabolas over a net, happy simply to keep the ball in play.

Fun need not disappear as skill and higher stakes tighten the strings of the nervous system. Steve Blass, after winning two World Series games for Pittsburgh, said that it had been tense all right, but he imagined tensions were greater in an operating theater since baseball was, after all, a game, and not open heart surgery.

Long ago when the "pay to hate me" style of Jimmy Connors and Ilie Nastase was not a financial advantage in tennis, a player at Forest Hills, Zenso Shimidsu of Japan, was about to put away set point against the great Bill Johnston. As the weak lob fell before the waiting Shimidsu, he gave too great a swing and whacked it out of court. Suddenly he grinned, then laughed. Quite properly it seemed to him richly funny to be reminded of cosmic banana peels in a situation where it wasn't really going to hurt, in a situation outside real life—a game. I wish he were around and playing now.

We don't, of course, expect the professional athlete to grin ruefully over disaster or to see the humorous side of defeat, since to him sport is not a game, but the repository of his ego and the means of his livelihood.

Sport for him is obviously not a relief from real life but real life itself, as long as he can sustain the high degree of physical fitness required in the gladiatorial world.

It is appropriate that coaches and managers should whip the scarred gladiator into a frenzy of possible overachievement and that he should be required to continue playing through the pains of assorted abrasions and contusions.

The appropriateness of outside pressure is in direct ratio to the pragmatic rewards that are appended to victory, rewards like cash, valuable scholarships—what an odd word that is, incidentally, for a grant to a young person whose time is too valuable to be wasted on study—or endorsements of products that will benefit from the athlete's réclame.

We are only grotesque when we apply the standards suitable

to the gladiator to our Little League children. It is unfair to make them the surrogates of our flab-shackled daydreams. The professional, after all, is well paid to hit our home runs, score our touchdowns, throw in the baskets we wished so much to make, and blast our dreams into the corners of hockey nets.

There is a great deal of grumbling these days over how much he is paid, but is it, in fact, such a muchness in view of what we ask of him and what he does for us? We must remember also that corporate executives can go on collecting even larger sums for doing things harder to understand until they are sixty-five or seventy, while few athletes interest the IRS for more than ten years.

My complaint these days is not about the money or the whole economic explosion in the sports world, an explosion that has seen expansion, stadium building, and professional sport brought to towns that have never seen more than an occasional troupe of traveling wrestlers.

It is the talk about the money rather than its actuality that depresses me. By the time an athlete and his agent have discussed the deferred payment, the business loan, and the insurance policy, they both seem as dull as any pair of young executives, and when they get into the matter of image ("We both feel that Sam's endorsements must be handled carefully lest the youth of America . . ."), I begin to wonder why I ever cared about their winnings and losings.

In the boom days of the twenties, Connie Mack, manager-owner of the then Philadelphia Athletics, was shocked to discover that his players had installed a stock ticker in the locker room. He predicted that this division of attention would hurt their baseball, and it did, but the damage was probably brought on by weakness due to boredom, the sapping boredom that results from endless discussions of buying and selling.

Statistics demonstrate that athletes, even at current levels, are not getting an excessive amount of the pie. Only occasionally do professional sport corporations release reliable statements of profit and loss, and the oddities of the tax laws make some of the losses useful tools in the owners' war on poverty, but the sums contributed by TV networks for the privilege of showing the games are in the multimillions, and by the simple arithmetical exercise of measuring published salaries against

15

these contributions, you will see why the rich are always ready to buy an available franchise. I want the players to have even more money if they will just stop talking and acting like characters out of Sinclair Lewis's *Babbit*.

Dave Kingman simply and bluntly demanding a raise is a lot less depressing than Reggie Jackson endlessly and ostentatiously counting it or announcing the cost of his shirts and ties, or Tom Seaver offering himself and his wife to the merchandising scheme where the Mr. and Mrs. image is needed.

I can, if I want, see this kind of behavior at a sales convention, for which tickets are much easier to get.

If it's true that we are driving our amateurs from pleasure to push, we seem to be acquiescing in the creation of a bewildering new hybrid in professional sport, a man who is peddling even before he stops performing.

I can readily understand that the successful pro will here remind me of my own argument about the briefness of his earning life in sport and the need to have something ready for the day of dismissal, but practical arguments are not always apposite when we deal with sport because we must remember that it is in large part a shared delusion.

In order for us to enjoy that illusion sufficiently to be willing to give our money and our attention to its mysteries, we must regard the participants with the appropriate superstitious awe. When Joe McCarthy managed the New York Yankees he continually lectured his players on behavior proper to champions. Champions always wore good suits, tipped liberally, did not engage in horseplay in lobbies or train stations, did not, in fact, do anything that would disturb the image of a Yankee as a godlike creature above the common herd. This sort of thing was so effective that it gave the Yankees a stature that not even the behavior of the present Yankees can entirely erode.

It takes skill and dedication to nourish a thing as unstable as delusion, but there are rewards. Look what the British pay for the comforting delusion that they are a monarchy.

I don't care about an athlete's politics or his private life, but I do wish he would put off behaving like a businessman until, in the fullness of time, he becomes one.

After all, one game is not really more important than another in the cosmic scheme of things, but it's wonderful fun to pretend, and we all have expended a lot of pretense on the Super Bowls, the World Series, the Triple Crown, and football games like Yale-Harvard, Ohio State-Michigan, or Texas-Oklahoma. If you think delusion doesn't play a part, however, ask a Harvard man about Texas-Oklahoma and he will express polite surprise that the two states now have colleges, while a Texan will tell you that interest in Yale-Harvard exists only in the Kremlin. Both men will impartially despise Ohio State and Michigan.

If, however, owners of teams keep denigrating the mystique of fan identification and talking about moving *my* team if someone doesn't take care of *my* tax problems, and if players keep insisting that they are really in a form of business not very different from making shoes and marketing steel, and if colleges keep up public squabbles about TV revenue and Bowl shares, it is just possible that bubbles will pop all over the place.

I remember an article a few years ago by a former bigtime football fan who, on impulse, drove one Saturday afternoon to an unpublicized game between a couple of unranked colleges. He discovered, quaint as a Currier and Ives, an old-time grandstand full of professors, students, children, and dogs, entertained at halftime by talking to each other and listening to small marching bands fleshed out with people who carried unplayed instruments while a couple of mediocre but well-matched teams played for the championship of nothing at all. He was so struck that he vowed to spend the remaining football Saturdays of his life at such games. It took him only a few minutes to puff up the delusion that it mattered terribly whether Northeast State Teachers beat County A & I, and there he was with his own bubble pipe creating his own classic.

When Alan Cohen of Madison Square Garden remarked that championships are all very well but it's primarily profits that make management's heart go pit-a-pat, he was making a very logical statement but not a wise one in bubble country, and when the furor dies to a grumble I would not be surprised if a few fans had found the odd charm of New Jersey college gyms and Pharmacy against Textile games under weak light.

If the pros and the collegiate semipros want to keep us all at fever pitch they must take a lesson from that fine old fencing writer Alexandre Dumas, and give us a lot of the old "All for One and One For All" stuff.

It is well to remember that Athos, Porthos, Aramis, and D'Artagnan were all mercenaries, gentlemen adventurers in the service of their king, and prepared to go against the king's own government if he wished and paid. For all their fortune seeking, and it makes up a large part of several volumes, we always saw them as romantic figures, good at their game, full of attractive arrogance, ready, under the Musketeer banner, to fight any odds, fascinated by gold but inclined when finding it to sweep it uncounted into a capacious pocket for division later over flagons of wine. Their perfection as professional men of action, athletes of a rough century when losers at fencing never got to play again, made them literary immortals, and they have given their name to innumerable groups of three or four ball players, to hockey lines, to polo teams, and even to exceptionally dashing groups of bowlers.

They represent the kind of impractical skill and overwhelming devotion that should be, with a fine carelessness in the matter of danger, the badges of the athlete we admire or want to admire.

My modern Musketeers are a mixed lot. One doesn't usually equate the austere Joe DiMaggio with the raffish Joe Namath, as one doesn't link long time great performers like Babe Ruth with men like old St. Louis third baseman Pepper Martin, whose reputation rests on one glorious October week in 1931 when he won the World Series by himself. Some of my Musketeers are legends, like Pete Reiser, the doomed hero of the Dodgers; and some are obscure, like Mike Ryba, who, after more than ten years in the minor leagues, finally pitched a mop-up World Series inning and announced he was one step closer to Cooperstown. Some are complex, like Mike Reid, who played tackle and Franz Liszt, or Bobby Brown, the third baseman-heart surgeon who told me that he was fearful that the World Series would keep him from his anatomy lectures. Some were simple men, like Hughey Casey, the old relief pitcher, who, when he was not mowing down batters, mowed down pheasants.

All of them had a quality that the French call panache, and I found special pleasure in watching them exercise their skills with the flourish that made me feel that something of tremendous importance was taking place before my eyes.

Returning to the Dumas Boys and Their Search for the Queen's Necklace, let me point out that Aramis never had an agent, Athos didn't talk about his family, Porthos didn't give a damn that his image was that of a hard drinker who only entered churches to hide from the authorities, and D'Artagnan never endorsed anything except Milady de Winter's eyes, and he lived to regret that. I'd give a lot for a ticket to see them play the Cardinal's men.

It has always been interesting to me that small children, more than their elders, demand a structure of immutable rules in their games. These kids, given a playground, a meadow, or a stretch of street free or unfree of parked cars, will at once begin to create a new sport based on the relationships of trees, posts, benches or whatever, and the availability and shape of objects to be thrown, kicked, pushed, or dragged through the mud.

When the code is complete and the sides chosen, woe to the child who makes an aberrant move in the subsequent game. There are cries of "You can't do that! *It's the rule!*" The odd phrase "It's the rule," shouted by children all over the world in different languages, is an impassioned demand for the maintenance of an orderly world.

To the child, after all, the world is a place of constant confusion and value shifts. Sleep, which is supposed to be an overwhelming virtue at night, is a sign of sloth in the morning when the school bus looms. Candy, available as an occasional reward, is suddenly a rotter of teeth when procured by the child himself. Things are done at the wish of the giant jailers for no better reason than "Because I say so!"

Is it a wonder, then, that the child loves a situation where the laws have been democratically chosen and are maintained even-handedly by everyone in the group?

This, at bottom, is for all of us, the whole fascination of games. They are the only activities of life where the rules are, metaphorically or actually, written out on the top of the box.

Jean-Paul Sartre, a skier as well as a philosopher, put it that "Play is an activity . . . for which man himself sets the rules, and which has no consequences except according to the rules posited." It follows, according to Sartre, that games are the only area in which man is free because they make up the only area in which he is sufficiently well informed to define freedom.

In what sporty clergymen like to call "The Great Game of

Life," we may play for twenty-five years, secure in the supposed knowledge that we are two wickets ahead of the world, only to discover that the game is not, after all, croquet, but a form of checkers in which we have just been double-jumped. Sometimes the game is exactly what we think it is, a form of cosmic bridge, for example, but suddenly and disastrously it is lost because our opponents produce thirteen green cards which take everything.

It is a relief to us, then, as adults, as it was to us as children, to escape into the small, known, well-defined structure of a game. We agree, for the time we play it at least, to its importance, and everything else is lost in the shadows behind the sidelines. So, men of Death Row play cards on tables in front of the cells and chuckle delightedly at fortuitous pairs of aces because life has shrunk to fifty-two possibilities on a wooden square.

I doubt that the murderers cheat, because if they do, they are back in the real world. When you break the "rule" you leave the magic orderly area of the game. The condemned men, like the children, live a life of very limited choice and many stern orders. Only when the clockwork of the rules is in balance are they, for a few minutes, free.

What of the rest of us? Have we lost the pleasure of sports and games because of the weights we load onto their essentially frail structures?

Obviously if winning is overwhelmingly important, and is the only reason for playing, we must break the "rule" if no one is looking, or bend it if someone is.

Pity the boy who grew up to love the wonderful justice of sports and who now finds himself endlessly running up and down football stadium steps, an exercise given him to assure that he throws up—ironic phrase—the scholarship his coach has earmarked for someone else.

Pity the Olympic athlete slowly puffing up on anabolic steroids and doses of his own just-thawed last year's blood, while old men lecture him on the value of a sound mind in a sound body, provided, of course, that it's a mind that agrees with all the prejudices of the current regime.

Pity the Little League pitcher who throws at the heads of his schoolmates to intimidate them and assure a victory not only because victory is so important but also because if he wins Mom won't cry and Dad won't get drunk.

Pity the young tennis player brought up on Richard Harding Davis and *Tom Brown's Schooldays*—"Play the game youngster, play the game"—and who is now learning how to break a shoelace and hang over it until his opponent's hot streak has cooled.

Pity all among us who have ignored the cry inside ourselves—"You can't do that, it's the rule!"—and having bent or broken it found that our victory, however sweet has, at last, a rather dusty aftertaste not too different from that of humble pie.

It is an odd irony that Vince Lombardi, the man most associated with the philosophy that victory is the whole and only reward of competition, would have deplored the things deplored above. Vince was Tom Brown carried to a nightmare length, but in his fierce and terrifying way he was a romantic. He manipulated his players like a master psychologist, but he wanted them to win games not with rule-bending but with will-bending, with the absolute dedication that brings victory in every boy's book, the quality Dick Merriwell brought to the Olympic marathon: "Morgan led by twenty-five yards, still, when the finish was less than a hundred yards away. And then Dick sprinted. A roar of amazement went up as the crowd saw that final effort. And then, in a last wild rush, Dick went by the staggering Englishman, and a moment later, broke the tape.

"He went down in a heap as he finished. Then a shadow fell on his face, and familiar music sounded in his ears. The band was playing 'The Star Spangled Banner,' and he struggled to his feet."

I suspect that Vince might have given Dick a sharp word or two about falling down, but substantially coach and hero shared an idealism without realism. Neither Dick nor Vince would have stooped, however, to the tricks that pass under names like "Psyching," "Intimidating," "Getting the edge," or just "Keeping the bread on the table," which presupposes that anything goes when you're protecting the loaf.

On the other hand they would have both been annoyed with the dictum of that hard-playing but clear-sighted athlete, Pepper Martin, who once remarked, "You can take an ol' mule and run him and feed him and train him and get him in the best shape of his life, but you ain't going to win the Kentucky Derby!"

Those words, from a man who went as far as courage and stubby legs could take him, should be pasted up in locker rooms next to all those inspirational slogans which suggest that only cowards lose and that the winner is not only the better man at the game but probably the better man at everything else that is going to happen for the rest of his life.

Most of us, after all, do belong in the mule races rather than in the Derby, and even within the ranks of muledom there are obvious differences in temperament and ability which suggest that we should choose our mule races with care. A proper sports philosophy is expressed for me by two old physicians from Worcester, Massachusetts, who each year huffed through the Boston Marathon. Lacing up their shoes, they spoke not of laurels, glory, or the TV exposure awaiting the champion. Rather they discussed hard-won but humbler distinctions.

"This year, Charlie," said the more optimistic one, "I bet you throw up before I do!"

How does that grab you, Dick Merriwell?

If games are properly outside "real" life, then it follows that they should be outside real time as well, or as Johan Huizinga more comprehensively puts it, "Play is distinct from 'ordinary' life both as to locality and duration. . . . It contains its own course and meaning."

When we come to the kind of play more organized than that of puppies, babies, and free-form Frisbie groups, I would add a notion. I think it's allowable, even desirable, to pretend within that time frame, set aside from actuality, that what is happening is of overwhelming importance. This gives tremendous zest and color to the proceedings and is quite harmless provided we abandon that belief within a few minutes of the end of the game.

The actual importance of the contest is immaterial to both spectators and players once the period of magic has begun. The level of excitement is subconsciously chosen by those present and after a time exists beyond their control. It is only harmful when, like some lingering germ from a tropical paradise, it darkens the future. All of us should play as if life and honor depended on it, and all of us should cheer as if it were Lucifer State versus Angel U. in the arena; but at game's end all of us should recognize that paradise was neither won nor lost. None of us should emulate those middle-aged men who stare glumly into the bottom of a highball glass when they think of a shot that failed to drop in the last second of some long-ago basketball game.

Oddly, the thought of basketball brings to mind one of the most exciting events I ever covered in many years of following sports around the country.

At first announcement there is not much drama in the phrase "Iowa State Girls' High School Basketball Championship Tournament" but then most of you have never been there.

Indeed, when I was assigned to do a TV feature on the event, I assumed that I would do it in the pose of Mr. Urban Sophisticate having a good laugh at the rubes in bloomers. I had, of course, forgotten my own dictum about sports as a shared delusion.

Think of the circumstances surrounding the ISGHBCT. (I guess you couldn't call that an acronym.) The towns from which the players come are those huddled crossroads communities with names as far off and lonely as train whistles—Winterset, Gravity, McCool Junction, and Promise City (What optimistic pioneer guessed wrong on that one?). These are the towns where the only winter sounds are the rustlings of dead cornstalks, where the leisure activities are not symphony concerts, musical comedies, dance recitals, or driving down the Grande Corniche with a Mediterranean wind in your hair and the prospect of roulette at Monte at the end of the road. The social centers here are the folding-chair circles around the dryers in the Laundromats.

Once a year, however, one gets, if not a roadster ride on the Riviera, a bus trip to Des Moines, called by some the Copenhagen of the upper Middle West.

The pipes of enchantment begin to play the summons to the game, sweeping one away from the real and into what should be, if Huizinga is right—and I've been there and he is—"A new-found creation of the mind, a treasure to be retained by the memory." This memory, of course, unlike that of the old basketball player, is of an experience so completely outside reality that it lacks the power to hurt.

By the time the girls arrive at the arena, seventeen-thousand-odd people have preceded them, have packed the seats and are beginning to build a bonfire of emotion.

Mr. Urban Sophisticate was, metaphorically, in overalls and

a straw hat within minutes of arrival in this maelstrom.

Perhaps the years I spent in the theater are an indication of my suggestibility, my not always desirable wish to belong to whatever possible extended family is around me, but no Iowa farmer with a daughter in uniform was more acrackle with the overflowing electricity of the occasion than the man CBS had sent to be a dispassionate observer, and by the time we arrived at the finals it seemed to me that if the girls from Union-Whitten, led by their dazzling star, Denise Long, her orthodontia gleaming like a Valkyrie's helmet, did not defeat the forces of Farragut, my heart would be broken. I am sure that Farragut produces nice girls, but at that moment their rather odd-looking sailor suits, modeled on those worn by the men who served under their namesake at the siege of New Orleans, seemed to me the very livery of Darkness.

Well, we Union-Whittenians lost, and my heart cracked, mending itself only when I emerged into the routine of real life outside the doors of the arena.

The happy ending, however, happened the following morning when all the girls, from those who had lost in the first preliminaries to the mighty maidens of Farragut, had breakfast with the governor. Everyone was alive with excitement, and the final flourish was a shower of gifts as each girl received a heap of local products including combs, compacts, and little bags of seed corn.

I'm sure none of us will forget that wonderful occasion, and on my wall still hangs an orange and black banner to remind me of happy days, no less happy for our loss.

How sensible are the girls of Iowa when compared to the grim puritans who grip our sports today. Indeed, it's well to remember that "today" has been a long one. In the early part of this century, when my father was an undergraduate at Harvard, an unfortunate sophomore dropped a kick in the Yale game, and thereby Yale won. For the remainder of his stay in the school the fumbler was known as "the man who dropped the punt."

In the fullness of time he went off, as Harvard men do, to law school or a bank, and a younger brother popped out of prep school and entered Harvard to be known for four years as "the brother of the man who dropped the punt."

Let it not be said, although I'm afraid it will, that young men are preparing for a stern world where mistakes are not forgotten, and that they should have a stern preparation for that world.

Sport is a preparation for more sport and not a businessmen's ROTC. Admittedly a few extra sales are made after someone says around his cigar, "Ed, I want you to meet the man who beat Michigan and is now in our software division," but you can't tackle economics or block logistics.

As to the pressures of competition, it is not their degree of severity but the extent to which they are permitted or encouraged to linger that is important.

Certainly there was pressure at the basketball tournament in Des Moines. Certainly there was feeling beyond what could be contained. Girls wept when they committed fouls and when they were fouled. They wept when they missed shots and when they made them, and at the end there was a giant weepout.

The feelings were all of the moment, however, and the pressures self-induced. Certainly no one told the girls that their success in life was likely to be in ratio to their accomplishments on the court. You may say that this is because girls were involved, and that their sports, at least until recently, have been treated with some patronization. This is wide of the mark, and if you doubt it, talk to some of the girls on the tennis circuit whose parents are hanging the heavy weight of their fantasies on young arms and legs, or talk (if you speak Japanese) to the members of that nation's Olympic volleyball team, who, unless times have changed, cannot marry without the coach's permission.

Boys and girls, men and women, can all be distorted by the philosophies that use games to grotesque ends.

To the endless positivism of the sports establishment, it might be well to oppose a little team of negatives: A coach is not a priest. Games are not life. Failure in athletics is nothing more than failure in athletics. There is no authority save the Rule, which all the players have agreed on, and there is no fun like playing a game for the sake of a game.

2

"NO MAN BUT A BLOCKHEAD EVER WROTE, EXCEPT FOR MONEY"

A long time ago, when I held the twin portfolios of manager of the Swarthmore College football team and secretary of the school's dramatic club, I felt like a Little League Siegfried Sassoon. Older readers may remember him, a man who spent the appropriate seasons hunting foxes with the bloodthirsty squires of England, and the remaining months of the year among the intellectual exquisites of London, writing poetry, listening to it, and chatting art, music, and theater in the salons of Bloomsbury.

Sassoon had, and has, many advantages over me in the way of talent and distinction, but the advantages I envied in my undergraduate days were the cloak of discretion by which he hid the gore and manure on his boots from his artistic circle, and the depravity of versifying—"damned juggery-pokery rhymes fit for parsons and women"—from the jolly Philistines whose vocabularies began with "Tally ho!" and ended with "Pass the port."

Everybody thought Siggy was a prince of good fellows and nobody knew that he had a pair of dreadful secrets which, if disclosed, would have made him a Mr. Hyde without hope of Jekyllhood.

In our little college in a little town, discretion was a kiss in a deserted classroom or a trip to Philadelphia. There was endless heavy jesting from the football players, particularly after they had seen me in a ruffled shirt and a Christmas card top hat as Mr. Bennet in *Pride and Prejudice*, while the drama aspirants made it clear that whatever glib aptitudes in the laugh-grabbing line had won roles for me, they knew me as an associate of the enemy of all that was elevated and beautiful.

A girl, with my best interests at heart, warned me that if I did not very soon make up my mind whether I was going to run with the athletes or the aesthetes, I would fall into a patternless existence which would lead to identity crises and regrets.

Of course I didn't take the advice but I think she was right, and certainly in the Great Game of Life I have suffered through landing on the squares of Indecision, Depression, and Who Are You?— Lose your next turn, take a role card, and return to Unemployment Insurance.

As to regrets, I have reached the age where the recognition of the part played by chance should preclude, in any sensible person, any acid hours in the dull company of regret. If you did the right thing twenty years ago, you might have been run over nineteen years ago. If you married that wonderful person, the honeymoon yacht might have been lost in a storm. If you're still moving in middle age, you can cheer yourself with the thought that longevity is an accomplishment, too. After a few more years of it, I shall be entering the Championship Flight.

One of the many chances that have made my progress so different from the up-the-mountain orderliness of the American Dream came right after I was considering taking the intelligent girl's advice and dropping my admittedly tangential association with sports.

Just graduated, I edited a book of my father's work, got involved in writing about the world of jazz, and went to New Orleans and assembled a band of old-timers to preserve on records that odd mixture of noise and needlepoint that was classic jazz. If I could have topped off this promising beginning with a couple of learned articles and some free-lance art criticism, I might have been freed of cultural schizophrenia, leaving sports behind in that cupboard of memory where one keeps the pleasures of immaturity—mud, loud noises, making rude phone calls to strangers, secret clubs, and all the pastimes that were a refuge from the terrifying shapelessness of life.

At this crossroads moment George Lyons, managing editor of the now departed newspaper *PM*, saw an article about my recording work and, filled with admiration for my father which I knew to be deserved and found to be depressing, offered me a job in the sport department of the paper. He was cauterizingly frank. He wished to see no clippings from the Swarthmore

Phoenix. The job was to be a memorial to the late, great Heywood Broun for a period of six months. If I stayed after that I was to feel it was because George liked me and I could then forget about the ego-eroding reasons for my earlier conditional acceptance there. Distinguished and unemployed graduates of journalism schools may well grind their teeth as they read this proof of the unfair nepotism they have long suspected to be the bar to the orderly advance of the meritorious.

I thought very strongly about taking their side and leaving the post vacant for a distinguished graduate, but it occurred to me that this was July 1940, that the United States seemed inevitably headed for an involvement in World War II, and that I, flabby and timid though I was, would be an obscure and probably disgraceful part of that involvement. In other words, I needed something to distract me while I waited to be drafted, and, feeling that whatever shame I might cover myself with as an inept young journalist would soon be layered over with the dark cloak of military failure, I went to work on the night sport desk.

I need not have worried about my inability to do the job, because as the distinguished graduates find when they finally achieve employment, one's first months on a newspaper are spent doing things a chimp or a child could do.

When the baseball season began, however, several members of our small sport staff became ill simultaneously, and there being no chimp or child available, I was sent off to Washington to cover the opening game of the 1941 major league season. I had a number of insufficiencies, among them an inability to keep a proper scorecard, but kindly older sportswriters carried me over the worst of the bumps. (My scorecards remained impenetrable, however, because a legacy from childhood left-handedness makes me send the runners around by mirror image from third base to second to first to home.)

Looking back, it seems to me that old sportswriters, like old actors, were always ready to give a helping hand to the young, the frightened, and the ignorant. If there is less of this now, it may be because there seem to be so few surviving old actors and writers, and such an overwhelming mob of the young, the frightened, and the ignorant.

Still enshrined in my memory is a fierce-looking old gentleman who bent over the seat in which I was cowering on that first baseball trip to Washington.

"Are you young Broun?" he barked, and I knew at once that the Baseball Writers Association of America had decided not to issue me a membership card on grounds of general fecklessness.

When I regretfully admitted my identity, the sternness of shyness melted from his face and he said, "I'm Sid Mercer of the *Journal*. I broke in your father in 1915, and if there's anything I can do to help you, let me know."

Poor, kind man, he had to show me everything except how to get the cover off my typewriter, an art I had practiced before leaving home.

For three months I enjoyed the cocoonlike life of the pre-World War II baseball writer, moving from hotel to ball park to Pullman car to diner on the road, spending long hours in pre- and post-game socializing among writers and players at home. We were, perhaps to the detriment of our objectivity, one big family. In August 1941 I was summoned away from the family in the first, or "Cream of Our Young Manhood," draft. This caused irresistible amusement to Brooklyn Dodger manager Leo Durocher, who felt that baseball writers had just about enough strength to depress typewriter keys and raise expense accounts.

"Hitler is smiling today!" cried Leo. "He heard Woodie Broun was the best the Americans could do and he knows he's won the war before it's even started."

Later I had my revenge when I visited the Dodger dugout wearing sergeant's stripes and entertained everyone but Durocher, who had been turned down by the army, with accounts of how I would have straightened Leo out if he had been fit enough to serve in my platoon.

Actually I had no platoon, having earned my stripes depressing the keys of a typewriter, but chances to strike back at the easy physical arrogance of athletes are rare and must be seized on.

Middle-aged men nowadays glaze the eyes of all with interminable stories beginning "We were with the old 379th outside Spritz-Bahnhof when Corporal Frazee said—or was it old Stinky Flint, the supply sergeant? Anyway . . . "

Wishing your eyes to stay clear, I will cover four and a half years of service by saying that the army improved my typing, taught me the Serbo-Croatian language in a nine-month crash course, sent me to Germany, and discharged me with five stripes and a determination—witnesses will tell you it has been unswerving—never again to make my bed.

There now arose a chance to solve the problem of my dual nature, and I determined that I would make a fresh start, possibly in some academic line. I fancied myself as a rather sophisticated and witty English professor, the one all the girls fell in love with, the one whose lectures were better than a show.

The only trouble with this daydream was that its accomplishment, if possible at all, would be preceded by several years of marching from class to class at the sound of a bell, and the writing of one of those doctoral dissertations with titles like "The Significance of Variant Spellings in Early Editions of the Lesser Lake Poets."

I had marched to enough places at the sound of a bell in thirteen years of boarding school before the army marched me to various places at the behest of varying imperious sounds, and I thought I'd like to sit a while and practice easy breathing.

I had hardly taken the first relaxed breath when the winds of chance puffed again and blew me right back to the typewriter. Ralph Ingersoll, publisher of *PM*, had been intrigued by several wiseacre remarks I had made in the long hours of the prewar night shift when I had opened all the mail and written all the two- and three-line column fillers, and he impulsively, kindly, and impractically offered to make me the sports editor of the paper. I pointed out that my experience was scanty, that as editor of the *Red Guidon,* official newspaper of the 411th Field Artillery Group, I had not had much experience in handling people, since I didn't have any staff, and that the people who would be working for me on *PM* would be all the people for whom, in the winter months of 1940–41, I had been the sandwich and coffee man.

Ingersoll smiled through all this, told me I didn't know my own capabilities, and sealed the deal by giving me the best raise, in percentile terms, I was ever to have. It brought me up to a living wage. I spent the next two weeks planning revolutionary changes in *PM*'s sports pages, accepting the insincere congratulations of my colleagues, and trying to think of a name for my sports column.

It is perhaps not wise for a man who has some working years ahead of him to advertise the fact of his jinxhood, but it is sadly true that those who interest themselves in my career seem all too often to suffer for their kindness.

Colonel J. S. Tate, who befriended me in the service and took me overseas with him, a man literally revered by his officers and men, finished the war as he began it, with a pair of eagles on his shoulders, while all around him pompous boobies were collecting stars as if they were beach pebbles. Two weeks after Fred Friendly hired me at CBS News in 1966 he was on his way to being a consultant at the Ford Foundation, dismissed in a confrontation with higher authority.

The theater director who gave me my first chance to be in a hit was dismissed from the show in Boston while crowds clamored to buy tickets to his successful production.

The director who gave me my last and best pair of Broadway parts was, in each case, gone by opening night.

The magazine editor who gave me my first extended chance as a writer—but enough! Suffice to say that two weeks after taking me on as sports editor, Ralph Ingersoll called me in and told me that the managing editor had caught the ear of the paper's owner, Marshall Field, and that as a result Ralph was to leave the helm of the paper he had created, and that those who had been closely associated with him probably did not have a bright future under the new regime. Ingersoll said he could probably save my raise, but that the editorial job would almost certainly end before it had fairly begun. Money has always seemed to me an agreeable substitute for power, and I thanked Ralph and waited calmly for the summons to the headsman's block.

I must say that the new chief, the late John P. Lewis, picked an amusing way of axing me, indeed the only amusing thing I remember his doing during his earnest stewardship of the dying newspaper.

Having summoned me to his office he told me that he had discovered that it was impossible to beat the horse races by playing the selections of newspaper handicappers, and he therefore wanted the new sports page to kick off with a hard-hitting indictment of these frauds who, posing as experts, were draining away the earnings of the gullible. I was to expose *PM*'s handicapper along with the rest of the vultures, so that the public would know *PM* did not care if the chips, falling where they might, fell all over me and my handicapper.

I pointed out with smiling reasonableness that if one could make money by backing newspaper selections, no one would work. When this argument was dismissed as frivolous, I did not ask why it was frivolous but noted that tables of success or lack thereof routinely appeared at season's end in the papers devoted to racing and that our feature would therefore not be breaking any new ground.

There was a pause and then Mr. Lewis smiled gently and said, "Since we are in such strong disagreement as to how things ought to be done, perhaps you would not be comfortable as sports editor." I smiled back and said I saw his point and wished my successor well.

The great exposé never was mentioned again and my brief taste of the executive life was not such as to encourage another try. I have not since been in charge of anything except, for brief and fitful periods, my own destiny.

I did get a column after a while and since we could never think of a name for it, it was identified for those who sought it by little drawings of me engaged in unlikely sporting activities. As the tubercular patients of nineteenth-century novels coughed away their lives in sprays of blood on quickly concealed handkerchieves, so the doomed newspaper coughed away its writers and reporters, and the suddenly empty desk next to yours was, like the handkerchief, not discussed in the hope, still existing among the most rational, that silence brings health and things not discussed don't happen. Somewhere along the way *PM* became, with new owners, the New York *Star*.

For those who remained, tasks obviously multiplied, as they did for Captain Smollett's crew on the return voyage from Hispaniola in *Treasure Island*. The only difference was that Smollett and Jim and the Squire and the Doctor made it, and we sank. Before we were finished I was, simultaneously, a three-times-a-week sports columnist, a once-a-week humor columnist, a frequent reviewer of books, and a rewriter of much wire service material, which I signed with that most anonymous of by-lines: "From Our Staff Correspondent." These things were done in addition to my covering, in person, one or two baseball games a day.

As a sports columnist I had the handicap that, owing to the insufficient facilities of our starving paper, I had to turn in my copy two days ahead of publication, which shut me off from the hot newsstuff that my colleagues could use to light their creative candles. Long before I became a miner of obscure moments for CBS, I was commenting on such otherwise uncovered sports as midget auto racing and indoor soccer for *PM*. The reward of diligence is frequently no more than the offer of more work on which to practice this admirable trait, and occasionally it occurred to me that if a Tolstoyan talent were hitched up with my weekly volume of words, immortality would already lie behind me.

My date with journalistic fame proved, however, as brief and sparkly as the glow of a birthday candle. My name and that of the late Tom Meany went up on the side of the paper's delivery trucks one day.

Tom, who had been my mentor and guide on the paper as Bud Lamoreaux was to be at CBS, was a prominent member of the sportswriting world and I was pleased to be linked with him on a three-sheet that said, "Read Tom Meany and Heywood H. Broun, Hard-Hitting Columnists in the New York *Star*"—To show that we were hard hitting, a boxer's fist jabbed across the space under my name.

That night the cold winds of fiscal reality puffed across the birthday cake and we emptied our desks and went home. I took one of the posters with me in case I should ever have a delivery truck of my own on which I could paste it.

Looking back on the sports I covered in those far-off forties days, the thing that strikes me most is that we, the sportswriters, were under the impression that an unexpandable big time had already arrived and that a puffed-up plateau of prosperity had been achieved which might be difficult to sustain.

In fact, of course, the salaries and hoopla of those days now seem as quaint as the cigarette-card images of the players whose highest earnings reached the four-figure level with a gasp of surprise and whose publicity dream was a line drawing in *Harper's Magazine.*

Most of the baseball players in my writing days were farmers from the south who wanted from the game enough money in savings to buy another forty acres or a tractor to substitute for a span of mules. The small-town types thought of employing the same savings to stock a hardware or grocery store, a store whose business might be slightly improved by a few photos in the window to prove that the fat man measuring out nails had once walked among the great and felt at home. Image had advanced somewhat from giveaway cards to occasional endorsements of cigarettes, usually rather discreetly worded. The players were now and then interviewed on the radio, and on rainy days we wrote feature pieces about them.

There were certainly a few celebrities of the Christy Mathewson, Babe Ruth, Joe DiMaggio sort, but most of their colleagues, whether they read the poems of Pindar or not, agreed with the old Greek sports odist that "Brief is the season of man's delight." The farm would certainly produce a better Christmas with that forty acres of bottom land added to the stony hills that broke Daddy's back, but the game was played with dedication not because of all the values with which sport has since been encrusted, but just because one didn't want to end up with a back like Daddy's.

Sports seem to have been somewhat more relaxed than they were to become, not because we were more rational people then, but because we had not yet weighted them with so much money and importance.

When Ross Youngs, in the year I was born, cried out one day, "It's great to be young and a Giant," he spoke for all the farm boys who, for the next twenty years, were just glad to get away from the plow and up to the plate, to have a good time, make a few bucks, and drink a few beers. I was around to meet the last of this lot. They did their best and were content with that and sometimes could find laughter in the circumstances of a loss. They were, after all, engaged in sport, which is play, diversion, frolick, and tumultuous merriment.

Then too, for a frosting on prosperity's cake, playing a game well is about as agreeable a way as possible to spend your time.

Certainly the music of morality through sport had been blaring with witless ardor ever since the stable of writers called Burt L. Standish had discovered that the public would believe that Frank and Dick Merriwell were perfect because they were athletes and athletes because they were perfect.

The legend of the newsboy crying, "Say it ain't true, Joe," to poor Joe Jackson after his involvement in the Black Sox scandal was endlessly repeated in newspaper columns with the notion that the youth of America looked to athletes for spiritual guidance, as citizens of more rational countries might look to philosophers, scientists, or artists.

The nice thing about the forties, however, is that though the river of guff was already in full spate, not many of us fell into its foaming nonsense. Few athletes governed their lives or their speech in ways designed to strengthen the image of the putative publicity campaign.

Somewhere in the sixties I discovered the truth of a statement of Raymond Chandler's. Real gangsters, he pointed out, went to the movies just like the rest of us, and seeing the improbable mobsters of the great iron- and stone-framed fantasies of the Cagney and Bogart era, they began to speak in the stylized monotone of the Big House and say the lines conceived for them in the pool house or the beach cabana, things like "See if bright boy carries a heater."

I'm afraid that the athlete is traveling the same road. The jovially profane men with whom I dealt long ago have given way to cautious straight arrows who act as if they had hired the firm of Rover, Rover & Rover as their public relations firm and have been given not the fun-loving Tom but serious Sam as their personal representative.

The first baseball player I ever interviewed offered to beat me to a jelly for asking why he had given up a couple of home runs in the late innings of a baseball game. He said that writers were all pains in the ass and that I was the worst of them, a comment I thought unfair since I had been one day on the job and hadn't had a chance to build up much nuisance value.

The irritable player was Luke "Hot Potato" Hamlin, a rough diamond who lived in a trailer in the Ebbets Field parking lot.

Later, after he had been knocked out of the box in Chicago, he put his arm around me and apologized, explaining what was puzzling to him but would have been clear to Sigmund Freud, that he always felt tense after winning and relaxed after losing. No modern-day ball player will admit to being relaxed at any time save, perhaps, when standing over the home barbecue cooking steaks while engaging in good-natured banter with his wife and children for purposes of a Sunday takeout.

If I had discussed image with Hamlin in one of his easygoing moods, say after he had walked in the winning run with the bases loaded, he would have been honestly puzzled. It certainly didn't occur to Luke, as it was later to occur to such as Billy Martin, the professionally disagreeable Yankee; Conrad Dobler, the football badboy; and more tennis players than you would care to meet, that if you couldn't sell yourself as the All-American Boy, there might be some money in being the All-American Pill. Wrestling, a sport closely allied to theater, knows what Noah Beery and Lon Chaney knew, that villains don't glitter like stars, but last longer. Luke was a hard-working ball player and as long as the Dodger management thought so, he could not imagine why he should concern himself with the opinions of the pismires of the press or the vast mass of people who were so unfortunate as to have to pay to see ball games instead of being payed to play them.

Long ago Maurice Barrymore, a great leading man when Cap Anson was a great first baseman, flew into a rage when his press agent put out a newspaper story designed to humanize the great man with homely details of his private life, an article including material of minor critical or artistic interest such as that Barrymore habitually breakfasted on ham and eggs.

"Who cares what I eat?" cried the exasperated Barrymore, unaware that in years to come magazines like *People* and *Us* would fascinate millions by measuring the yogurt intake of movie stars and showing athletes and their wives concocting the kind of thing often called "fun foods for patio parties."

Faced by the constant curiosity of the new journalism, a curiosity made deadly by the irrefutable tape recorder (Long ago James P. Dawson of *The New York Times* made me put away my pencil and paper at an interview. "Who the hell says anything worth hearing when he knows it's being written down?" said Dawson) the athlete has, perhaps understandably, erected around himself a shell as impenetrable as an armored car.

The ball players who talked to Jimmy Dawson and me, after I pocketed my pencil, were certainly rarely profound and often spiteful and narrow. They discussed the weaknesses of themselves and their colleagues freely and often informatively. The journalists to whom they spoke were the same small bunches who either traveled regularly with them or who met them at each stop around their league. To some they spoke more freely than to others, but the general assumption was that some things were obviously off the record and that secrets of the trade and stories of their sex lives, or lack thereof, would not show up in the papers.

Today there are a lot fewer papers and a great many more journalists. At any ball game of any importance the big microphones of the TV people and the little microphones of radio, newspapers, magazines, and, most dangerous, the verbal paparazzi, make the Birnam Wood that menaced Macbeth look as puny as a sapling planted by a politician.

It's time to button up the tank and set the turrets to firing streams of clichés. When I was an artilleryman we used to have a concept called "interdiction fire," the idea of which was to keep dumping dynamite on an unoccupied crossroads to make sure that it remained unoccupied. So, today's ball player will begin, often before any question is asked, with the ritual tribute to his teammates, his manager, the concepts of team play as a unifying force, and finish off with a tribute to the opposition which "Gave a hundred percent but just didn't get the breaks that we did today."

When the going gets tough and the questions specific, the tough get going—into the shower room or the trainer's room, or into such an inexorable repetition of the early good sportsmanship as to sound like some sort of dial-a-joke gone mad.

I do not blame the athletes of today. They have as much at stake in the image game as do office holders and they must be as cautiously dull. It's just that sometimes holding a microphone in front of a pitcher whose eyes are full of misery because he's been knocked out of the box and listening to him say, "For myself, I don't care. I'm sorry I let the gang down but the eventual victory wipes out my unhappiness" (and they really do talk that way now), I want to shout an unthinkable word—unthinkable at least for TV—and ask for two cents worth of honest ego.

Once, in the days before anyone cared what ball players ate, drank, wore, or rubbed under their arms, I asked old Dodger Kirby Higbe for his opinion of Bob Feller, then in his blinding prime. A pitcher today would immediately have paid tribute to Feller's curve, courage, and citizenship, but Kirby took a somewhat more personal view. "Feller," he said, "he wouldn't get a loud foul off me."

Of course, good old days put under a microscope show the little ugly things that microscopes are so good at finding. There were, until the last couple of years in which I was a baseball writer, no black players in baseball, and their arrival brought forth some memorable bursts of meanness from players and managements of the national game.

I remember an evening with Branch Rickey at the Havana Stadium in 1947 in which I had a brief glimpse of the bared fangs in the darkness of closed clubhouses and unreachable offices.

Jackie Robinson had spent the 1946 season with the Montreal Royals of the International League and had a sensational year, ending with his selection as the league's most valuable player. He had so obviously earned a tryout with the parent Brooklyn club that when he appeared on the '47 spring roster of Montreal there was a great outcry in the press against the apparent injustice. Both teams trained in Havana that spring and the Royals, with the celebrated Robinson in the lineup, were rousing more interest among Cuban fans than were the Dodgers, but the two clubs did not play each other and when Brooklyn went off to Venezuela for a series of exhibitions I stayed in Havana and went with Rickey to see Montreal play the Cuban All-Stars. Branch's stated purpose was to look at a daring base stealer from the lower minors who turned out to be so terrified at the great man's presence that he took no leads, stole no bases, and won no smiles from Rickey.

41

Robinson, meanwhile, was hitting the ball, dancing on the base paths, and generally looking like a talented adult joining in some schoolyard game.

After watching silently for a few innings Rickey suddenly said, "You know, young Broun, you writers haven't been entirely fair to me in this matter of Robinson. Pressures have been brought to bear on me, pressures which I'm not at liberty to tell you about, but pressures which have been considerable."

I did not nudge him, knowing his delphic manner, and a couple of innings later, when Jackie had executed a dazzling play at second base, the oracle spoke again. "Did you see that play?" asked the man we called the Mahatma. "Robinson has the greatest pair of hands I ever saw."

I knew he was telling me, in his oblique way, that Jack would be in Ebbets Field on opening day, but that it was going to be a trip through the mine fields to get there.

The St. Louis Cardinals and New York Giants had planned to strike rather than play against Brooklyn with a black, and some fast work by Stanley Woodward, the great sports editor of the old *Herald Tribune,* turned the light of publicity on these pustules of prejudice and shriveled them.

A high official of the Chicago Cubs told me that his team had intended to join the strike, but had been deterred when he told them their pay would cease at the moment they acted. He told me he would deny it if I wrote it, but by now it arouses no more emotion than any of the other old entries in the archives of injustice.

Aware of the never-announced pressures of which Mr. Rickey had spoken, I admired the masterful misdirection of the Mahatma's maneuverings, by which Robinson, apparently doomed to flower only in French Canada, suddenly appeared in the Dodger lineup in the final exhibition series of the spring, then broke through to triumph and public acceptance before the relaxed opposition could reknot its fists.

Jack was enjoined by Mr. Rickey throughout that '47 season against taking offense at the many ugly remarks made to him by opposing players in the hope of provoking the fight that would prove that blacks and whites could not, in the mothers-in-the-playground phrase, "play nice" together.

Since Jack was at first base because of the strategic needs of the team, he had the leprous distillations of many small minds poured into the porches of his ears by base runners. If he was not, like Hamlet's father, "soon barked about by a loathesome tetter," he was filled within by a rage that had no outlet save in headlong base running.

It was perhaps some of that rage that impelled him, in the first game of the '47 World Series, to leave the base paths on a routine double play and throw a full football block on Phil Rizzuto, who had already thrown the ball and should have been immune. Jack was, by nature, a hard, clean player and this uncharacteristic act caused a good deal of muttering and booing in the stands.

The apparent opportunity for Yankee revenge came a few innings later when Joe DiMaggio hit a routine grounder to short. Pee Wee Reese made a good throw, but Jack, uncertain about first base technique, came out to take it and then, fumbling backward with his foot, placed it not at the corner of the base, but across it, making it possible for DiMag to bring the full weight of his spike-tipped nine-foot stride down on Robinson's instep, breaking the foot, perhaps, but not the rules of the game, since the base belongs to the runner, not the fielder.

DiMaggio, in the last flying leap, swerved to the right and avoided landing on his opponent's Achilles' toe, which later led the late Jimmy Cannon to ask DiMaggio why he had not struck, or stepped, a blow for his friend Phil.

"I thought about it when I saw what he was doing," said Joe, "but then it occurred to me that I'm Italian and Phil's Italian and I didn't want people to think it's the guineas against the niggers. To tell the truth, if Phil had been black or Robinson Italian, I'd have spiked the s.o.b."

This is complicated sociological thinking for the last four steps of a ninety-foot run, but the odd anecdote, with its ugly words and practical simplistics, is an illustration of the strange nobility that set DiMaggio off from others and made him, for me, at least, the *chevalier sans peur et sans reproche* of my sporting life. He was a man for whom an ignoble act was impossible, but, more importantly, the appearance of an ignoble act like the spiking of Jackie Robinson, would be impossible.

There is occasional speculation today as to why he alone of

living old athletes seems to be recognized and treated with a kind of King Arthur reverence. To me, it is simple. Joe, from the moment he appeared in Yankee Stadium, an agonizingly shy boy with brittle legs and an iron will, to the moment he refused his last Yankee contract with the riding-into-the-sunset remark "I didn't think I could give them a hundred-thousand-dollar year," acted out in life the things we had read in those impossible books about "Baseball Joe," things we may laugh at now but wish were true.

No sensible person recommends giving back to baseball's owners so much as the synthetic skins of their cold frankfurters, and Joe's gesture is not a reproach to a modern ball player fighting for a good contract. It is just that sport must have some element of romance, or its color is as meaningless as the panoply of the changing of the guard in front of some tacky dictator's palace. The drums pound, but hearts don't, the colors are bright, but watching eyes are not.

Joe DiMaggio did not create an image, he was one. Even today when his rather limited purpose in life seems to be the sale of coffee makers and the joys of a savings bank, tasks he performs with more earnestness than flair, I am sure he has picked up none of the easy self-excusing cynicism of the advertising crowd, and that solemnly he insists the coffee he drinks come from the maker he speaks for on television. If you are some kind of insider who knows that he makes it in a saucepan or drinks instant, don't tell me. I need Joe DiMaggio. My pantheon has too many crumbling figures, too many empty niches.

I remember my first talk with him and my last, and each was characteristic of this *preux chevalier* from the San Francisco fishing docks. Just back from the war, I joined the Yankees in Philadelphia and was standing in the lobby of the Ben Franklin Hotel, an unknown baseball writer from an unknown paper, when DiMaggio invited me to join him for coffee. Our chat was desultory and amiable, and I kept wondering why he, a notably reserved man, had sought me out. It was certainly neither my charm nor a desire to plant a story in my paper. It was only after we parted that it occurred to me that he was fulfilling a leader's obligation to make those associated with the organization feel at home. Joe *was* the Yankees, and I was to spend the summer with them, hence his thoughtful gesture.

When I last saw Joe he was a vice-president and coach for the Oakland A's, and as we were setting up our cameras for an interview about the elaborate electrical hoopla of the Oakland scoreboard Joe said, "Heywood, do me a favor, don't ask me any questions about Charlie Finley."

I agreed, of course, but asked him why and got a reply whose first sentence should be engraved over the door of every legislature in the country.

"If you ask me," said Joe, "I'll have to tell the truth. The truth is that I think Charlie is a terrible man, but he is my employer and it wouldn't be proper for me to speak of him in that way."

All during the interview I toyed with the forbidden question as one might tongue a hollow tooth. I kept imagining the look of reproach, and then the reluctant statement, putting the honor of truth at war with the honor of courtesy. I didn't do it, of course, and I hope that Joe will forgive me for telling the story now. After all, he doesn't work for Charlie Finley anymore, and I suspect nothing happened to change his opinion.

Neither has anything happened to change my opinion of Joe. Romance and tumultuous merriment may not seem to go together, but they are essential ingredients of sport as it ought to be, and DiMaggio, too magisterial, perhaps, for laughter, is as romantic to me as any creation of Doyle, Dumas, or Richard Harding Davis.

I began to notice in 1948, my last full year as a baseball writer, that the moist, limp hand of public relations was beginning to pat and push at the shape of the ball players' personalities. Perhaps it was the appearance of more and more microphones, perhaps just the slew-footed march of the pied piper which, for lack of a better name, we call progress. In any case, I found that even my old friends were inclined to chant sporting mantras—"I didn't win it, the guys did," "I leave those decisions to my manager," "If hustle can win it, we'll win it," "They put on their pants one leg at a time"—and I realized that no one would again achieve the glorious frankness of Rogers Hornsby, who one spring was given the St. Louis Browns to manage and said to a questioning newspaperman, "Get out of the cellar with this bunch of bums? I'll be lucky to stay in the league!" They did, but he didn't. He never learned to call a spade an instrument which properly used can dig a gold mine, make a child happy on a sandy beach, or prepare eternal rest for the dear departed.

Greater, I think, than any of the personal or personnel changes in baseball in the half century of my attention to it, is the physical circumstances and surroundings of the game.

In the rickety odd-shaped stadia of the past, often built to advantage of the strengths of a particular player, like Ralph Kiner or Hank Greenberg, for whom homer-catching "Gardens" were run up, there was an old-shoe quality of intimacy which is rapidly disappearing.

Economic realities, which seem uniformly to be aesthetically disastrous, decree that old ball parks must be torn down because of their limited capacity and replaced with cement saucers, which are as efficient and as inviting as the stainless steel washbowl in an operating room. The new stadia can accommodate baseball, football, a rock concert, and a born-again rally, all of them profitably, none of them comfortably or pleasantly.

The tax structure, another economic reality, decrees that when a corporation buys tickets for a sports event, the sum spent is a deductible entertainment item, and corporations therefore routinely purchase season boxes which extend from the edge of the playing field to a last iron ring far from the battle, a kind of final immobile ripple in the concentric pattern of privilege that extends outward from the dropped stone of the baseball game.

Were these boxes filled with enthusiasts, matters might not be so bad, since the rich can be as worked up about baseball as the poor, but since the boxes are status items they are rarely occupied on nonstatus days, that is those days that have not been given the imprimatur of importance by the press. The ordinary ticket buyer thus usually stares across a void dotted with occasional idle executives and misses the fierce personal involvement of the Rorschach-shaped old parks.

Gone are such beloved cheerleaders as Brooklyn's Hilda Chester, with her cowbell and hoarse war cries; Bruce, the

46

screech-owl man, in Pittsburgh, and St. Louis's combative Mary Doyle.

In their place is the witless electronic bugle and the electric lights that spell out their "Charge" message for the tone deaf and the inattentive.

But enough of this curmudgeonry. Of course, sports have changed, and not surprisingly, they have changed in exactly the same way as the whole tenor of American life has changed. Perhaps, however, because of their almost indestructible magic quality, they are expected to exist in a dream world outside of time (and they do in the sense that a group of old fans reliving an ancient inning, quarter, chukker, or stretch drive are transported in time as completely as if they had entered H. G. Wells's machine), there is more disappointment among the sentimentalists.

Politics has its disillusion built in, ("Just for a handful of silver, he left us") and the expression "business is business" is an indication that most Americans do not expect of industrialists the honesty they would take for granted at a card table, but sport—well, sport is supposed to be different and its present insistence on emphasizing its alliance with business is hurtful.

We can be philosophical about the burial of our dreams under the advancing asphalt of dynamic growth but things like the amputation of Ebbets Field bring phantom pains on every sunny day when association jogs the memory with bat sounds and the distant shouts of the devotees.

That was part of the world of my first sports adventure, a world where pro basketball was played in armories by ordinary-sized men in high sneakers, where pro football players drove trucks to augment their incomes, and where there were enough poor boys to fill innumerable ramshackle boxing "clubs" with smoke, sweat, pain, and excitement.

TV had not yet done its phoenix act on boxing in which it first burned it out and then brought it triumphantly back from the ashes, crying its triumph in the voice of Muhammad Ali, that most telegenic of sports personalities.

Inside its attendant current hoopla this most primitive of all sport remains the least changed of all. When it shifted from London prize ring rules to Marquis of Queensbury, it became, contrary to popular opinion, more brutal (for instance, rounds in those old endless battles ended with every fall, sometimes a voluntary collapse, substituting wonderful sixty-second vacations for the terrifying ten count. Gloves and bandages, it should be noted, protect the fist and not its target. Bare-knuckle fighters couldn't hit as hard), and it has stayed as elemental as ever.

In my boyhood I attended innumerable fights, sitting in the distant balcony seats appropriate to my purse, and I thought of the bouts then as a kind of knockabout chess. The smallness of the fighters as perceived from the dim distance of the cheap seats made it difficult to understand their power to hurt, and I was as lighthearted about their lilliputian scuffles as I was about the repeated deaths of my recently abandoned toy soldiers, who toppled at the touch of a finger and were restored to life with equal ease.

I was, therefore, quite shocked when I attended my first bout as a writer and sat with my nose against the rough canvas edge of the St. Nicholas Arena ring on West Sixty-Sixth Street.

Two preliminary boys crawled through the ropes to fight for their share of a hundred-dollar purse which was going to be sliced like one of those pie graphs that tell you what happened to you but not why. At the bell they shuffled forward and jabbed listlessly at each other. After about a minute of this there was some restlessness in the audience, and looking down to make a note, I became aware that my lapel was sprinkled with drops of blood. Those jabs may have been casual, but the nose is a delicate vessel, and I was to discover that a mist of what delicately used to be called claret is commonplace in the press row.

I reached down to rub at the ghastly dew when the ever-helpful Jimmy Dawson seized my wrist.

"Wait till it dries," he advised, "and then you can flick it off with your fingernails."

I discovered, too, in the years I spent writing about fights, that those inside body punches, which set the untouched to shouting "Waltz me around again, Willie!" evoke gasps and grunts of pain, which, punishing to the protagonists, become depressing to those who are trying to make it all sound like a festive evening.

Stanley Woodward used to say that after five years one of two things happened to a sportswriter. He either plunged deep into his subject, never to return to a rational world, began, for instance, referring to local teams as "we," or he ran from his typewriter with a shout of boredom and went off to some other occupation.

My five years were not up when the choice was taken from my hands by the failure of the newspaper, but little bubbles of ennui had already begun to form on my lips, and I was uneasily aware that I was beginning to use, in my work, the sportswriter's antacid, hyperbole. Looking bleakly at the task of writing about a doubleheader in which second division teams had divided two games by one-sided scores, I was taking refuge in things like "Pitching reputations were mowed down like Pickett's men at Gettysburg in yesterday's Polo Grounds action, but when the smoke cleared, battle honors were even. . . ."

Well, maybe not as bad as that, but certainly I was increasingly employing verbal amphetamines as typewriters literally fell apart under my endlessly bobbing fingers. The S key fell off my portable during the 1948 World Series between Cleveland and Boston and made my work difficult since PM had changed its name to the Star, making my dispatches headed " pecial to the NY tar," difficult for the press box telegrapher.

Nobody feels good about the death of a newspaper, and I shared the shock of my colleagues, a shock made more painful since we knew that but for top level indecision at critical moments in our history, the brutally sudden stilling of a lot of good, strong voices needn't have happened.

This book is not about newspapers, however, so a story that would make the Ancient Mariner's account seem as tragic as the mishaps of the Five Little Peppers will have to be told elsewhere.

Behind my anger at the ineptitude that had sunk our ship was the comforting thought that there waited for me a metaphorical lifeboat in which I was going to bob off to the magical islands of the theater, or to put it less flossily, I was letting the success I had enjoyed in the annual baseball writers' shows convince me that the world was waiting for a character actor of my kidney.

When you got to about the twenty-fifth volume of Tom Swift,

it used to take almost a chapter to tell what had happened on the way there, adventures from the motorcycle days, through the electric rifle, and the Caves of Ice, to whatever he was doing in the current volume. I'll make the account of my theatrical career shorter, partly because Tom's adventures were more exciting, although I spent lots of time in those Caves of Ice which house flop shows, and partly because a summary of most of it can be found, I am ridiculously proud to say, in the pages of *Who's Who in the American Theater*.

During those theater years I believed that my sports background, like the ringside blood at St. Nick's, had dried thoroughly and could be flicked off with a sweep of the fingertips. I was to discover, seventeen years later, that, like Lady Macbeth, I was beyond the help of fingernails or even the perfumes of Araby. How the damned spot wouldn't out will be told in the next adventure, "Heywood Hale Broun and his Magic Jacket."

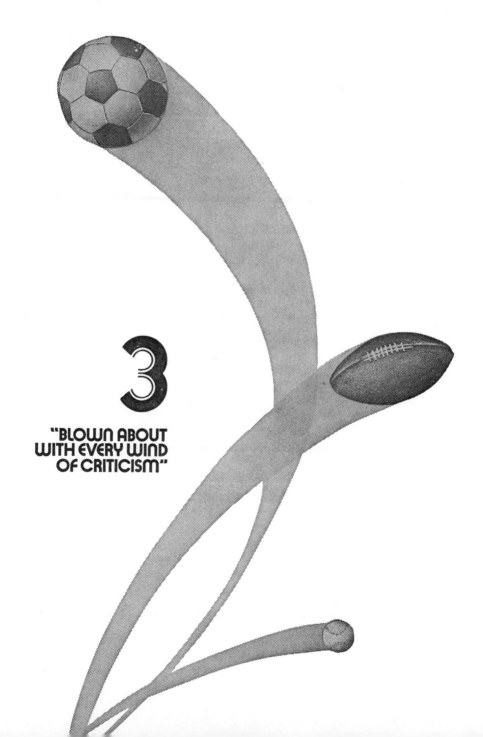

3

"BLOWN ABOUT WITH EVERY WIND OF CRITICISM"

George Abbott, that wise and wintry realist, once told me that ability got less recognition in the theater than in any other art or profession.

"People wouldn't know a good actor if they saw one," is the way he put it, "but they can recognize a good part. If you play a bad part in a good play it will do your career no good, nor will a good part in a bad play—no matter how well you do it. If you have a good part in a hit, your whole life will change, you will become a success, and you will pay a price for that success. You will play the same part all the rest of your life under different names."

When I discovered that I was going to have a splendid supporting part in Jack Richardson's *Xmas in Las Vegas*, the doors of the golden cage of success seemed to open before me, and it was in a buoyant mood that I set out for the fateful dinner in the winter of 1965 which was to bounce me like a pinball back among the jocks.

The dinner was a club affair at which I was to preside, and when after the coffee cups were cleared and I had launched my speakers, finished my cigar, and drained the last drops of the superior head-table wine, I felt as smug as was possible for a middle-aged man with more hope than accomplishment.

It was at that moment that Gordon Manning, a vice-president of CBS News, caught me by the arm and suggested that if I would let him drop me off at home, I might hear something to my advantage. To humor him and to save money—I never took cabs until the New York reviews were out and seldom then—I agreed, and during the ride Gordon proposed what seemed to me the least interesting idea since I had been offered the role of a man hit by a car in a low-budget movie.

"You were a writer, and you are a performer," Gordon said, "and that seems to me an ideal combination of talents for a TV newsman. We are starting a new Saturday news show and I think you ought to audition for the job of sports correspondent."

Haroun al Rashid, offered a crust by some ragged companion unaware of the caliph's disguise, could not have been more kindly and condescending than I was to Gordon. I explained that my role in the new play came with a thick layer of butter and jelly, eye-catching eccentricities that guaranteed audience attention. I was to portray a lecherous, asthmatic, alcoholic trombone player, who finished up with a near-death farewell scene in a class with Little Eva's departure to a better world.

Under such circumstances, I explained to Gordon, the chance to try out for his show had no appeal. If he had caught me a few months earlier, when I was back from a disaster in Bucks County—a new play in which the heroine, through magical powers, turned me into a lizard while the critics, through the power of their opinions, changed the play into a turkey—I might have been receptive but not now when the Great Moment, for which I had waited through seventeen years of bank clerks, deputy sheriffs, and druggists, was at hand.

Gordon was quick to realize that under the circumstance his proffered feast was a stale ham sandwich compared to the banquet of blazing fame and money a la mode that awaited me, and we parted the best of friends.

I am glad we did because *Xmas in Las Vegas* opened on a Thursday night and closed on Saturday of the same week, after a matinee performance to which we were bidden to ask our friends since almost no one had bought tickets, and a final evening before a grim little group unleavened by friends.

A day or so later I ran into Gordon and with that brisk directness which actors must employ to grab the coattails of ever fleeing opportunity, I asked at once if the audition were still open. He assured me that many had been tried and none chosen and that I was welcome to draw my bow at the venture.

Shortly thereafter I presented myself in a dark green coat and a mood of gray resignation. I read three little scripts of my own devising in a vacant studio, wrote Gordon a note of thanks for the chance, and went out to look for a job.

Vast wheels at CBS turned in different directions and a few weeks later I was taken on for a four-week trial period, concurrent with the beginning of The CBS Saturday News with Roger Mudd in February 1966.

For the first two weeks I did what I had done at the audition, went to an empty studio in my dark green coat and read my pieces off a teleprompter. Compared to my previous TV work, trying to remember lines in the silent boiler factory of a live production in which, just out of camera range but not out of sight, the walls of one's castle are being removed to make way for a little paper battlefield, this kind of thing seemed agreeably easy.

I didn't know whether anyone liked my work, since, as a free lance and an outsider, I didn't go to the office until just before the taping when I handed in my script for approval.

Then in a scene that had all the coincidence fiction tries to avoid, I was handed a memo that said that news director Fred Friendly thoroughly approved of my work, and I was savoring the assurance of its contents when a shout came echoing down the off-white intestines that pass for corridors in the CBS News building: "He did it! He quit!" cried the messenger of doom. The famous set-to in which Friendly took on Jack Schneider, the newly anointed crown prince of CBS, on the subject of Senate hearings versus soap operas was now a part of TV news history, and Fred was part of the Ford Foundation.

The entire staff was then summoned to the newsroom, a place I found with difficulty, and standing out in the corridor I heard Mr. Schneider announce that the new senior vice-president of news would be Richard S. Salant, a former holder of the office.

The next day Mr. Salant moved into the executive chair and, according to spies, announced that one of the first orders of business was to "Get rid of that funny-looking guy that Fred just hired."

Paul Greenberg, who had been given the job of producing the new CBS Weekend News, is a proud and stubborn man, and he decided to be proud and stubborn about me. In an effort to make me more palatable to the new powers he took me out of the studio and sent me to cover a dog show at Madison Square Garden. Such "in the field" stories are the bread and butter of TV news but I was obviously and utterly ignorant of the means of putting them together. A patient and silent young man named Bud Lamoreaux was assigned to supervise the picture taking and the putting together of the piece. In the next ten years we were to do about six hundred pieces together and Bud grew a good deal less silent, but never less patient, which was a very good thing, because after teaching me the business he had always to deal with the fact that my patience span is about the length of the fuse on a cherry bomb.

Despite Bud's best efforts and because of mine, our first collaboration was a disaster. Mr. Salant had disliked me as a talking head, and when he had a look at me full length his distaste grew proportionately. His opinion was reinforced, again according to spies, by the fact that his twelve-year-old child had, with the quick intuition of the young, sensed something sinister in my character.

A day or so later I met an old college friend, Eliot Asinof, on the street and he told me he had just auditioned for the job of sports commentator on the CBS Weekend News. I told him I would call him the moment I was fired and thereby give him a running start on the others I had heard were submitting themselves and their samples for the job.

My four-week trial was now up but Salant, although when he thought of me did so with a shudder of distaste, was not giving me much thought among the multitude of problems a news operation presents, and Manning and Greenberg were keeping me on a week-to-week basis in the hope that I would get better at the job and that Salant's child might descry, behind the cold and brittle facade, the better side of my nature.

In the first week of this new phase Greenberg decided to put me back in the studio and told me that he felt some comment was obligatory on Michigan's decision to strip Muhammad Ali of his heavyweight boxing title because of his refusal to accept the military draft.

"Look, Paul," I said uneasily, "I haven't been here very long and it doesn't look as if I'll be here much longer so I'm not making a heroic career sacrifice, but I have to tell you that I can't condemn Ali even though I presume it's the network policy to do so."

"I'm not telling you what side to take, I'm just telling you to say something," said Paul, thereby beginning a policy that never varied. In later years I said a number of things that various executives didn't like, but I never had to retract or apologize and I never was instructed to say something I didn't want to.

The Ali editorial finished with a flourish of borrowed fire since I quoted Mr. Justice Jackson's great "No official, high or petty, can prescribe what shall be orthodox in politics, nationalism, religion, or other matters of opinion, or force citizens to confess by word or act their faith therein." I braced myself for a torrent of denunciation and a trickle of support and got nothing at all from either the powers above or public. The sole response was a phone call from an English newspaperman who wanted to know where he could get the full text of Jackson's opinion (West Virginia Board of Education v. Barnette 319 U.S. 624).

It is not that people do not pay attention to TV, it is, I think, that they do it in odd ways. I have received congratulations for a great many features in which every detail is remembered except one, that Charles Kuralt was the correspondent, while Charlie has been good enough to tell me that he hears an occasional good word on his sports work. Maybe the viewers thought I was defending Mr. Justice Jackson.

It began to disturb me that I was possibly jeopardizing the positions of Manning and Greenberg, whose continued championship of me must by now be considered a considerable reflection on their judgment, so I devised a face-saving scheme to get us all off the hook. I had been offered the part of Uncle Willie in a Palm Beach Playhouse production of *The Philadelphia Story*, which was to star Richard Chamberlain, TV's Dr. Kildare, in his stage debut.

I would accept the job, I explained, and they could put it out that I had left CBS in order to accept this golden theatrical opportunity—if a three-week job can be so described. Meanwhile, if they decided they wanted any more work from me, I would be in Florida, the ideal place for spring sports features. Lamoreaux could pick me out of rehearsal when I was needed.

I went off to Palm Beach, off again with the raggle-taggle gypsies, forgetting TV and presumably by TV forgot. I was making my failure into a funny story for the other actors when Lamoreaux called and asked me to meet him at Gulf Stream Park racetrack in Miami to do a story on Buckpasser, Greentree Stable's great three-year-old, who was at that moment languishing in his stall with a fever and a cracked hoof. The story was to be built around the possible use of a new method of patching hooves.

My wife, an actress in the classical tradition, who tends to think of almost every situation in life in terms of maximum dramatic impact, then made a suggestion that was profoundly to alter the course of my life and rob the theater of a man I still think of as a character actor of infinite color and variety.

"Horse racing," she said, "means loud clothes. Coats made out of horse blanket material, diamond stickpins, things like that. Since you don't have a stickpin or a horse blanket, wear that crazy madras coat you got from the play *Send Me No Flowers.*"

I pointed out that such garments were more likely to be worn by manic grave-plot salesmen, like Mr. Akins in the play, than by television correspondents, but she replied crushingly and sensibly that I wasn't likely to be on television much longer anyway so I might as well wear the jacket and go out in a flourish of color.

Dressed to brighten the mood of burial ground buyers, I joined Bud in the backstretch and together we ran into a wall of difficulty, objections to our presence from Johnny Campo, then assistant to trainer Eddie Neloy, and now a distinguished trainer on his own. Johnny was polite but unyielding and to my amazement Bud did not accept the obvious and retire. He made some small sign to the camera crew and began a long, quiet speech to Campo about what we planned. Feeling that I should be equally brave in the face of defeat, I went off to winkle out Mr. Bain, the inventor of the hoof patch, who was laired in a little room at the end of the barn. He didn't want to be interviewed because he was (a) shy and (b) had no official standing, not yet having been hired to perform his special podiatry. Dressed in my Mr. Akins coat, I summoned all my Mr. Akins sales fervor, and about the time Bud's persistence won the day with Campo, I towed Mr. Bain out into the sunlight while Buckpasser, after an amazed look at my jacket, stood up in his stall and came forward for a closer inspection, affording us a splendid camera shot.

Mr. Bain didn't get the job in this case but I was now on my way to getting mine, several important things having happened that morning. Lamoreaux and I had found a way of working together, which was never to change in any important way.

In terms of jazz I would describe Bud as the trombone, building the foundation of the counterpoint, while I, as clarinet, ornamented the theme with flights around the melody line. Should you ask who played trumpet, or lead, I would say it was the eye of the camera, that recorder of actualities.

Of course, human nature is too complicated for the narrow pigeonholes of imagery, and if we had been simply bull and butterfly he would eventually have stepped on me or, alternatively, I would have fluttered away.

In more practical terms we began that day to learn the process of communicating without speaking, that cerebral and emotional *pas de deux* that is found among good sonata players, shortstops, and second basemen.

The lively jacket subtly assisted me with another problem. Bud had told me that the years I spent as an actor seemed to have conditioned me to assume a role at the opening of the camera shutter and that the character I had chosen, a sort of Sam Newsman, was not without unhappy elements of caricature.

Send Me No Flowers, a semihit or semiflop, depending on whether you acted in it or invested in it, had been among my happiest experiences in the theater, and its costume carried in its folds traces of that gaiety and confidence, traces that seemed to rise inspiritingly around me, breathing ghostly echoes of laughter and applause. Certainly Sam Newsman didn't wear anything like that, and he began to fade away.

On a much less mystic level, the spies reported that the Fates on Fifty-seventh Street still didn't care much for my style but were delighted with the jacket.

Still on a week-to-week basis, I returned to New York after the closing of the play in Palm Beach and did a couple of cold-weather jobs unaided by the magic madras.

In one of these I went to Yankee Stadium in a drab, warm tweed from Scotland and did some on-camera connective bits for a pair of interviews on the theme of the old order changing and yielding its place to the new. Bud had interviewed Bobby Murcer, putative star shortstop of the Yankees, in Florida and then gone to Wisconsin to interview Tony Kubek, just-retired Yankee shortstop, now inspecting cheeses in Wausau. When the piece was put together Murcer's career and mine took a turn for the worse, while NBC hired Kubek as a sports commentator largely because of the lucidity and charisma he displayed standing among the cheddar wheels in a white lab coat.

The ups and downs continued for some weeks, spies reporting disapproving head shakes and occasional judicious nods while Bud and Paul pruned my flamboyant style but, at the same time, wouldn't let anxiety leech out originality and leave me with the cautious flatness of "Here on the practice field where the Green Devils ready themselves for a stern test. . . ." At one point there was a premature champagne party when CBS sent me a great bundle of contracts to sign. In the civilized world that would have been the offer of a job, but before we could open the second bottle somebody pointed out that nobody had signed the papers on behalf of the company, so we put the rest of the wine back in the icebox and stuck the contracts in a file cabinet. The next day somebody else auditioned for the job.

Then the critic for the old *Herald Tribune* said something nice about the jacket—which, as my principal asset, was now worn on all jobs irrespective of the temperature—and the seesaw tilted my way again.

As the season of summer stock approached and no final decision about my future with the network had been made, I reminded Gordon Manning that packages were being assembled at that very moment, Uncle Willies and Mr. Akinses being chosen to make the rounds of the Massachusetts beach resorts, and if I was not to be a famous TV personality I would rather be floating on the brine than filing for unemployment insurance.

He told me that opposition was waning but that importunities at this point might cause it to flare up again, and ended up counseling patience.

As I have indicated, my normal daily supply of patience won't last through a crosstown traffic light, but I realized that Gordon was playing the chess game of corporate maneuver on my behalf and that it wouldn't be very gracious of me to kick over the table, so I went on working and wondering whether each Saturday's piece would be the last, while the packages were being sealed up and sent off on the strawhat circuit.

Summer theater's contribution to American culture is about the same as cotton candy's contribution to American diet, but for the actors, weaving their way among the playgrounds of millionaires, dispensing easy laughter in plays about infidelity, mistaken identity, and other surefire howlers, it is as close to heaven as vagabonds are likely to get. To be paid to run up and down the sands of Cape Cod, to lie under the palms of the beach named for those romantic trees, to listen to the loons skittering over the lake at Skowhegan, to gorge oneself at the Ogunquit lobster pound—the chance for all this was glimmering away while producers chose other actors, and I waited to see if I was going to be allowed to fly to some bleak manufacturing town to talk to a basketball coach.

The patience finally popped while I hung in a pattern over Washington National Airport on an evening when I had been scheduled to give a speech on theater to a group of doctors who had put aside their knives for a night of fun. When I finally got on the ground and called them to explain my lateness, the fun was about over, and I apologized and began to wonder why I was disappointing those who liked me at the same time I was disappointing those who couldn't wait to see the last of me at the network.

The next day I asked that the sword of Damocles be un-threaded and sheathed, or allowed to drop through my head. I then packed a bag and set off with Bud to do a story about the much-traveled baseball Braves, once of Boston and late of Milwaukee, my mind less on the story than on the prospect of some character man getting sick enough to give up his summer job to me. Knowing actors as I do, I realized that sickness wouldn't be enough, and that I needed a dead colleague to assure myself of a living. The thought of what I was asking depressed me further, and I was therefore both pleased and surprised when the public address system in Atlanta began calling for a "Mr. Brown" to go to the telephone. The call was from Greenberg, who told me that my haberdashery seemed to have won the day and that I was going to be offered a contract.

Thus, through the accident of a gaudy old costume coat and my wife's sage suggestion about its use, I was to have, for ten years, one of the most envied jobs in television news. One of the principal reasons for that envy was the fact that my time was assigned and sacrosanct. Few viewers realize the agonies of news correspondents whose work dies on the spikes of that Iron Maiden, the schedule. There are technically thirty minutes in the evening news broadcast. Of these, six or seven are taken up with selling you things to make you sleep well, smell good, or go to the bathroom. Six or seven minutes more are referred to as "golden time" and are reserved for the resonant tones of the anchorman. That leaves sixteen minutes or so to be divided among about a hundred correspondents, each of whom has many times had the experience of working up a first-rate piece that is in the advance lineup until 5:30 of the day of broadcast and is then scrapped when some film arrives by satellite of the carnage at a nursery school blown up by some group dedicated to freedom and the elimination of false religious faiths.

Sometimes the story doesn't make the schedule at all because the President of the United States has said something profound or purporting to be profound.

Sometimes a correspondent discovers that a piece patently inferior to his has been run because the "mix" of light and dark, of good news and bad, was considered to be better served without his very possibly outstanding work.

There is nothing to be done about all this. Clocks are not cruel. But there is rich material for paranoia, and the telephones of news show producers constantly reverberate with complaints from those who feel that they have been shut out through simple unfairness or the not-so-simple machinations of underhanded colleagues who regularly stoop to misrepresentation and worse. Often the callers are right, but nothing changes the fact that the anchorman's "good night" comes just thirty minutes after his "good evening."

Politicians and terrorists, both much concerned with publicity, learned long ago that the leisure-oriented weekend is not a good time for anything big in the way of talk or action and, as a result, the only major stories on Saturdays and Sundays are likely to be natural disasters in the flood and earthquake line, Mother Nature not being a sabbatarian.

It was with this phenomenon in mind that the CBS Saturday News was created, for good or ill the first of the new burgeoning magazine shows. After a brief report on fire and flood we used to settle down to the examination of folk music festivals, ethnic gatherings, bird watching trips, the plight of the American Indian, and, for ten years, to be dislodged only by cataclysmic disaster or his own broken ankle, Heywood Hale Broun on sport. I had not, therefore, the heartache of the correspondents who fought for their minutes and envied me my custom-armored slot. They envied me less when it rained in Peoria, finishing my planned story and forcing Bud and me to a flight and a drive through the night to Ottumwa for some secondary item that could be made palatable only by prodigies of verbal and pictorial pyrotechnics.

I remember an occasion when I went through forty minutes of film trying to get the athletic director of the University of California to repeat an unguarded and interesting statement—the only unguarded or interesting statement that I can remember being made by an athletic director—which he now declined to utter or unguard. After our hollow "thank yous," we whirled off the San Francisco airport in time to make a plane to Pittsburgh and a baseball story.

Still we did produce the pyrotechnics and can be proud that we missed but five shows in ten years, two weekends when the news was too terrifying and somber, and three while I was in the hospital with a broken ankle. Parenthetically, the break cost me a trip to the America's Cup races and a meeting with the man that Ike Pappas, who replaced me, found as difficult and off-putting as anyone he had met in a news career that included a full measure of wars and riots. It seemed in tune with our political times, therefore, when Bus Mosbacher, the man who awed Ike with his rudeness, was made chief of protocol in the Nixon administration.

As the world is not yet ready for Dr. Watson's account of the Affair of the Aluminium Crutch, it is probably not ready or even very interested in how I fell off a big piece of sculpture in High Woods, New York, and smashed up my ankle. Some reference should be made, however, to the months I spent thereafter on a pair of wooden crutches, testing Lamoreaux's considerable pictorial ingenuity to hide from our public the fact that I was wearing a plaster cast from hip to toe under trousers extensively slit to leave room for the bend in the cast. This curve made balance awkward but kept my bare toes from dragging in the snow.

For our first week of work with three legs between us, I was placed in a golf cart and did a story about Ralph Terry, a Yankee pitcher who had become a golf professional, but it was obvious that we could not carry the cumbersome cart around with us, nor stick exclusively to the game that employed it, so

Bud began to seek out locales where a handy chain link fence or pillar could be gripped or leaned on by the hand that wasn't holding the microphone.

As movie actors learn to begin revving up their energy at the cry of "Roll 'em," so I cleared my throat and started my smile when I heard Bud tell the camera crew's electrician, "Okay, take Woodie's crutches away."

There were a few lagniappes in my lameness, among them the fact that during the four months I wore the full cast, Bud and I traveled first class since it was impossible to store all my plaster in a coach seat. It was, and probably still is, a network rule that correspondents travel in the back of the airplane, and the millions that are saved that way are no doubt constructively used, though they can never repay for the innumerable hours I have spent sitting between drunken sailors and women with actively ill babies.

The cries of my usual infantile companions and the snores of jolly Jack Tar were, however, no more than the murmur of waves in the brief era of hors d'oeuvres and semimobility, and I enjoyed those rides among the rich with the fervor of one who knew that the bones were inexorably knitting and that when the last purl returned my ankle to service I would be back feeding on dried pot roast in the Forest of Elbows.

Indeed the only time I felt my cast to be a real handicap was when Lamoreaux balanced me on a barrel on the edge of Niagara Falls to do the on-camera close of a piece about Calvin Murphy, the basketball player, then attending Niagara University. A crouching soundman steadied the barrel and the invisible hand of the electrician held my toes against the steel drum's top, but I was as relieved to hear "That's a take," as I was to hear the same wonderful phrase a few years later when I was balanced on a snowbank in Minnesota while the wind howled and the cameraman tried to thaw out his machine, his film, and himself in a heated car after several efforts had been wiped out by whirling sleet. The hardiness of the Viking football team was the subject that time.

These on-camera opens and closes seemed to bring out a D. W. Griffith spirit in Bud, and over the years he devised a great many spectacular settings for me. One of my favorites in retrospect, although it gave me a wretched time in the making, was an underwater appearance in a Bloomington, Indiana, swimming pool.

A clear glass wall in the pool permitted the coaches to examine natatory techniques, and since among those displaying their techniques was Mark Spitz, we talked to him and his coach, Indiana's "Doc" Counsilman. The final flourish was to be the appearance in the window of a body rising slowly from the bottom like a waterlogged cork, and mouthing, as it passed, the words "This is Heywood Hale Broun at Indiana University."

Each time I did this, and it seemed to require more repeats than a Buddhist prayer, an attractive spray of bubbles came out of my mouth and about six ounces of chlorinated water went up my nose. Indeed, the last time I had some difficulty rising and hung in front of the window like one of those little red devils suspended in old-time novelty pen barrels.

Later and drier, I burbled the words into the top of a glass of water and the effect, after synchronization, was the talk of the industry for a day or possibly two.

On another occasion a whole Harvard crew was dragooned into service in order that I might ape a coxswain. Coach Harry Parker gave us the combination boat, a rowing group of has-beens, never-wases, and disciplinary problems that loses its breath and sometimes its lunch racing in lonely splendor on the day before the varsity, jayvees, and freshmen have their well-publicized regatta.

The combination boatmen had already had their post-Yale party and were in various stages of morning-after disarray as they took up the suddenly leaden oars, but their systems were electrified with fear when the middle-aged man with mega-phone and floppy hat nearly stepped through the bottom of the boat. We finally got going downriver and I enunciated my bit of script into a wireless microphone taped to the side of the boat. I then enunciated to the crew that we were about to go aground since my steering was rudimentary, and with a skill that might have shamed the varsity, they avoided disaster and came neatly back beside the float.

A story with a wonderfully sentimental close, which also demonstrated how far Bud and I traveled from the publicized big time of sport in search of its primal simplicities, was the Swarthmore-Haverford football game of 1967. These two small

Quaker colleges, in one of the country's oldest and least-known rivalries, had been putting aside the Friendly tradition and battering each other in an earnest, amateurish way. In a day when the semipro tradition is totally accepted by American colleges, they still permitted only actual students to play.

At the end, the camera focused on the back of a huddled figure in a sideline hood and we heard: "It is fitting that as Swarthmore completes the second undefeated season in its history, on the bench should be the manager of the first undefeated team, the 1939 eleven," and then, turning and beaming an old grad smile, "This is Heywood Hale Broun in Swarthmore, Pennsylvania." Elsewhere on that Saturday, Notre Dame and Michigan State played their famous 10–10 tie with the National Championship at stake.

It might be a good idea at this point to explain to those ignorant of the techniques of TV news (a large group, which for a couple of years after I got into the business still included me) how stories like the ones Lamoreaux and I did for CBS News are put together.

Most of our work was not done against time in the sense of covering an event for same-day broadcast, although some blood-chilling examples will shortly be given, and our usual calendar included Tuesday departure for the place of interest, and one or two days of filming in which Bud, as producer, was shaping the story by the shots he chose. During this time I would write, usually on the flyleaf of whatever paperback book I was reading, the fifteen-second open and a close of the same length. I would memorize these and do them in whatever bizarre background had been chosen, and I would interview, on camera, from one to five people, about a third of whom would subsequently have their hearts broken by telling all their friends to watch a show they weren't going to make.

Back in New York Bud and I would sit with Greenberg in a small room filled with air of a fuglike nature that was almost tactilely palpable, and look at what sometimes resembled a rough cut of eternity, the raw material of four or five polished minutes. Shortly thereafter I would be shut up in an even smaller room, where the fug felt like invisible burlap, with some blank paper and an outline as rigid in its demands as those old-time poems whose lines, by their length, had to come out in the shape of hearts, wine glasses, or bunches of flowers.

From time to time I would burst out of my cell, groaning, to find Lamoreaux and Greenberg chatting with friends, reading interesting magazines, or dozing dozes from which they would wake to drive me back to work.

When the script was finished, late in the afternoon, it would be checked against the outline and a thousand wonderful phrases removed, over the years, by the unanswerable statement, "We have no pictures to cover that." When it was agreed that the words were a perfect wine glass or mug or whatever was required by the timed outline from which I had worked ("Fifteen seconds of your opening, nine seconds on the origin of the game, five seconds to introduce the captain of the caber tossers, thirty-two seconds for his interview . . .") I went to a recording room and read my script onto tape, falling briefly and thankfully silent for the captain of the caber tossers, after which tape and reels of film were given to a film editor, who makes it into what is seen on the air.

This relatively leisured sort of thing permits searches for *le mot juste,* long jolly lunches, and lots of pacing. True, the clock is ticking but it is the reassuring ticktock of some easy old grandfather in a Victorian hallway.

When one works in the afternoon for broadcast in the evening, as at the World Series, the clock tends to sound like a machine gun. Live broadcasting is much easier because there is no need for editing, and eloquence, though welcome, is not demanded. Reducing a game to from two to four minutes is like running a watch repair shop on a roller coaster.

In 1968 Harvard and Yale reached their annual football war with equally unblemished records and the CBS Saturday News decided to contrast the unbridled hoopla of the Ohio State-Michigan game with the bankers-gone-berserk atmosphere of this ancient rivalry, with Lamoreaux and Broun assigned to Harvard Stadium.

As is usual, we left the game before it was over, speeding to the nearest CBS affiliate station at the end of the third period with Yale holding a comfortable 29–13 lead. On the way we verbally began laying out a story line based on Brian Dowling, the wonder quarterback, a young man on whom we had done a personality piece earlier in the year.

When we arrived at the studio Bud inspected film that, rushed to the lab by motorcycle rider, had already been developed, and began shouting from the next room, "Six seconds of Dowling fading to pass, four seconds for the first touchdown," etc. while I began obediently fitting my words within those walls. We had substantially finished the work when a scream from the local news staff drew us to a set showing the game still in progress. Incredibly in the last forty-two seconds of the fourth quarter Harvard scored sixteen points to bring about a tie and destroy a nice little essay on Brian Dowling.

It was now about four-thirty in the afternoon and the story was in the film magazine on top of Dave Marlin's camera some miles away. Here a kindness of Bud's proved useful. When we left the stadium he had surmised from the motorcycle rider's metal-studded outfit that a gift of gauds would not be out of place, and he had given the young man our elaborate button and ribbon game credentials, sunbursts of authority equaling a Ruritanian Order of the White Eagle. Gratitude gave our rider wings and he arrived with the necessary footage a lot faster than common sense or the law would dictate, but even with this help we were still constructing our piece when the measured tones of Roger Mudd in New York announced the evening's bill of fare, including "a report from Heywood Hale Broun in Cambridge."

"Don't be too sure," I shouted at the screen as I crammed another strip of seconds into my allotment.

When the piece was finished we were to feed the words and pictures to New York by telephone line, a process I have never tried to understand, and do not wish to have explained to me now.

New York had instructed us that since feeds were also coming in from Saigon, London, the Vatican, et al, we were, short of libel or accidental obscenity, not to stop and go back to seek a perfect match of script and image.

My eyes are set rather close together (proof of dishonesty in old-time novels and, in the opinion of some, still proof) and I find it difficult to keep one eye on the script and one on the monitor screen to see how closely I am meshing. Indeed, only a frog would be comfortable at it, so Lamoreaux had devised a technique by which he conducted me via a series of kneadings and tappings on my shoulders, signaling for everything from presto through allegro assai to largo as the occasion demanded. We launched into this one about five minutes before its actual scheduled appearance and were proceeding smoothly when the kneads and taps were broken by a convulsive grip and a cry of "Stop!"

The telephone gabbled protests from the open line beside us, but as Bud hastily explained, I had left out one touchdown in my narration and was therefore and thereafter ascribing Crimson successes to the Blue and vice versa.

"Roll back the film," I cried, "I'll write something between the lines," and seizing a Magic Marker I squiggled a spastic conga line in the narrow white alley where the missing touchdown belonged. The film began again, accompanied by kneadings and tappings, and as I approached the black thicket of new material I realized bleakly that my years of progressive school free-form learning were here now to haunt me, and that I could not read my own writing. Hastily I made something up and hoped that panic had not reversed reality, and then proceeded with the typescript. We finished with "in Cambridge" and a last thump on my back, and before I could wipe off that sour sheen of oil with which fear coats the forehead, Roger announced us, and like Little Sir Echo, I came bouncing back from New York.

When one is doing this sort of thing—and all TV correspondents do lots of them, some of them actually live because there wasn't time to take the feed on tape—there is a strong wish to be elsewhere, to be, perhaps, that medieval journalist, the scholarly monk, sharpening quills for the day's work, the illumination of the first capital letter of one of the Venerable Bede's editorials.

That taste in the mouth, the rusty iron flavor of immediacy, can, however, become an addiction, and after a few weeks of leisurely lapidary work on some Tuesday, for an event which we were readying for Saturday, I found myself longing to get back to making card houses in a hurricane.

Sometimes all the ingenuity and dedication one can bring to a task are struck down by the malfunction of a cog, an equivalent of Ben Franklin's horseshoe nail, the want of which proved so extensively disastrous.

I remember the excitement of Sackets Harbor, New York, when it discovered that CBS News was coming to cover its ice fishing tournament. Sackets Harbor likes to boast that a major naval engagement of the War of 1812 took place off its shores, a boast that is constantly renewed because, since the carronades and long nines fell silent, nothing much else has happened in Sackets Harbor. And now the whole country was going to see Sackets Harbor on a Saturday night.

The TV station in nearby Watertown had, all the previous week, been heralding our imminent arrival. It was news that might have been less riveting elsewhere, but in a territory where the big subject of conversation is the depth of the snow, the announcement "Heywood is coming! Heywood is coming!" was repeated with a fervor usually reserved for heads of state and dress designers.

For a few hours, as we moved over the ice inspecting and filming the mechanically drilled holes, the tip-up fishing gear that signaled a bite with the snap of a blank cartridge or the tinkle of a bell, and the snug shelters full of chili and whiskey in which the contestants huddled, I had a little of the feeling of what stardom is like and why it is so agonizing to have to give it up when the pinwheel of publicity goes dark and becomes the wheel on which happiness is broken. I won't say there was any reverential touching of the hem of my garment, and no one asked me to put my hand on a child to ward off the king's evil, but I posed with innumerable people for pictures that were to prove intimacy with the mighty, and gave out autographs no less treasured because they were barely legible, since my aforementioned handwriting loses something more when inscribed on an unbraced paper napkin.

My wife, playing Elizabeth Taylor to my Richard Burton, found it hard to believe that on the trips she didn't get to take I was more used to hotel clerks saying, "No reservation for you, Mr. Brown," and to people on the street wondering if I was the comedian in the movie whose camera had attracted their curiosity.

The adulation, on this occasion, so filled the frame of anything we tried to shoot that Jane and I were banished to the edge of the lake, there graciously to receive the populace while the crew got on with its work.

That work returned to New York with us, was given to the lab and shown to us in the viewing room, where ten minutes during which we kidded ourselves that we were looking at the world's longest strip of clear leader film was succeeded by knowledge, colder than the ice at Sackets Harbor, that we had three thousand feet of celluloid window pane—that owing to some accident in the developing bath, our whole story existed only in memory and in those photographs which, I am sure, were torn up when the news of the disaster was broadcast. Bud had the unhappy task of calling Watertown and telling our new friends there that Sackets Harbor could go back to gloating over the disasters of the British Navy. There was a pause after he conveyed this, and then the Watertown news director said in a wondering voice, "I thought mistakes like that only happened at little stations like ours."

"No," said Bud with sad wisdom, "at big places like networks, we make big mistakes."

Some years later I went back to Sackets Harbor for the ice fishing tournament, endured the jokes about the possibility that the camera was empty, and at last gave air time to the men and women who, with alcohol and ear flaps as their only advantage over the emperor penguin, sally out on the ice in search of sport.

Thinking back on the ten years of Saturday stories, however, I do wonder sometimes whether television, by its very nature, doesn't quickly fade from the bright-colored pictures that preserve excitement to the steady, clear, meaningless light of oblivion. There is so much TV, piling memory on memory until the whole thing falls through the attic floor and drops to the cellar, where mildew mars it beyond recognition.

Sitting and reminiscing about the ten turbulent years that followed the cold disapproval of my first weeks at CBS News, I often find terrifying gaps in the progression, as if six months at a time had stayed too long in the developing bath, but with the help of many more memories than mine, a lot of those gaps will be filled in the following chapters, with others left to the ultimately merciful mantle of the mildew. Since it is unhealthy to live too much in the past, I am happy to report that the pendulum that began swinging when I was simultaneously the football manager and the secretary of the Little Theater Club is still moving through its graceful arc, and that recently several people, unaware that I ever had any connection with sport, have asked me, "Aren't you the man who married Chuck and Donna on the soap opera 'All My Children'?"

It may be too late for Hamlet but I have a lot of bright-colored coats if any summer theater producer needs a Mr. Akins. And later, of course, there'll be Lear.

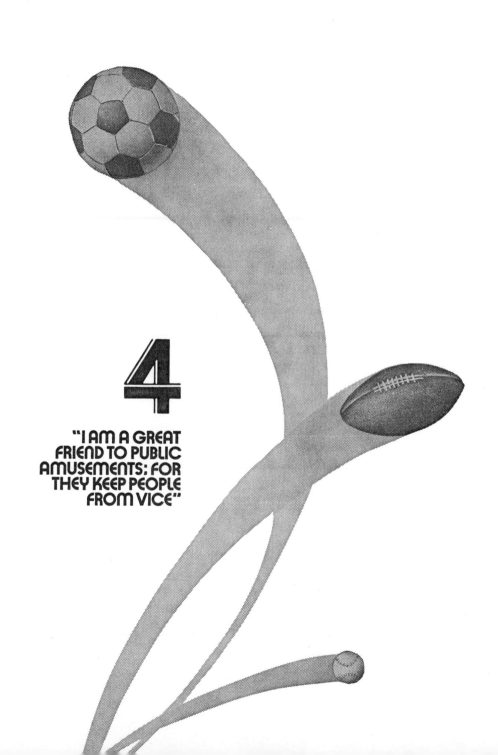

4

"I AM A GREAT
FRIEND TO PUBLIC
AMUSEMENTS; FOR
THEY KEEP PEOPLE
FROM VICE"

Baseball was CBS VP Gordon Manning's favorite game, and from TV's "bland is beautiful" point of view, there was much logic to the blizzard of memos in which he urged the virtues of the national pastime. The Gordograms, as they were called, would be particularly numerous and pressing after stretches in which the Broun Saturday essay had concerned itself for two or three successive weeks with the kind of fringe-sport pieces—horseshoe pitching, the national marbles tournament, or Japanese aikido in a Manhattan dojo—Lamoreaux and I delighted in. Gordon felt that such stuff added distinction to TV news in the way that oregano spices up a stew—and that it should be used just as sparingly. Meat and potatoes are, after all, the bulk of the dish, and Gordon felt there was a whole world of solid stuff about earned run averages and slugging percentages that we seemed to be passing right by on our way to the Indian Rodeo and Root Festival.

When the Gordograms began to come with clippings attached extolling individual diamond performances, Paul Greenberg would call in Lamoreaux and say, "I guess it's time to do a Bill Bradley."

(Just back from Oxford and apparently made up of equal parts of rectitude and ambition, Bradley had given us the dullest interview we had ever recorded. To be fair, he has since become a suave and polished sort of fellow, but our interview was pretty much Cotton Mather in satin shorts.)

Subsequent to his basketball career Bradley began the climb that early on had been predicted for him by winning election to the United States Senate. Political writers can now, from time to time, "do a Bill Bradley," but I suspect that the stuffiness we noticed will go unremarked in Washington, where it has the kinder name of statesmanship.

We would, in such cases, be off for the stand-up opening on the dugout steps, the interview behind the batting cage: "There's no substitute for hustle. . . . I found I'd been trying too hard for home runs. . . . I've picked up a screwball . . . a palm ball . . . a fork ball, and it helps me keep them guessing. . . . I think I can play another five years if I keep in shape. . . . I play where the manager tells me. . . ." and then, mercifully, "I have to hit now."

When I did my first baseball piece for CBS News, when I was still acting in *The Philadelphia Story,* I was reminded again of the wisdom of Jimmy Dawson's remark about putting away that pencil.

I did an interview with Eddie Mathews, then closing out a distinguished playing career with Atlanta, and when it had plodded to its predictable close, Eddie saw the cameraman remove the magazine and immediately launched into a sparkling and witty monologue, filled with anecdotes of the most engaging sort and finishing off with a series of imaginatively erotic questions, which he suggested I might have asked him. Inside that cookie-cutter image the game encourages, there is, after all, some real yeast.

To use the bakery image once more, it could be said that our interview with the late General William Eckert, the Millard Fillmore of baseball commissioners, was, as far as yeast was concerned, sheer matzoh.

The commissioner, after the announcement of his appointment and the requisite accompanying fanfares, had found that he was getting about as much publicity as a New York City Water Board member and, perhaps for the same reason, that he wasn't doing anything. He let it be known among the networks early in 1966 that he was open for a hard-hitting interview in which he would speak plainly and with refreshing candor. The only requirement was that questions must be submitted in writing some days in advance so he could decide what matters he was going to hit hard and with what degree of refreshing candor.

We succeeded in persuading him that the written questions business wouldn't wash, pointed out that he could always refuse to hit hard if he didn't like the question, and prevailed on him to let us take him to the ball park and interview him in a field box. Once he got over the shock of being picked up in a taxi instead of in a limousine or staff car, he thawed a bit and began hinting that things would go more smoothly if we could rehearse the interview a few times on the way to the game. Talking him out of that one took until we were ready for the interview. This proved an exercise in missed bunts, the real meat of which was that he liked baseball better now that he had good seats.

Poor man, he did his job as well as he was let, but he does exist in my mind as the example in excess of the flannel that once clothed the athletes and now seems to swaddle the game.

In fact, of course, baseball is among the most emotional of sports. That very slowness of which some fans complain is twisting the nerves of players as they seem endlessly to contemplate the possibilities of triumph, defeat, or disgrace that are possible with every pitch. It is true that the very length of the season seems to even out the emotional strain and, except for a little yapping at the beginning of the game, there is none of the battlefield prayer-meeting atmosphere that goes with weekly football, but the beautiful balances of the game produce a sawtooth of success and failure. The agonies of Tantalus are as nothing compared to the frustrations of a hitter feeling the air where, a millisecond before, a curveball had irresistibly invited him.

It was, however, the frustrations of a pitcher that most painfully illustrated for me the emotional pressure behind the professionaly blank faces and the mandibular rhythms geared to tobacco or bubble gum.

Robin Roberts pitched in the major leagues for nineteen years and unlike most colleagues of similar professional longevity never picked up any of the guile that can be substituted for the inevitable dimunition of youthful power. In other words, he threw pretty much nothing but fastballs when he came to the Phillies in 1948, and he was still doing it in 1968, when, at the age of forty, he was pitching in Reading, Pennsylvania, for the Eastern League, in one last try to find the lightning that had so long illuminated his life.

The whole atmosphere in Reading was Wagnerian. It's an old town with a lot of graceful formal architecture, buildings once fashionable but now likely to be housing consortiums of feeble little businesses and desperate little lawyers. The analogy between their decline and Roberts's depressed me all the way to the ball park, a place that depressed me not because of any high-toned imagery but just because it was so starkly seedy.

To the young players who staff such teams this seediness is incidental, like the ugliness of bus stations from which one goes to the beach or the mountains. For Roberts, the gritty dressing room ornamented with oozing water pipes might well have seemed like that place where went those warriors who had been denied Valhalla.

When the game began we were on our way to an inspiring piece about determination defeating advancing age. The smoothness of the old star's delivery and the simple aura of his reputation fuzzed the keenness of young batting eyes and the camera recorded an expanding Roberts, a man enjoying his job, as he always had, and not caring that he was doing it on the edge of baseball's outback.

Ambition soon sharpened young eyes, however, and suddenly and horribly Roberts was being relentlessly battered, his not-quite-fast balls rattling off the tin fences, while the kids circled the bases in curiously embarrassed silence. The ordeal seemed endless. The minor league manager was reluctant to relieve Roberts, while Roberts could not bear to walk off the mound and out of his dream into a world of executive training, sales meetings, and speeches at sports banquets. The young players felt sorry, but not sorry enough to quit belting those fatally straight pitches. It was like seeing Manolete being knocked repeatedly into the dust and blood of a provincial bullring.

All the while the camera was recording the now sadly altered story, and it was toward that camera that Roberts eventually walked, his face that of a man whose heart is caught between blocks of dry ice, to say with awful politeness, "I'm sorry I couldn't give you a better show." I don't remember my reply, but I assume it to have been kind, thoughtful, and quite meaning-less.

In baseball, more than in any other sport, the loss of a place in the game is the loss of a complete life. Infinitely more demanding of skill than any other of our physical pastimes (I don't count hockey because we haven't done much with it), it takes up the waking hours of its practitioners from small boyhood till the moment one is sundered from the last of a succession of families by that "get out" official letter, which, in a characteristic baseball euphemism, is called a "release."

Sometimes it comes early, sometimes late, but it almost always leaves a long stretch of life in which the endless attention to the nuances of craft are suddenly pointless, resulting in too many hours for fishing, drinking beer, and working at the dull trades of the rest of the world.

Once we did a story on a last chance tryout camp run by the Montreal Expos. Young bonus players who had been dropped by other baseball organizations were invited to come at their own expense and have a try at proving that human judgment had been fallible. Remembering that Proust's work had been rejected by publisher's reader André Gide, that George Meredith had told Thomas Hardy to stop writing, and that the Detroit Tigers had given up on Carl Hubbell, the kids swarmed to the camp, some sleeping in their cars and pretty nearly all of them fueling their hopes on the fatty tissue of fast-food hamburgers.

I think three of the hundred-odd finally signed minor league contracts, but one of them remains in my mind for the simple starkness of his approach. Jim Hefflinger, one of a pair of brothers who had spent two years trying to find out what happened to the flicker of their early promise, had been turned away from every level of organized ball but was still grinning and running out hopeless ground balls when I asked him why he was spending money on a chase as futile as his hitting.

"That's easy," he said, "I'm only twenty and I got a whole long life to pile furniture in a warehouse."

At forty, Robin Roberts had better prospects than Hefflinger in the business world, and enough behind him to merit his eventual elevation to the Hall of Fame, but at the moment he walked off the diamond in Reading he might have considered trading all of it for the optimistic outlook of the young stock clerk.

Remembering that Gordon Manning always used to point out that people turned to sport to escape gloom, I'll now stop spreading it, and tell a cheerful story which took Lamoreaux and myself four years to film, at the rate of two days a year.

A four-line item in the *Washington Post* brought to our

attention a black high-school player in Ruston, Louisiana, who pitched no-hitters and hit home runs. There are a great many such high-school players, most of whom end up in furniture warehouses talking baseball, but Ruston is hard by Shreveport, maybe the best town for food in America now that New Orleans is fooling conventioneers with "La Viande Glacé a la mode de Kapoque," and we decided to have some crayfish and a look at the young prospect.

Ruston is a remote town, and Lincoln, the then all-black school for which James Rodney Richard pitched, seemed remote from Ruston, a building set down in the middle of a big farm. The games we saw played on the bumpy field had crude farm-boy strength, but Richard had the grace that makes strength the agent of art. The camera showed that he released the ball too soon and displayed a number of other deficiencies not unnatural in a seventeen-year-old, but his six-foot eight-inch body moved with an assured and purposeful arrogance that comes with the genes or not at all.

We visited the Richard home and met the parents, who toiled at the back-breaking rural jobs that look so good in TV commercials where work is just a means of working up a thirst, and we inspected the meadow where J. R. learned to play.

I would like to spend a year bringing Little League coaches to this field and making them sit silent and observant of the proceedings. At some point in years past a game had begun here, employing two old apple trees as bases and an embedded stone as home plate. An apple branch, polished with use, was employed in hitting rubber balls in varying states of repair to all corners of the field and as nearly as I could tell, players who hit a long shot could, like cricketers, make more than one run while the ball was being pursued through the weeds.

From first light to dark on every possible day, teams of various sizes made up of players of various sizes were in continual action, and the score was roughly calculated at the end of the day, usually being in the two or three hundred run range.

Older girls and boys, including even the mighty J. R., who had now been seen and approved by numerous major league scouts, played and used the dignity of their ages to settle disputes, so that no umpires were needed. No parents were present and no hardware stores advertised themselves on the children's backs. On the other hand, considerable skills were learned which are unavailable in the minipro atmosphere of organized infant sport. Jumping over cow flops and leaping off hummocks in pursuit of a flying tennis ball makes, eventually, some awesome outfielders, while fielding ground balls that carom off boulders like the steel spheres in a pinball machine is the way to become a shortstop for whom infield pebbles hold few terrors.

To those who believe that TV correspondents are constantly tempted by bribes and favors to use their magic lanterns in the causes of special interest, I must confess that James Rodney gave me a lamp which he had made in shop, and that it still stands beside my bed, but I defend myself by saying that he gave it to me after we had done the story, and anyway, I am saving it to give to Cooperstown, where I expect, eventually, to see him honored.

The following year, Richard, who had signed with the Houston organization, was at Cocoa, Florida, in the lowest minors. We continued our story there and found him pitching through swinging rubber tires and taking care of a wife and baby. He was just emerging from the cocoon of a fairly uncomplicated boyhood and a few threads of awkwardness still clung to his social manner. We were told that Houston had paid him a substantial bonus and thought well of him. This was borne out in the third year of our serial when he jumped up a step to the top minors with the Triple A Oklahoma City team. Changes were now visible in more than J. R.'s pitching style. He had grown an Afro, bought a dashiki, and learned to play pool. His sense of himself extended beyond the simple prides of strength and agility, and the eye of his mind could see a world much bigger, if perhaps somewhat less pleasant, than the apple tree meadow in Ruston.

Few of us run very far from home, however, and J. R. prepared Louisiana-style meals from his mother's recipes for his teammates and when the smoking platter came to the table he asked a traditional family blessing on it with none of the slightly self-conscious piety of those to whom faith is akin to good manners and proper dress.

We went to see J. R. again when he had risen to the top with the Astros, and found him brooding slightly under the vigorous instructions of Leo Durocher, whose lectures often made up in energy what they lacked in clarity. Richard and Durocher survived each other, however, and as I write, J. R. is leading the National League in strikeouts, has had a twenty-game winning year, and is, I hope, still cooking well and blessing the product. I doubt that I'll be there with a camera crew when he walks off the mound at his personal Reading, Pennsylvania, and therefore I send a message in advance. You were always a treat to watch, J. R., agreeable to talk to, and the lamp works fine. I hope, too, that the last day will be one of your choosing and not one circled in black by Father Time.

I hope, too, that your inevitable twilight is not as awful as that of Larry Bearnarth, a pitcher we interviewed in Evansville, Indiana, the county seat of Vanderburgh County, birthplace of race caller Chic Anderson, world headquarters of Atlas Van Lines, and home of the Evansville Triplets baseball team. Bearnarth was thirteen days short of eligibility for the major league pension when—"The manager of the Milwaukee Brewers told me that there was no further use for me there, and he said I should come down here and pitch the rest of the season . . . and they had an exhibition game here the other day, and they left me here and went to Detroit without me. I came out of the clubhouse after the game and had to cross these railroad tracks and I had these two suitcases in my hands, and just as I was about to cross the tracks a hundred-car train came by. . . . I was standing there when the Milwaukee Brewer bus pulled up to the same interchange and I guess it looked kind of sad for them to see this guy that was just let out, you know, Tobacco Road type stuff, standing there with my two bags and they're waiting to get across the tracks, too."

There is a splendid understatement in Bearnarth's remark about the sadness of the sight as seen from the bus. What the great cold metal side of the departing future looked like to him is left unspoken and is therefore more painful.

Bearnarth made it across the tracks, but he never got on a bus to Milwaukee or to any other town where thirteen days meant more than just treadmill time.

Baseball is, of course, more than anything else a game of statistics, the most measurable and the most measured of sports. If Bearnarth had had a better earned run average than

18.00 for the three innings he pitched for the Brewers in '71, if his lifetime mark had not been 13 and 21—although for a man who had done almost all his pitching for the Mets that wasn't too bad—he might have gotten his thirteen days and been entitled to $175.00 a month at the age of forty-five.

Yet I think it is the endless figures of baseball that are largely responsible for its fascination. Aldous Huxley once wrote a story called "Eupompus Gave Splendour to Art By Numbers." It appeared that in his fascination with the mystic nature of numbers, Eupompus, a fashionable portrait painter in classical Alexandria, took to painting huge canvases covered with identical small objects, which his followers, called philarithmics, reverently counted.

"To count and to contemplate are the same thing," they proclaimed, and thereby set the tone for most modern baseball scholarship.

The late Tom Swope, a Cincinnati baseball writer, used to have in his cellar every box score of every major league baseball game ever played, and on rainy days, or even on some good ones, he used to go down there and read them, a perfect Eupompian pastime.

Ask a question about the arts and you cannot help but get a lot of round, imprecise words that are hard to sort into a pattern; ask about politics and you will get sonorous abstractions; ask about life and you get a subjective lecture from someone who probably hasn't lived enough of it to be worth listening to; ask about baseball and there it is, crystal clear.

"He hit .320, with good power, thirty-seven home runs and ninety-three RBIs, had a good arm, eight assists on the year, but lacked speed, stole only two bases."

Frank Conroy, an actor with whom I worked in his old age and my youth, had, in his youth, gone about asking people who had seen Edwin Booth, the Laurence Olivier of the nineteenth century, what was so special about him. They all said he was the greatest they had ever seen but when pressed by Frank could only come up with unsatisfying stuff about how "natural" he was or what a "nice" voice he had. If Booth had been with the old Cincinnati Red Stockings or the New York Knickerbockers, teams that were contemporaries of his, we would have had a pretty good line on Edwin and could have stacked him up against Beerbohm Tree or Edwin Forrest when picking our All-Star team.

By our identification with baseball we acquire these reassuring numbers at secondhand. Look, for instance, at the old service elevator man in your office building who wears the cap of the team he loves. On winning days he hums as he pursues his shapeless work. His team has shape, a winning streak that has carried it to first place. He will tell you about it, beginning "We are hitting all through the lineup. . . ." If things are going badly he will be depressed, but there is always some individual player who is doing well and can form the matter of his discourse. If the worse comes to worst, as in the days of the old Mets, one can enjoy Eupompian black humor and cry, "We are number twenty-four!"

Numbers, then, dot baseball conversations and baseball literature as raisins dot the better rice puddings, and the baseball broadcaster depends for his between-pitch material on that clipboard of ready-reference statistics, many of them odd and arcane but all of them vaguely comforting in their precision.

Clipboard morsels run from the purely professional, "You'll be interested to know that Randy has the seventh best record in the league for hitting against left-handers with men on second base," to the warmly personal, "Last year Randy was chosen Baseball Father of the Year in his hometown of Tainted Forks, Texas. Teammates say he's the best chili cook in the bigs." After all, one cannot continue to say "The count is two and two" ever and ever until it becomes three and two, although sometimes it seems as though that is happening.

This then is the traditional stuff one talks or writes about the game or describes on the air. Logic dictates that the more impressive the numbers the more time and space is given to the players involved and the flow of advisory Gordograms was always directing our attention to some temporary demigod low in ERA or high in RBI.

What does an interviewer do, however, when he discovers that the demigod is a dead bore and that there is a fascinating and amusing subject who must be done quickly before his numbers drop him out the bottom of the game?

Such a one was, of course, Larry Bearnarth. Another piece I

enjoyed doing concerned itself with the career of Eddie Stanky as a college baseball coach at the University of Southern Alabama. I had interviewed Eddie when he was managing the Chicago White Sox and found that he resembled a boiling pot on the edge of a rickety stove. Make a wrong move and there would be crashing, scalding, and steam. He was voluble and interesting on that occasion but a routine postinterview discussion on the art of film cutting suddenly dissolved into an intense and menacing warning of what would result were we to edit his words in such a way as to alter his meaning.

"Remember," he cried as we departed, "I'll come after you with lawyers, do you hear me?—lawyers."

I couldn't think of any possible distortion that could be made of our discussion, which had been an all-of-a-piece talk about managerial tactics. To rearrange it would have been no more than to stir a spicy stew, but I realized there existed in Stanky a need for combat which playing had fulfilled but which sitting in a covered ditch watching other people play sometimes left unsatisfied, hence the need to mock up an occasional OK Corral.

When Eddie renounced all the high-level calculation and contention of a major league command post for the red clay campus of a school whose principal distinction was that it could put USA on its athletic uniforms, it was as if some swaggering Florentine bravo had walked out of Piazza dei Signore to turn up after a while running an orphanage in Calabria.

We found Eddie actually gardening at his home in Mobile, Alabama, he who had always thought of grass as something to rip up with spiked shoes, and I thought the whole story worthwhile just for the magic moment when, with a gentle smile, Eddie drew a student base runner aside and began his instruction with the soft phrase "May I make a suggestion?"

Later in the piece he is seen disclaiming distress at the sight of an outfielder dropping the ball: "I've seen the great Willie Mays and Mickey Mantle drop routine fly balls. . . ."

Only at one moment did the old Stanky peep out, when, in a doubleheader with Kalamazoo, in town for four games in two days, a visitor hit a perfect double-play ball that would have ended a bases-loaded situation except that it bounced directly in front of Eddie's shortstop, appeared to pass directly through him, and bounced many times behind him. For a moment

Stanky's face was a mask of molten iron. His incisors seemed to grow and curve and I thought he might leap on the boy and tear out his throat, but in a moment the fangs withdrew, the iron cooled and softened, and there, growing slowly and painfully, was the smile you see on Saint Sebastian's face as he speculates that his rough past as a Roman soldier may be atoned for by the arrows that dot his torso.

I once did a fairly straightforward interview about pitching techniques with John Maloney, which was lent some piquancy by the fact that Maloney was ninety-two years old at the time and about to take the mound in a Kids and Kubs game in St. Petersburg, Florida. To be a Kid or Kub you have to be seventy, and John, about to achieve twenty-year status in what is obviously a tough league for such an accomplishment, had lost the edge of his speed and had to depend on guile to get by. He had quite a lot of guile, but then so did many of his lively old teammates. On one soft grounder a second baseman, whose knees gave off a flourish of castanets as he moved, managed to get in front of the ball, but having clawed it up, suddenly fell motionless on the grass. Full of solicitude the base runner went over to the fallen man.

"Are you all right, Sam?" he asked, and possible tragedy suddenly became low comedy as a suddenly active Sam triumphantly cackled, "I'm okay but you're out!" and tagged the samaritan.

If it seems time for a few numbers I can tell you that Jack Wernz was leading both Kids and Kubs with a batting average of over .700 and that it seemed a little unfair for him to go racing around among those genial creakers, looking like a greyhound among bulldogs, but since he was seventy-five, there was no way to make him wait until time slowed him up a bit.

A number that seven major league teams believed would never happen was the record 1,070 games in which Hoyt Wilhelm appeared over twenty-one years in the big leagues, a record that puts Hoyt up there with John Maloney in the sheer dint department. Released or virtually given away by the Giants, Cardinals, Indians, Orioles, White Sox, Angels, and Braves, on the grounds that old age had finished him, Hoyt was just under fifty when he reached the record thousand with the Cubs, throwing as he had for many years the effortless knuckle-ball which he called a fingertip ball.

I mention Hoyt because our piece about him was perhaps the only contribution that our part of the CBS Saturday News ever made to science. To my limited, liberal arts mind, science has only one useful role to play in our time: to discover how to get rid of the garbage that its abundant technology has created. It has already fulfilled its other two great roles, the invention of pain killers and the printing press.

You can see that I am not the man to say something learned about the laboratory, but I did at least provide the commentary for some super-slow-motion film that proved scientifically what hitters have already learned painfully, that a knuckleball wabbles in flight and once wabbling, no one, including the pitcher, can predict its course. This is obviously a chance for some philosophy about the wabbles in the road of life, but most people who deal with the knuckleball are too busy bathing bruises for such abstract speculations.

One abstract speculation that shouldn't be allowed to wisp away without consideration concerns the regional and national differences in baseball. It first occurred to me in 1947 in Havana when the Cuban population resolutely ignored what was supposed to be the big event, the arrival of a major league team for a whole season of spring training, something that hadn't happened since the days of John McGraw's Giants.

The reason for the lack of interest in the Dodgers was the fierce finish of the local professional season in which four teams were tightly locked. Watching the Cuban teams play, I realized that there are many areas in any game that are governed by the ambience in which it is played, almost as much as by the rule book with its international universals.

One of the social crimes in American baseball, until black and Hispanic players committed it so often as to gain it grudging acceptance, has been "show boating," or "hot dogging," that is, playing with a defiant flourish that eschews the safest way of doing things in favor of the most dashing. In our sports fiction, the measure of our ideals, the hero, is always both modest and earnest, and the colorful characters who supply the humor are relief pitchers and utility infielders.

But can one imagine a modest, earnest bullfighter? But then can one imagine Dick Rover patting the bull on the nose, then turning in his ballet slippers to let the sun flash on his sequined suit while he accepts the tribute of tossed roses?

Cuban baseball was full of veronicas executed with the glove, and batter's box pirouettes that would have brought olés from Andalusian gypsy dancers, but it also had a fierceness that led to a good deal of gunfire during the season's deciding game.

I saw the same fine metamorphical capework when, for CBS, I went to Hiram Bithorn Stadium in San Juan to have a look at Puerto Rican baseball, but the turns in the game that would have set off a battle in Havana seemed more likely to start a conga line through the aisles. The San Juan Senadores and the Santurce Cangrejeros, representing different sections of the same urban area, were the equivalent of the old Brooklyn-New York rivalry between the Giants and Dodgers, but the atmosphere was as far from the Polo Grounds or Ebbets Field as the *pastelillo* (burning coals wrapped in dough by the taste of it) is from the ball-park frankfurter. The raucous sounds of the old Dodger Symphoney performed the same function as the modern electronic bugle call. They were spurs to action, war cries arranged for instruments. The music at Bithorn was almost always of a celebratory nature and indeed, if the drumming was particularly good, the dancers might miss two or three hitters in their pleasure at the progress of the choreography through the aisles. The players were aware that although victory was paramount, winning without style was meat without gravy, and they tried to be as colorful and unpredictable as the Cangrejeros' mascot, a giant ribbon-bedecked crab who scuttled about on top of the dugout at the end of a leash. Cangrejeros means crab catchers, and the symbol put Santurce ahead of San Juan, who had not persuaded a senator to scuttle about on top of their dugout.

Sitting imperturbably amid all this Caribbean revelry was the Santurce manager, a small man who had spent nearly two decades in baseball without getting near the big leagues and who, three years later, was to win the first of three straight pennants with Baltimore. Earl Weaver is, when not in a tearing temper, a philosophical man aware that when he took the big job, he had surrendered security.

"I would always have had a place in the Baltimore organization as a minor league manager, and always a winter job in Puerto Rico," he once said to me wistfully. "Now if I don't keep producing, I'll have a lot of time to spend in my vegetable garden."

Of course, highly motivated people like Weaver always go where destiny calls them even if it be to the top of some uncomfortable Everest, where there is nothing to contemplate but one's own success, but I think what he misses most about the old days may be those tropical battles that were half baseball and half block party.

Even within the American baseball structure there are startling differences in responses among the fans, with the inevitable concomitant differences in player attitude.

I think it is important that a team represent a definable community, and suspect that the relative lack of success of such outfits as the California Angels and the Texas Rangers is that they do not engender any violent neighborhood support. Doing stories about the Angels I always seemed to be running into orange juice and tennis types who were studying to be investment counselors when baseball was over. I don't imagine Gene Autry's scouts sought out just this sort of man—although what Autry's scouts were looking for has been the subject of much discussion—I think it is rather that the players were fitting themselves into a sort of endless suburb, in the middle of which they played to a revolving collection of fans largely made up of those who were going to Disneyland tomorrow or had been yesterday and wanted to see a ball game before returning to the Middle West and real life.

The most intense example of community identification was, of course, the Brooklyn Dodger team, which was the lance point for the frustrations of a community besieged by the armies of derision. When the Dodgers played the Giants, representing the hated world across the river, it was Ghibellines against Guelphs, Spartans against Athenians, or, depending on which side you supported, Good against Evil.

Shreveport, Louisiana, to me is the place where you can get the best food in America, which seems distinction enough, but I remember the touching pride of the town when, during the brief life of the World Football League, it had its own big-time club, the Shreveport Steamers.

Teams seem to polarize a town's sense of itself, so that New York, in some of its darker days, forgave and reelected its mayor, John Lindsay, for the irrelevant but significant reason that the Mets had won the World Series. That governors will benefit from the successes of state-named teams seems dubious. States, except Delaware and Rhode Island, are too big.

Until a series of mean-spirited administrations rooted it out, the Yankees had a quality that was definitely geared to the sophistication of the city in which they played, even though they may have stepped away from the plow to get there. Tailored suits, beer in glasses, bridge instead of poker, and power baseball were part of the Yankee picture. Bunts, hits and runs, and stolen bases were considered more suitable to scrambling little teams from scrambling little towns.

Once when Charley Dressen, newly a Yankee coach, was protesting an umpire's decision by throwing towels out of the dugout, Joe DiMaggio told him to stop it and go out to collect the towels.

"When the Yankees don't like a decision, Charley," said DiMaggio, "we don't throw towels, we go out and hit some home runs."

Strong personalities like DiMaggio's, Babe Ruth's, or Ted Williams's leave echoes behind that affect the way teams play long after the hero has fumbled through his Hall of Fame acceptance speech and has begun to limit his exercise to celebrity golf tournaments.

When Ted Williams was casting flies with a good deal more skill than he had employed in catching them, the Red Sox continued, temperamentally at least, to come from the mold that, unfortunately, had not been broken after Ted was made. This meant a team made up of strong individualists who thought largely about hitting, men to whom a glove was just something you had to wear between chances to get more hits. The pitching staff got little attention and had earned run averages that looked like the inflation rate.

Moe Berg, the scholar-catcher, once recalled an archetypical Red Sox moment for me, a day in 1939, Williams's first year in Boston. With the elderly Lefty Grove pitching one of his last great games, the Sox had gone into the ninth inning with a 2–1 lead based on two homers by Ted. In the visitors' ninth Williams dropped a fly ball in left field and Boston lost, 3–2. In the grim dressing room, Grove, a passionate man, was relieving his feelings by bending the steel door of his locker and shredding his uniform when a lark-happy Williams bounded in crying, "I certainly belted those two right on the nose!"

In the shocked silence that followed, Berg, then a coach, was heard to plead with manager Joe Cronin to send Williams back to the Pacific Coast League.

Managers do not take kindly to suggestions that are not packaged in deferential whispers, and the next season Moe was gone, while Williams remained to hit many more right on the nose and play the outfield like a Buckingham Palace sentry.

The Red Sox have changed since those days, but the last I saw of Williams he was as idiosyncratic as ever, giving managing a try at Washington with a ragbag collection of players, many of whom, in the early days of spring training, he seemed to know only by number.

During our interview I asked the natural questions about how a man who had concentrated so completely on one phase of the game could teach or direct the areas in which he had taken no interest. I noticed that although the agreeable smile still hung undisturbed beneath his nose, his neck seemed somewhat thicker and pinker. I tried to soften the rasp of my persistence with the oil of tact and was in the midst of a question so gracefully circumlocutory that Talleyrand could have used it in his dealings with Metternich, when Lamoreaux suddenly announced that we were out of film. Williams unhinged the smile and went off across the field as I turned to protest.

"I'm not much of a technician," I said, "but I think I've learned the time span of a four-hundred-foot magazine and I doubt we were halfway through."

"You're right," said Lamoreaux, "but I was sure he was going to hit you."

As the neck had continued to grow into a pillar of fire even during my diplomatic ditherings, the same thought had occurred to me, and I had planned a spectacular fall as the blow was launched, feeling that this would have guaranteed a whirlwind finish to a not very interesting piece. Now, of course, I'll never know the action that the blazing nape presaged. Perhaps he would simply have said, "I find, sir, that this discussion is unfruitful and beg leave to withdraw, since further talks would only tend to polarize our respective positions." Or perhaps not.

Much is made by baseball's poets—a group that includes

columnists who like to have something in the bank against emergencies, writers who want to get a day's jump on their vacations, and everyone on rainy days—of the leisurely nature of the game, and, drowsing over my scorebook on a hot August day, I've seen the force of their argument, but World Series time used to be as frenzied for me as it was for ticket scalpers and hot dog men.

In the days before sophisticated tape editing made it possible for a news program to pick selected highlights of the broadcast of the game, CBS News used to take several camera crews, twenty messengers, and a squadron of motorcycle riders to the park, while a group of film editors and lab technicians stood by at the local affiliate station. We had enough walkie-talkies to conduct the Louisiana maneuvers, and at each critical play Bud was calling his camera positions to find out if any of them had been jammed or engaged in reloading as history was being made.

At the end of each half-inning the unfinished magazines were taken off the cameras and carried by the messengers to the rim of the stadium whence they were dropped to the waiting bike riders below for rushing into the bath. The flow of film was endless, and when slow motion, with its prodigal speeding of reels, was being used, heavy.

Once, when we had carved fifteen seconds more than two minutes out of the Cronkite News time and were feeling good with ourselves, Bud and I came out of KMOX-TV, the St. Louis station, Bud dangling a small reel from his finger. A motorcyclist delayed by repairs to his machine looked at the reel and asked about it and Bud said, "That's what we got on the air tonight."

"Do you mean we rode back and forth all afternoon for that?" asked the messenger, unaware that crowding two minutes fifteen seconds of congressional rumination off the Cronkite show is akin to getting a tap dance contest into a cathedral.

On another occasion, in Baltimore, a vital reel fell off the motorcycle and was held for ransom by an old lady who ran out and grabbed it from the street. There were frenzied phone calls to the legal department about the propriety of spending a hundred dollars to free the film—refused whether on grounds of precedent or penury, I don't know—while the police department said they preferred not to be seen wrenching things from old ladies in poor neighborhoods. I believe that the filmnapper was persuaded to take ten dollars out of somebody's pocket on the grounds that in another ten minutes her prize would have been rendered worthless by that principle that condemns yesterday's journalism to serve as wrappers for today's fish.

In 1967, when Boston churches were playing "The Impossible Dream" on their campaniles as the Red Sox struggled toward a final day pennant, we did a daily on-the-spot report from Fenway Park and my spot was a little iron basket that hung from the mezzanine and was designed either for a small photographer, a big child, or as a torture cage like those in which medieval dissidents were kept neither sitting, standing, nor lying down. It continued to be my home during the Boston games of the World Series. I got quite used to it and would have introduced a few of those little touches we bring to our nests, except that my plaster cast made even a notebook an impractical extra bulk.

For a couple of these games the Cronkite News assigned a young producer named Irv Drasnin to work with me, and Drasnin, an athletic intellectual, had done something daring and foolish in a softball game that left him with a cast halfway up his forearm.

When the two of us struggled away from the ball park to go to the studio we looked like a work in progress by the plaster wrap artist George Siegel.

When the Mets won the Series in 1969 Lamoreaux reached a career landmark when his five-minute piece actually led the regular evening news broadcast. It included Ike Pappas, looking like *The Stoning of St. Steven* under a hail of clods in Shea Stadium, Sal Marschiano, sticky with champagne in the dressing room, and Heywood Hale Broun as overall coordinator and pontificator.

This was a tremendous accomplishment, as the serious-minded men who put together the week-night news shows classed sports as somewhere between features about the doings of gifted tots, and interviews with rock singers. Ernie Leiser, one of the more wintry of the news chiefs, had a joke at which he always chuckled, repetition costing it none of its freshness for him.

"We've had sports on the show," Ernie would say with a pale, puritanical smile, "Mao Tse-tung swimming in the Yangtze."

I was glad to see us achieve an eminence usually reserved for committee hearings, but a little sorry that the occasion had to be in celebration of a triumph by the Mets, easily the most graceless organization we had to deal with in the years of our World Series coverage.

From time to time the fact that New York City is the center of the communications and advertising power structure is the subject of a thoughtful study on the business pages of the newspapers. I was less thoughtful about it when the whole power structure descended on Shea Stadium and filled to overflowing that area of the press section not occupied by the regulars from the big papers. Endeavoring in any organized way to cover that World Series in New York was as difficult as trying a Scottish sword dance in the bar of "21," and pretty much the same people were getting in the way. Escape to the comparative decorum of the field and the clubhouse was rather a relief.

Covering the Series was, of course, much easier and cheaper, once we did no more than borrow tape, but there are times when I miss the vast creative hooraw that used to go on as Bud struggled for the right footage in a heap of tangled film while I struggled for the right wordage in a heap of tangled thoughts. I think they were better pieces, too, but old stagers are always saying that.

Among the tangled thoughts that remain with me from ten years of baseball for TV news are things like the inspired locker room lunacy of the Pittsburgh Pirates under the leadership of Steve Blass and of some lunchtime shots of Blass's crew in funny hats and an advanced stage of good fellowship that so shocked the Establishment that the funny hats were forever put away.

The stated reason for clamping down on the horseplay was that some of the players had worn World War I German medals, which, according to some sportswriters, made them apologists for the horrors of World War II. This seemed to me a bizarre accusation, but any accusation will send those who depend on public goodwill to cover, and the Pirate management instructed its players to be as dull as their colleagues. I suspect their real crime was in having fun, something that in modern character-building sport is deplored. Much of Joe Namath's bad press, for example, was based on the obvious enjoyment he got out of football.

I remember our covering those same Pirates in one of the first World Series night games, our coverage coming largely from a neighborhood bar with a TV set. The excitement there was much more intense than among the expense accounters at the ball park.

Adding up ten years of baseball for TV news, I remember some odd byways, like watching Japanese minor league rookies as they were led into a real Japanese garden in back of a little department store in Lodi, California, and covering the serious but unsuccessful tryout of a girl first baseman in Connecticut, while the teenage rookies who were her prospective teammates struggled between hostility and that automatic deference to the ladies that so maddens the modern liberated woman.

I'm proud of putting Henry Aaron on the air, a man with the most to lose, in eloquent defense of the baseball strike, and later watching him hit his record 715th and being glad that his splendid disinterestedness had not cost him this triumph.

I remember the voluble good humor of Tug McGraw, who played the game with the high spirits of the kids in the Ruston meadow but was serious enough about his integrity not to take money for his "You gotta believe!" slogan in a TV commercial.

I remember watching my cameraman run out of film during a triple play; I remember filming the odd double life of Nick Colosi, who in winter was a deferential nightclub captain at the old Copa, and in summer a flintily unyielding big league umpire; and I remember a hundred-odd graceful and ungraceful movements on and off the field which sometimes flicker through my mind as if a high wind had run through all the strips of film we had pasted together in our hope of turning out essays as final and graceful as a good double play.

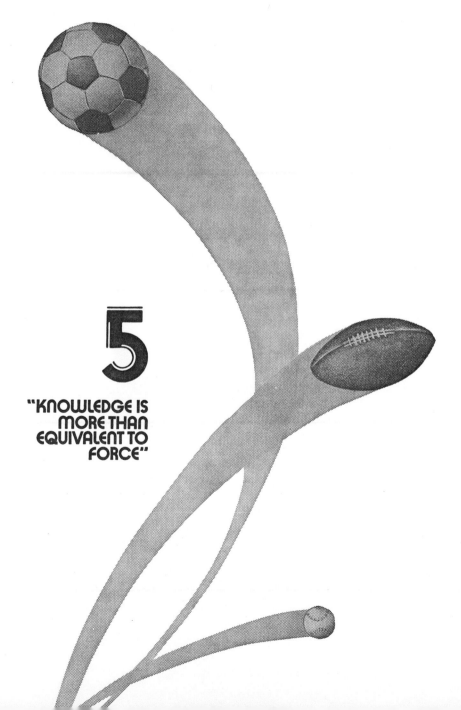

5

"KNOWLEDGE IS MORE THAN EQUIVALENT TO FORCE"

Football has been rousing emotions for hundreds of years in a variety of forms, all having in common the idea of moving a ball from one place to another with varying degrees of violence as the means of propulsion.

When, in 1314, Edward II tried to ban the game "Forasmuch as there is a great noise in the city caused by hustling over large balls, from which many evils may arise," he was tilting at windmills as were Greek moralists who pulled their beards over the roughnesses of the game then called *episkyros*.

Football is, after all, a wonderful way to get rid of aggressions without going to jail for it. I thought of this while watching the game of street football the Florentines put on every year in the Piazza dei Signore to commemorate some civic triumph which now escapes me.

Teams from the four quarters of the city march into the square in gorgeous Renaissance costumes; referees flourish plumed hats at each other, and fifteen minutes later someone from the Western section has been kicked in the shin and has retaliated by tearing an East's ruffles and bloodying his nose. Within half an hour there have been quite a few scores and some of them are being settled in sanguinary fashion as the ball eddies from East to West.

Intellectual cynics think of modern American football as just a ruffianly way of making big money, but this is an oversimplification. I would agree with Bill Curry, the old Green Bay Packer, who said there wasn't enough money to pay for the pain of plunging at Dick Butkus late in a hard-fought match.

Curry said he kept getting up and bouncing off Butkus again because of the strong sense of fellowship that the joint shedding of blood and adrenalin engenders, the desire to throw one's arms around comrades at the end of a successful enterprise. The wish for this strong, if temporary, family feeling will make some men push through constant pain to play a game.

The intensity of the desire simply to play was brought home to me early in my stay with CBS News when a ramshackle minor league team called the Brooklyn Dodgers was assembling a roster. They had picked up a number of NFL old-timers and failed rookies, and as a last gasp held a one-day open tryout at the old Gaelic football field in the Bronx, a barren, bumpy stretch where grass dies under the blank-eyed stares of old subway cars lined up on an adjacent elevated structure.

More than seventy men showed up in varying states of dress and physical readiness, most with football shoes hung round their necks, shoes in which briefly they had felt the ground turn to fiery clouds beneath their feet in some high school or college triumph, a triumph that drives them to one more try for the feeling.

Coach Andy Robustelli was honest in his opening speech, pointing out that though this was a chance, it was a last chance and that those who did not make it here should put the dreams away with the shoes and find some earthbound occupation. It was not the expression of a high opinion of Andy's league, but he's always been a realist, and as a realist he warned the candidates that when they were doing something marvelous he might be looking the other way and that in an unjust world this would be a not unexpected addition to an endless list of injustices.

For two hours we watched, wondering at the self-deception that led most of the men to this minefield of humiliation, and marveling at the fierceness of desire and its tragic inability to overcome such handicaps as shortness of arm, heaviness of foot, and pervasive clumsiness. I saw men leap up for passes with the strained concentration on their faces that turns up in pictures of runners breasting an Olympic tape, and I saw the men miss the passes by as much as two feet.

One perfect football player turned up who passed a spiral as tight as a coil spring and spotted his passers with the ease and accuracy of a carnival shill knocking over wooden bottles. Unhappily, although he gave his height as five feet seven, he came only to my shoulder during our interview, and I am five feet eight. He would have fitted nicely into a pickup game of jockey room personnel.

When it was all over, one soccer kicker had been signed to a trial contract, and whether the unsuccessful took Robustelli's advice, I don't know. I suspect that those old football shoes had a few more futile steps in them.

Nobody, of course, epitomized the fanatical nature of competitive football more than Vince Lombardi, who made of the game a symbol of a life bearing the strange device Excelsior.

I first met Vince in December 1966, when, in search of a little warm weather in which to practice for a playoff game in Dallas, he brought his Packers to Tulsa, Oklahoma, and ran into the same frost that stopped Longfellow's young Excelsior bearer from getting across the Alps. The Swiss mountains, however, are accustomed to snowbanks, while Tulsa had no more snow removal equipment than has the city of Honolulu. The CBS Saturday News was there to do a feature on how the Packers were wrapped and braced for combat, and, with the leader's permission, we were all set up in the bowels of the stadium when the Packer bus arrived—and all the lights went out for five blocks around.

As the players stumbled down the dark stairs, our electrician, on Lamoreaux's instruction, shone a battery lamp on the light-colored ceiling, providing enough illumination for people to move about and enough for us to see Lombardi's face, which looked like the fright mask on a samurai helmet.

Seeing a group of strangers in his dressing room, Lombardi shouted—I interrupt here to set up some ground rules. In these permissive days I could reproduce all of Vince's words without fear of being arrested but they would have a shock value beyond what he intended. I could also use blanks but these take up space and start lurid guessing games. You must just accept that every other word on his side of our ensuing conversation (and of many of our later conversations) was what Penrod Schofield used to call "a vile oath," or in Penrod's spelling, "oth," although many of the words were oaths I hope Penrod had never heard—Anyway, with oaths stripped away, Vince shouted "Get out!" Bud pointed out that we had been given leave to be there by him and that anyway we were providing the only available light. Vince said he didn't care about the light, he just wanted us out of there.

He indicated that he wished we would leave Tulsa University Stadium, the city of Tulsa, and even the state of Oklahoma. He then turned on his heel and dashed into the office provided for him, or to put it more accurately, he dashed into the wall of the office provided for him. The subsequent sounds seemed to be vile oaths in purest form, if that's the right modifier, but at last a request for candles rang through the room, and a terrified janitor scurried off to fumble through a dark storeroom.

I pointed out to Bud that Lombardi's instructions to us were clear beyond the possibility of mistake and that we were still standing within range of the coach's formidable anger. Bud, a better psychologist than I, or perhaps more eager for the story, counseled patience and a waiting game, and in about three minutes Lombardi emerged from the office calm and smiling, told us that he knew he had behaved badly, thanked us for the light, hoped we would be able to supply it for a time even though filming would be impossible without full power, and asked us to join him and his coaches at the evening cocktail ritual where it was known that Lombardi—for a few minutes— actually relaxed.

The evening was an agreeable one, even though at rest Vince had that look of potential danger that one sees in a contented carnivore full of red meat—for the moment.

The next day the lights had been restored, and we were able to guess the coach's dominance as we watched the walking wounded parade as the Packers entered the trainer's room. There, aluminum braces were fitted over knees purple with scars, swellings were pressed into an appearance of normalcy with little corsets of adhesive tape, and a group of men who had been shaken and battered into the rattling looseness of beloved old toys were tightened up for one more Sunday.

Quarterback Bart Starr stood before the trainer with his arm upraised so that a spongy rubber doughnut could be taped against his ribs to protect some torn cartilage. As the gentle fingers softly pressed the resilient rubber against the bruised skin, Starr gave a full-throated shout of pain. The Comanche code of stoicism that forbids groans on the field didn't apply here, but as I looked at Starr, biting his lip as the tape tightened the pressure, I realized that in a few days he would be prepared to stand with that arm upraised in a game, looking for his receiver and waiting, even as he was aware of the onrushing shoulder of a monster lineman, a shoulder armored like the ram of an Algerian pirate galley. If he didn't get the ball away soon that shoulder would hit the doughnut with the effect of a steam hammer on an egg, but one mustn't think about that. One must keep looking for the receiver. Vince wouldn't like it if you didn't keep looking for the receiver.

Victorious in the NFL Championship game—Vince wouldn't have liked it if they lost—the Packers moved on to the Super Bowl in Los Angeles and chose to practice away from the public eye on a field in Santa Barbara. Lombardi announced that no pictures would be allowed, so I was somewhat surprised when Lamoreaux told the crew to get ready for a trip to Packer practice. When I pointed out that for most people, the ukases of Lombardi had the force of the wishes of Genghis Khan, Lamoreaux said, "He owes us something for those lights in Tulsa and he's not the kind of person who forgets."

When we began unpacking beside the field Lombardi ran toward us with the gait and sound effects of a phobic rhinoceros. When he came close enough for recognition he rumbled to a stop and growled in a voice one would use to profaners of the inner temple, "Oh, it's you guys. Okay, but twenty minutes. Got that? Twenty minutes and OUT!" We assured him that this time would amply fill our needs and we were going to go into some further thanks when he turned on his heel and marched toward another cameraman whom he ordered off the field in a tide of scalding words.

"But Vince," protested the man, "I work for you. I'm the Packers' cameraman."

"One camera is enough," snarled Lombardi, "and right now, it's theirs. OFF, OFF, OFF!"

(Like a coloring book, the preceding conversation, like the one in Tulsa, comes ready for you to decorate from the depths of your vocabulary.)

We hurried through our work and on the stroke of the twentieth minute, Lombardi, like the late Zero Mostel, was again visibly turning into a rhinoceros, and only subsided into his normal fury when he saw us pell-melling things into the car.

We met again from time to time and I always felt from him a

certain cautious affability, a remembrance of a difficult day on which we had been helpful, and it became less cautious as it became obvious that Bud and I did not intend further to presume on the small obligation.

Our last meeting occurred on the day he took over the Washington Redskins at their Carlisle, Pennsylvania, training camp. The Skins had the reputation of being a rather jolly and sophisticated bunch who took winning and losing with the insouciance of oil sheiks at a roulette table, and the world was waiting to see how Lombardi, who regarded insouciance as something appropriate to games like lawn bowls, would do with his new charges.

His first words to me on arrival were, "No sound, Heywood. GOT THAT? I want you to shoot everything silent or get out. IS THAT CLEAR? No sound!"

I gave him the pleasant meaningless smile of a poker player looking at a raise, and Bud busied himself with some small task that would keep him away from the conversation. As soon as Vince had returned to his chores, planning began as to how we were going to achieve sound under the eyes of a man who can see a caterpillar yawn and hear a gnat belch.

One could easily see Vince's reasons for wishing to be presented as a vigorous Trappist. It was his obvious intention to use a volume of noise and abuse that would make the rhinoceros no more than a happy nightingale, and although he wished it to burn the Redskins' spiritual flab as Savonarola's sermons burned the hedonisms of Florence, he didn't want the whole nation to hear him in full cry.

Our methods were those of ingenuity rather than underhanded engineering. No ingenious bugs were taped inside helmets or gummed to the water bucket; all that was used in our subsequent piece were a few full-throated roars and such coachly advice as "Throw the ball here. That's where I want the ball thrown. I don't want the ball thrown way the hell up in here. I want you to throw—throw it in here." These admonitions accompanied by illustrative gestures. The vile oaths, although plentiful, were obviously not for the foreseeable future of television.

We knew that Vinnie was watching our soundman to see if he wore the headphones with which the levels are checked when sound is being recorded. The soundman in this case worked by guess, his ears proclaiming their innocence by their nakedness, and occasionally we withdrew from the equipment altogether for a conference, a moment after the cameraman had flicked with his toe the switch on the machine as it lay on the ground. The pictures of shoes were of little use but the sound was there. What we wanted was simply the cutting edge of a voice that could and did drive men to prodigies of physical effort.

I didn't think of myself as some sort of auditory paparazzo or sinister stealer of civil rights, but just as a man completing a portrait, a portrait which was, in fact, highly laudatory, since I always thought of Lombardi, given the philosophical framework in which he worked, as a great man. Setting great store by obedience, however, he never forgave me.

Months later, when Irv Drasnin, a CBS producer, wanted to do something about the Redskins, Vinnie cursed the bewildered Drasnin as if he were an underworld emissary with some unclean proposal about throwing games. It appeared that Irv's corporate connection with me made him unacceptable to Lombardi.

"What did you do to him," Drasnin asked me later, expecting to be told I had stolen a playbook or told dirty jokes in front of Marie Lombardi.

"I recorded his voice," I replied, and my colleague went away shaking his head in wonder.

Vince was iron-hard but basically fair, and when he became something of a conservative idol, I used to wonder what some of his admirers would think if they knew that the rooming lists at Green Bay were made alphabetically and entirely without respect to race. None of the euphemisms about compatibility, which other teams employ, would do for Lombardi. Any Packer should be proud to room with any other Packer.

In our last interview, when I asked whether fun and relaxation were not a necessary relief to the training grind, he said, "I think there's a place for laughter, but certainly not on the field. This is not a laughing business, and out here there's no—there's very little fun on the field. And I might add this: There's no laughter in losing, either."

That's vintage Vinnie, and whether you agree with it or not, you must admit that it marches with the iron tread that took Lombardi's ancestors, in their disciplined legions, to the corners of the known world.

One of the places the Romans never got to was Ireland, which may explain why Duffy Dougherty, despite success in the blood and iron competition of the Big Ten, managed to find a little laughter in his coaching job at Michigan State. When I first met him I noted a white-dabbed cold sore at the corner of his mouth, but he waved away sympathy with the cheerful explanation that the white was the residue of the foam that was natural to the snarling frenzy of coaching. Duffy was full of one-liners, an attribute that the sour philosophy epitomized by Leo Durocher's "Nice guys finish last" ascribes to the unsuccessful. He also encouraged, in R. L. Stevenson's great phrase, "A little judicious levity," among his players, and the first day of practice each week was given over to relaxing horseplay in which tackles were allowed to catch passes and guards to throw them.

Despite all this Monday merriment, Duffy's clubs, playing a big-time schedule, won far more than their share of games, proving once again what most Americans now find so hard to believe—that laughter does not lessen physical prowess. After all, the Scarlet Pimpernel was always all-smiles just before he pinked the gloomy representatives of the guillotine, and in real life Babe Ruth roared homerically all the way to the Baseball Hall of Fame.

Ara Parseghian of Notre Dame, Duffy's great rival, would never have permitted such fun, since he treated each practice as if it were the last chance to perfect the techniques necessary for brain surgery in an open boat.

When I went out to South Bend to interview Parseghian, the only grim Armenian I ever met, the occasion was carefully chosen to minimize strain. In the days of his ascendancy, Parseghian preferred to deal with the press by recording daily interviews which could be heard by calling a machine. Feeling that this would not film well, we asked for an audience during a week when Notre Dame had an easy game, one that could only be lost through food poisoning at the training table. After negotiations of a length and delicacy suitable to high-level border disputes, we were granted a day and, arriving at the locker room, found Parseghian still irritated that we weren't satisfied with his packaged wisdom. At last, in what can only be described as a condescending bark, he said that in about a half hour we could have exactly three minutes, no more, and please be ready. We were, and he was reasonably responsive, after which he went off to lead his players in cheers, which seemed an odd occupation for a man past thirty.

A college coach, after all, is supposed to be a guide to youth, not a classmate or a fraternity brother. For a counselor to join his pupils in the excesses of youthful enthusiasm seemed to me as grotesque as if wise Nestor, the elder statesman of the Athenians at Troy, were to join Achilles in his bouts of pouting and sulking.

You may charge me with inconsistency at this point, since I spoke warmly of Vince Lombardi for displaying the same gritty characteristics that I deplore in Parseghian, but there was a magnificent consistency in Vince, who would never, as Parseghian did, have played calculatedly for a tie against Duffy's Spartans in the so-called National Championship game.

For years disapproving romantics sent pun-intended ugly neckties to Parseghian as a reproach to him for running out the clock in the 10–10 1967 game which was to decide who was mythical Number One. At the end Michigan State was taunting the ball-holding Irish. It was the kind of cheerless efficiency one might expect of Parseghian, whose team was, in fact, awarded the championship MacArthur Bowl.

In football, with its constant imagery of war and atmosphere of sweat and suffering, the Laughing Cavalier seems always something of a fribble who is failing in dedication, yet Lombardi was uneasily aware that Paul Hornung, a veritable D'Artagnan when it came to slashing through great odds to improbable victory, was also a veritable D'Artagnan when it came to wine, late hours, and what, in a less enlightened age, used to be called wenches.

Joe Namath, a veritable apotheosis of fribblehood in the public mind, was, in my experience, a romantic square with the calculation and common sense of a desert dervish in a Holy War.

Joe once said to me with puzzled wistfulness that when he was serious people thought he was kidding, and when he made a joke he got in trouble because it was considered a statement of his philosophy.

A single, now forgotten action of his stamps the man as no statement ever could. When, in a meaningless exhibition game, he was the only New York Jet between the opposing runner and the goal line, he launched himself from the uncertain fulcrum of his patchwork knees, brought down the runner, and finished himself for the year. It was certainly not a mature and thoughtful act, but is sport the place for mature and thoughtful acts? Of course not. Real life is the place for them.

We once did a football piece of such romantic nature that, I have it on the best authority, it made Mike Wallace cry. What was it that brought moisture to the agate eye of the great investigator?

It concerned a man as romantic as Namath and a good deal less talented, Ed Krysiak, who, after twenty-three years of navy service, was a forty-three-year-old grandfather, an undergraduate at the University of New Hampshire, and a candidate for the football team. The coach and Krysiak's wife had said the sensible things to him and he had smiled and successfully gone through the set of physical tests that separate out the impossibles before they can even suit up. His fellow footballers, one of whom had played in high school with Krysiak's son, went through a stretch of addressing him with the condescending "Pop" and, as he persisted in being bruised and beaten up as a third string defensive back, had begun calling him, somewhat more affectionately, "Crazyiak."

Now, it's clear that on the squad or no, Ed was not truly a story unless he actually played in games, and he had, before we arrived, having gotten a respectable number of minutes in contests either widely won or hopelessly lost. Still we had no film of this. You often hear that TV distorts sport to its own purposes, and I guess it was the pressure of the situation that persuaded Coach Jim Root to put Ed into the waning moments of a game that New Hampshire was winning by only 12–7. I like to think that the coach was as romantic as Ed, and put him in not for us TV people, but in the knowledge that competition lacks zest without 'the raw kick of danger sauce, and that after his long and dogged try Ed deserved that bellyful of fire.

The first play after he entered the game was a successful pass over his head and then, thank God, he broke up a go-for-all with a dash and agility that should have brought happiness to every middle-aged man who saw the film. The score remained unchanged, Ed had won a letter on his heart, if not on his chest, and I said, "For the successful in sport, the rewards are fame, fortune, and the symbolically precious crockery of the trophy case. For Ed Krysiak the reward is something else, the sweet surprise of the dream deferred." Mike Wallace wept.

We seemed, Bud and I, for people who were doing light, cheery features, to photograph a lot of tears. Some of the most copious came at the end of the Jets' 1969 Super Bowl triumph. The game will be knowledgeably discussed elsewhere in this book but suffice to say here that at the very end, as the Jets ran off the field, a security man, one of those people who say "Can I help you?" just before they hit you, threw me against the wall with what seemed to me unnecessary violence. Losing my head, I kicked him sharply in the calf and then, as he turned to do the job that brutality training had fitted him for, I recovered my head and ran into the Jets' dressing room. Bud and the camera crew followed, and suddenly we were all alone in the middle of the celebration to which the press was not yet supposed to be admitted. Thus we were able to film one of the great scenes of our decade together. It was Joe Namath, one architect of victory, hugging a little old man in a funny straw hat while he and the little old man beamed love at each other and cascaded tears. The hat was on top of Namath's father and when the two Hungarians had finished laughing and crying, enough emotion had been expended to fuel two gypsy orchestras and a czardas competition.

It has always seemed odd to me that football players who bring high emotion and intense dedication to the game, and who recognize the need for constant sharpening of their skills, are so casual and so inept in their frequent forays into acting. Perhaps the arrogance that sustains them through the agonies of competition gives them the belief that they can do anything, but Joe Namath on the field had the fearful grace of a hunting leopard while on the screen he displays the nervous aimlessness of the leopard's trapped victim.

So, too, O. J. Simpson and Jim Brown, whose perfect timing on the field took them through opposing lines like mercury on a tilted table, do not show a concomitant deftness with the lines of a Hollywood script.

My firsthand look at football players as actors occurred a couple of years ago when a movie was being made from George

Plimpton's book *Paper Lion*. Bud and I went to Boca Raton to make pictures of Alan Alda and the Detroit Lions making pictures.

The sequence being shot when we arrived entailed a good deal of movement as a group of Lions decide to take the young writer masquerading as a quarterback to dinner, and there were a number of crosses and recrosses that had to be done so as to reveal specific speakers at specific moments. The drill was not, however, any more complex than the average end sweep with pulling guards, and the amateur actors' inability to get it right was due largely to the fact that they were treating the whole thing like the first rehearsal of a fraternity musical and convulsing each other with primitive ad libs and physical improvisations that made hash of the necessary patterns.

The director, Alex March, was an old friend of mine. I had met him when he was an actor and I a sportswriter. I had been amazed that this sensitive young man was a sports fan at the uncritical level of the bubble gum card collector, and I was sorry to see that now the bubbles of those early worshipful dreams were bursting into a sticky mess and ruining take after take as the Lions continued throwing chaos at the choreography.

At last, by some miracle, everything went perfectly to the final line, which was spoken by Alex Karras. He was to say simply, "I've got the coat," and put it over Alda/Plimpton's shoulders. The cameras rolled, the players moved so that no line or action was covered, Alex arrived and added an adverb of obscene and unlikely description to the coat.

Gray-faced, March got up from his director's chair and walked off the set, leaving the laughing Lions to pummel Alex in playful rebuke. I followed March and found him leaning his forehead against a cool metal sound truck. In my acting years I had worked under his direction and knew him to be a patient man but one who could be deeply angry when his patience broke. I didn't think it would help to be deeply angry with people like Karras and Roger Brown, who between them had about six hundred pounds of muscle and two ounces of common sense.

"I can't bench them," groaned Alex, "I can't fine them, and I can't trade them. What the hell can I do with them?"

All I could do was to suggest breaking for lunch, a suggestion which, for lack of a better one, he accepted. During the break I sought out John Gordy, a thoughtful man who was, at the time, the head of the NFL Players' Association, as well as a first-rate guard of ten years' experience. I pointed out that when Plimpton had joined the Lions there had been an undercurrent of resentment on the discovery of the masquerade. The players had been told that George was a legitimate candidate for the team, a quarterback from a college sufficiently obscure to have escaped sports page notice.

They felt that Plimpton's pretense was a put-down of their profession and they grumbled at his making a joke of a solemn calling.

Now the roles were reversed and I asked Gordy if Alda resented the fact that an art to which he had given his life, an art in which he was, in their terms, all-pro, was being treated like recess on the last day of school by a bunch of untrained Punchinellos.

Gordy gave it some thought and then came up with a complex but revealing answer.

"I don't think he resents us," he said, "because he would rather be a football player than we would want to be actors. Look at him out there, he's practicing his passes and skipping lunch."

Sure enough, Alda was patiently tossing footballs at a jacket on the ground, paying a respect to their skills which they denied to his. Later I asked him the same question I had asked Gordy and found him as tactful as Daniel or Androcles and for the same reason. He did wistfully admit, however, that he would like to bring off a few plays in first-class style before the movie was finished, and I hope that he did. They seem to have been called back in the cutting room.

The daydream of being a player, the thing that drove Krysiak and finally caught Alda by the arm, was illustrated even further by an otherwise sane, successful family man, a forty-seven-year-old fashion photographer named Al Barrett, selected by Lamoreaux as a fan exemplar. He attended every Giant game and every football luncheon. When the Giants were unreachably on the road, he would set his children up in front of the TV screen in Giant sweat shirts to throw their unheard piping against the far-off cheers of the partisan crowd, while he and his friends hung tensely off the edge of the sofa and the wives lurked in the background ready to rush forward with the halftime cold cuts, as out there trainers would pass through the locker room with the halftime Gatorade.

Bud and I spent several days with Barrett contrasting his mingled lives of firsthand elegance in the high-fashion world and vicarious violence at the Stadium, and I still remember the light in his eyes when he said to me, "When a Giant runs down the field with the ball I sort of run with him, and somewhere inside I'm saying to myself, if I were a little bigger, a little faster, a little braver, it really would be me out there."

For the people who watch it, then, football is often the food of fantasy, and for those who play it there are a variety of fulfillments.

In 1971, after fourteen years of playing linebacker—in school, college, and in the pros—with a savagery that awed even his fellows in ferocity, Dave Meggysey had a change of heart, quit the St. Louis Cardinals in mid-career, and wrote a book called *Out of Their League*.

I had read portions of the then unfinished book before we sought out Meggysey in a Northern California hideaway where he was working on the final chapters and living the Berkeley life of natural foods and designedly noncompetitive exercise like jogging and a little free-form no-score soccer. The chapters on his childhood were bleak accounts of loveless, joyless years on a farm, years in which the anger built inside the boy like smoldering embers under the crust of a forest floor. Then one day in high school he made the great discovery that anger could be ritualized in football, a game which permitted you to do things on the field that you'd get arrested for off it.

In his years at Syracuse and with the Cardinals he earned such attractive nicknames as Mad Dog, and let loose the bottled flames of his rage until suddenly and oddly he was on the revival trail. It was with the highly self-conscious heaviness of the reformer that he opened our interview with "Football addresses itself, or talks about, or articulates—symbolically articulates—some of the worst values in American society. Certainly it is a militarist organization and the glorification of violence within that organization, and if we talk about athletics as a means of self-expression and a means to achieve competence, then it seems to me a little bit inhumane to achieve that notion of competence by defeating another person continually."

He seemed serenely sure that his volte-face was a revelation and that he could leave behind him all that had driven him through the whole of his youth. Remembering that youth, I finally asked him the obvious question: "Dave, the conflicts of your childhood are still in you, stoking up the fire. If you quit playing football, how are you going to express that anger?"

The question was so obvious that he had, as all of us do, kept it just over the rim of consciousness. A troubled look ran over his newly mild features, and he sighed.

"I guess you're right," he said, "but I haven't given it any thought."

He was a kind of test-tube perfect example in the endless debate about whether brutal sport is a release of dangerous repressions, a substitute for war and violence on a larger and more dangerous scale, or a subtle corrupter that makes us view pain and its infliction as too commonplace to justify shock. I hope that Meggysey's new zealotry has been hot enough to keep the flue of his psyche in working order.

There is a phrase in psychiatric jargon, "Well compensated," which means that the cracks in a personality are being papered by some external circumstance such as fame, power, or money. Should these things be withdrawn the cracks may widen into splits, and the person would do well to seek help toward the goal of being "Well adjusted," a state that suggests that one can deal with anything except the basic unreasonableness of life.

Sport, with its fantasies and intensities, obviously is as useful as acting, with its opportunity to win the attention and even love of strangers, in arranging that the flawed are, for a time, well compensated. It should be pointed out, however, that the nature of the two occupations dictates that there are more old actors than old athletes, and that there's usually a lot of life to get through after the uniform has been turned in.

I once had a long talk with another troubled player, George Sauer, Jr., the brilliant pass catcher of the Jets who drifted out of football in search of fulfillment as a writer. I had warmed to him on a day when a couple of loud voices on their way to a hangover had stopped to watch practice. Burping out a disagreeable mixture of whiskey, steam, and venom, they kept shouting that he would never be the man his father, a great all-American, had been, ringing a number of uninteresting changes on this theme.

Sauer ignored them and continued to run his pass patterns, but as he left the field he veered to run past me and murmur, "I've heard of your father, too."

During our subsequent talk I asked how a man of his considerable sensibilities got along in the aggressive world of football.

"You forget," said Sauer, "that I'm not expected to be aggressive. Just the opposite, in fact. As a wide receiver I'm always running for my life, learning that to be an outsider is the ultimate achievement."

In the end, this rationalization was not enough, and George, the loner who was not that well compensated by gladiatorial oneness, drifted out of the game while still at the peak of his athletic power.

It's true, of course, that when we speak of football in other than simple fan terms our approach is almost always a debate on the merits of its martial aspects. The fact that a dancer's sureness of foot and a cheetah's speed are also essentials tends to get lost.

Certainly the most unlikely looking football player that I ever interviewed was Noland Smith, who used to be a kick returner for the Kansas City Chiefs. Noland was about five feet six and weighed about 150 pounds. Despite this he was successful because, skittering downfield like a water bug, he escaped the behemoths as mosquitos escape the ham-fisted slaps of weight lifters. When we took a picture of him feeding his tiny baby a bottle while his wife, who made him feel comfortably large, stood by, and it looked like a domestic scene in Lilliput, and when he sat next to big Buck Buchanan on the Kansas City bench I suddenly thought of a forgotten story from my childhood. It appears, according to this cautionary tale, that Richard the Lion-Heart, meeting Saladin the Saracen in a prebattle conference, endeavored to impress the Arab leader by cutting an iron bar in two with a blow of his broadsword. Saladin then took a silk handkerchief from a pocket, hung it over the blade of his scimitar, and with a flick of his wrist sent the blade upward to freedom as a pair of silk fragments fluttered down.

Of course, Noland and Buck, like the broadsword and the

scimitar, were contrasts toward the same end, victory on the field. In the character of Mike Reid, a tackle at Penn State when I first met him, delicacy and strength were blended in an odd way which I never saw in any other person I met.

When he was not practicing knocking down people, Reid hung over the keyboard of a piano, which he played with considerable distinction. He was, as an undergraduate, just a shade below concert level, interested as well in composition, to which he devoted a good deal of time, and obviously torn between the promise and diversity of careers in music or professional football.

Interestingly, pictures we took of him during a Penn State game did not in the least resemble pictures we took of him on the way to his music lesson or at it.

Game pictures taken on the bench showed his short hair standing up in traditional crew cut style, his jaw thrust forward with a menacing jut; in short, the traditional movie Marine whose buddy has just been killed and who is now going to take apart a pillbox with his hands. Unlike the Marine, Reid begged the indulgence of our cameraman while he went behind the bench to throw up, but in the game he displayed terrifying quickness and ferocity, an agility that film editor Marty Green beautifully orchestrated with short rapid passages from Mozart, which Mike had played for us.

Going to the music building we saw the firm but kindly face of one of those fresh-air curates who used to bring spiritual comfort and cricket coaching to the English poor. The hair lay flat, and a large pair of horn-rimmed spectacles eased the blocky contours of an aspect further softened by some preparatory humming of the romantic music of Franz Liszt.

Reid had, naturally, considerable power as a pianist. Indeed, in our interview, when asked his favorite composer he said unhesitatingly that it was Liszt because, "I'm not the best pianist in the world, but I don't think there's any doubt that I'm the strongest, and Liszt is a composer who demands a lot of muscle."

He said also, with a rare and wry insight into the duality of his nature, "If I prepared for a concert the way I prepare for a football game, I would begin by throwing the piano out the window."

With the confidence that comes to youth and strength he

professed to be untroubled as to what might happen to his hands in the churning, stomping Laocoön of mid-scrimmage. With unconscious arrogance he seemed to feel sure that he had sufficient control of events to preserve the tools of his other trade.

That season Reid was an all-American and a first round draft choice of the Cincinnati Bengals. He was to say to me six years later, "Some thought was given to the possibility of a concert career, but it would have required giving up football at the time. I never regret the decision but very often wonder about it, though."

At the peak of his success with the Bengals he suddenly retired, not because of injuries, a salary dispute, the inchoate discontent of Sauer, or the revulsion that drove Dave Meggysey from the game, but simply because he had decided to do something else.

I found him at a nightclub in Upper St. Clair, Pennsylvania, playing his own composition with a small electronic music group he had organized. The five years of football had not damaged his hands but he felt that they had by interrupting the continuous practice necessary to a concert career, ending the possibility of full-stretch playing. He hoped to broaden the horizons of this simpler style with the complexities of composition.

Did he miss football?

"I'll miss the kind of bond, the strength of the bond that builds between players. I'll miss that, and probably never have that again in anything else, I don't imagine."

The uncertainties of popular music being what they are it may be that by the time you read these words Mike Reid will be fighting off crowds that want buttons and locks of his hair. Equally he may be playing in the weary vinyl lounge of a mom-and-pop motel. Wherever he is I suspect he'll be uncertain about where he is going next, but I'll always admire the firmness with which he made his choices at each crossroads on the way.

Two football careers that began as sensationally as Reid's and briefly marched in parallel, eventually moved down very different roads indeed.

Gary Beban, quarterback of UCLA, and O. J. Simpson, halfback at USC, performed brilliantly under the blazing spotlight of California publicity, each, as one might expect in a city so successful at shaping fantasy, playing a well-defined and popular role.

Beban appeared the quintessential college hero of the movies. Handsome, self-assured, engaged to a campus beauty queen, he moved over UCLA's showy campus with the springy step of one of those leading men who knows that no comic dean or villainous gambler in a deplorable fedora can halt his triumphant march because the producer has told him so.

In his Heisman Trophy year the university printed a glossy brochure resoundingly titled "Gary Beban, the Great One," which pushed his claims with the relentlessness of an encyclopedia salesman, and about which he was, naturally, disarmingly modest and amusing. "A football player doesn't play the game the way a writer writes it," he told me, "but publicity is part of the enthusiasm."

Simpson was, when I interviewed him in his junior year, the shy young black player whose mother had worked to get him an education and who, after two years of junior college, was having difficulties with the rah-rah complexities of a big school. These difficulties did not extend to his play, which was sensational, and one sensed in talking to him that his relative inarticulateness was not caused by inferior intellect but was, instead, a cautious but steady approach to that larger world in which he wished to make no more missteps than he was making on the field. He seemed ideal casting for the friend of the hero, Little John to someone's Robin Hood.

Their competition, the runner against the passer, was replete with honors for all, and Simpson matched Beban's Heisman Trophy. The subsequent developments had the crisscross effect of a Henry James novel as Beban, who had never failed at anything, struggled through a marginal four-year professional career, while Simpson, whose speech, when I first met him, had a soft diffidence that had the sound man desperately twiddling his knobs, not only continued his sensational play, but became, at last, the bell-voiced salesman of rental cars and a movie star.

I think his greatest accomplishment, now buried in his scrapbook, was to have made the breakthrough into the commercial and endorsement world for the black athlete. In April 1969 he came to the New York auto show to represent a General

Motors division, and only two years after our first meeting, I found him a totally different person. The cloak of shyness had been cast aside like Clark Kent's business suit, and the attractive arrogance that has marked O. J. ever since was harnessed successfully to a realism that kept him from being discouraged when General Motors dropped him because catch-up football in Buffalo had given him a season or two of statistical letdown. In an interview at the auto show he told me that it might be unfortunate that in America success was gauged almost purely by financial standards, but if that was the case, he was going to have the right numbers as a leadership base for the future. It was grandiose talk for one's early twenties, but charm washed off its pomposity.

"I knew inside that I had tried the best all the time," said Beban two years after he had left pro ball. "It wasn't good enough and therefore there was something else to be done in life."

Beban married his college sweetheart and is a successful salesman of industrial real estate. After all, Dick Powell didn't even try for the pros, yet in the strange, cruel world of the sports fan who throws a grappling hook into an athlete's heart and expects to be towed along, Beban is the one Heisman Trophy winner in a decade who didn't Make It. When we sought him out at his realty office, a colleague giving us directions asked, "Have you come to inverview 'The Failure'?"

Beban's Heisman Trophy stands on the mantle in a guest room, the little bronze runner rushing toward a dark corner, but a last interview with the little runner's owner showed me a man who knows where the daylight is.

"Maybe," he said of his glorious UCLA days, "we were a combination of young men who were really strictly collegians and could, whether it's for father or school or girl friend or whatever motivated us—maybe we were strictly collegians who were inspired to that one peak time."

Perhaps that's what football ought to be. Perhaps that's why we sometimes feel a sudden weariness as the scarred old pros bash at each other on the way to the leaden hoopla of the Super Bowl. Perhaps if sports have their inner rhythms, that visceral knowledge that one day sends kids onto the street with footballs instead of baseball gloves, there is a larger rhythm, like

Ecclesiastes' list of the times for this and the times for that. Perhaps if baseball is the game that runs its leisured way through the whole of hopeful spring and lazy summer, football should be the game of brief intensity, a search for a great day.

What can there be after that one peak time, whether it be Ed Krysiak's late moment or Gary Beban's early one?

After all, if you've had it, you will have achieved what Joseph Conrad described as "Something out of life, that while it is expected is already gone—has passed unseen, in a sigh and a flash—together with the youth, the strength, with the romance of illusions."

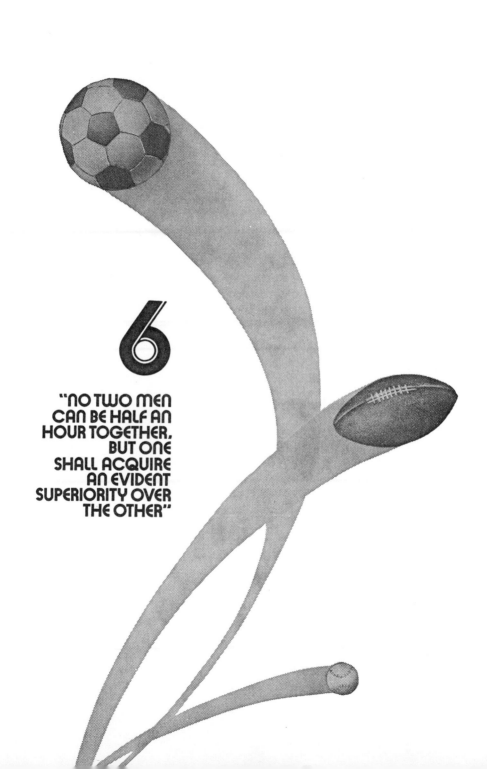

6

"NO TWO MEN
CAN BE HALF AN
HOUR TOGETHER,
BUT ONE
SHALL ACQUIRE
AN EVIDENT
SUPERIORITY OVER
THE OTHER"

In a dynamic society like ours, where careers rise and fall with the rapid irregular beat of that bouncing ball that used to guide us through movie community sings, one person's drop is very often the propellant for another's rise. So, the old *Herald Tribune* dropped the cautionary "guest critic" from Walter Kerr's by-line when Kerr, after seeing a play whose star had commissioned it, wrote: "Jay Robinson has delusions of adequacy."

So also the mournful story of a golfer blinking in the sunshine after eleven years in the shadows of neglect, shadows that were immediately to reclaim him, was the springboard from which I won, for a time, the unqualified approval of CBS's higher levels.

In 1955, Jack Fleck, a municipal course pro from Davenport, Iowa, came birdieing out of the twilight to tie Ben Hogan in the National Open at San Francisco's Olympic Club. Defeating Hogan the next day in an eighteen-hole playoff, he found himself one of the most unpopular men in the game because his victory was built on Hogan's defeat. This deprived the sainted Ben of a record fifth Open title, and vindictive idolators spent a lot of time in the next few years dwelling on Fleck's subsequent lack of success. At last, discouraged and bitter, he dropped off the tour and went back to the club pro's task of silkening sows' ears and selling sweaters.

In 1966, when the Open was again played at the Olympic, Fleck, perhaps remembering the champagne side of '55, qualified and returned to the scene of his big moment.

Bud called and arranged a pretournament interview, but by the time we arrived Fleck had changed his mind, perhaps reasoning that his collection of media scars was sufficiently large already. When I spoke to him at the beginning of a practice round, he announced that he was dining with friends directly the round was completed and could not see a minute clear for any talking on TV. He turned on his heel and departed, and Bud, who wouldn't give up if the heavens opened and a great voice told us that Our Credentials Were Withdrawn, said we should set up on the hillside by the eighteenth green and then go get some lunch.

When Fleck returned in the afternoon I waited at the edge of the green, and then did what rich people so often and so successfully do.

The rich, you may have noticed, don't bother with questions. In a restaurant, for example, the silver spoon set says, "We will be four," not "Do you have a table for four?" Questions lead to negatives as inexorably as "Just a glass of beer" led to a bed in the gutter in the popular songs of the Gay Nineties.

When Fleck picked up his ball—sinking a good putt helped, I'm sure—I did not ask if he had changed his mind, but simply told him that the camera was on the right of the hill and that we were ready for the interview. Obediently he walked across the green, which had been a bed of green fire for him long ago, and gave me a wistfully articulate interview in which he said that at forty-four he found the hills of Olympic much higher, that he had left the tour he loved simply because he wasn't good enough, and he was not really expecting another miracle.

The next day, after the camera crew had followed Fleck at a discreet distance, while Fleck, unhappily, remained at discreet distance from par, I grabbed a lull in the activity to drop into a sand trap with my lightweight typewriter and start the script. A passerby, hearing the raspy rattle, leaned in and remarked, "This is a hell of a time to be writing to the folks at home, buddy," but like the good golfer, I kept my head down and with easy wrist motion, kept swinging away at the machine.

Fleck failed to make the cut, Hogan, full of memories more acrid than Fleck's, failed to win his fifth Open, and I heard from the spies that Mr. Salant had pronounced my piece on the tournament to be a model of what a sports news story should be. The bouncing ball was on the rise for me.

The degree of concentration required in tournament play is endlessly talked about in golf books but, like virtue, it is easier to talk about than to achieve, and is never really understood by the nonplayer and the fun player unless observed at close range over a considerable stretch.

My chance to see a man's nervous system on the rack of this grim game—An invention of we Scots as typical as our medicinal tasting whiskey and our offal-heavy national cuisine—was a stroke by stroke observation of Deane Beman's first professional round.

Beman, now the commissioner of the pro tour, is a personable man who had built a considerable career as an insurance agent, playing championship amateur golf on the side. At the age of twenty-nine, he closed his desk, locked his office, and set out to wrest a living from an occupation where there is no insurance against the agony of a shanked shot or a rimmed putt.

He celebrated the change of course with one last joke-a-stroke round accompanied by three friends and a CBS camera crew. It was good golf but there was easy laughter at occasional ineptitude and nobody glared at the camera as if it were some cyclopean basilisk with the power to steer a shot off line.

A week later we conferred with Beman the night before his professional debut in Houston, Texas.

"I know I'm not going to have a gallery tomorrow," said Beman, "and that it's just going to be you guys and me, but I hope you'll understand if I don't talk to you or pay any attention to you as we go around."

We assured him that we would be as anonymous as possible, and I remembered that another golfer, Rives MacBee, had told me that stepping up to take his first shot as a pro he had not been afraid that the drive would be merely bad, he had been so hysterically nervous that he thought he might swipe the ball into the spectator group around the first tee.

Beman showed no outward signs of perturbation, but for fifteen holes he played steadily and mechanically, often coming within a couple of feet of us as we moved to a new setup, without any apparent awareness of our existence.

Crossing a bridge to reach the sixteenth tee he looked at me with an eye filmed by the membrana nictitans, or second lid, which hid the eye of Fu Manchu, and which indicates an inward gaze. Suddenly the shutter raised, and although I didn't see the lambent green fire that marked the gaze of the sinister doctor, I caught a moment of recognition.

"Hello, Heywood," he said, and with equal terseness I gave back "Hello, Deane," before the lid dropped again and restricted his vision to flags and the distances therefrom.

Beman completed the round at even par, and I asked him if he felt relieved that his debut had been a steady and respectable one.

"What's to feel good about?" he replied with the long-range agony of the tour golfer. "I have to play again tomorrow."

Obviously there are vast satisfactions in the game, as anyone who has heard the devotees interminably describing rounds to each other can attest, and as I visited with Deane off and on during his tournament career I found him happier than he had been in the insurance business. For Beman the happiness lay in precision, but I suspect for most amateurs, the joy lies in the inherent acceptable violence, the striking of something with what is revealingly called a club.

"It is the vehemence of the blow rather than the consequences that produces the ecstasy," wrote Bernard Darwin, that most literate of all golf writers.

Granting that a disastrous hook or slice will skim the sweetness from the aftertaste, the primitive joy of savage impact can still be savored, and the cautious player who drives a straight hundred fifty yards to avoid the risk of the rough is a person to be pitied.

"Hard-hitting," continued Darwin in the same essay, "has some of the great qualities of obloquy. It is like telling a man for once in a while what we really think of him."

Those who never say what they really think, like the dab-down-the-middle drivers, are deprived of a great, if dangerous, satisfaction.

I did not set out to say anything devastating about the Masters Golf Tournament when the famous 1970 brouhaha involving myself, the tournament's chairman the late Clifford Roberts of Augusta, and half the lawyers at CBS began, but before it was through, obloquy—"evil speaking against a person or thing" as the *Oxford Dictionary* defines it—was flowing in a blood-red tide like wine on Bastille Day.

The whole affair began in innocence as so many homeric quarrels do. Paul Greenberg had been given a half-hour early Sunday evening show to go with his Saturday enterprise, and since the Masters finished on Sunday, Paul planned to put a tape of the final putts on the air. The tape would be easy to obtain since CBS Sports did the Masters, and in order to have a little pad on top of the bare bones of actuality, Bud and I were to go to Augusta early in the week and do a little scenic stuff on the beauty of Augusta National in spring.

"Get me two minutes of that canned nostalgia that you can do in your sleep," was the way the order was put to me, and with no thought beyond how much I enjoy grits for breakfast, I began my packing. Almost immediately, however, I emptied my suitcase again. Bud had called Augusta to get credentials for the informal par three course tournament which preceded the real thing, and had been refused on the grounds that I was not acceptable. It appeared that everything had gone swimmingly until Bud told Colonel Somebody-or-other, the press chief, the name of the correspondent. (As the quarrel burgeoned, it sometimes appeared that everybody at Augusta who wasn't in a white coat serving drinks, was a colonel serving confusion.)

Pressed as to the reason for my unacceptability, the colonel said that I had never visited the course before and was therefore unqualified. It was pointed out that four years earlier I had toured the course with Jack Nicklaus to do a piece on how Jack prepared for the Masters. He won it that year and the less knowledgeable executives at CBS were convinced, not of my luck, but of my percipience.

That objection taken care of, the next came in view, the claim that I was not a genuine golf correspondent. Ever patient, Bud explained that the PGA had issued me a gold badge with my name engraved on it, but that in any case I did not intend to cover the tournament itself, but simply to do a little background work the day before. The colonel then got down to the real reason. It appeared that tournament chairman Roberts considered me "irreverent." It did not matter that my previous visit had resulted in a respectful recitation of a champion's preliminary exercises. There had been other occasions at other events where I had apparently permitted an unacceptable sense of humor to show.

At first we thought there was a misunderstanding and that Roberts, who, like other forthright men, was not a great listener, was under the impression that I was to take part in the actuality telecast by the sports department, something he had been controlling down to the most tiresome detail for years. Whether he knew this or not, he made one thing clear. He didn't want me to come to Augusta, and no argument that said personal feelings about qualified journalists were insufficient grounds for a ban would sway him. Indeed, describing Cliff Roberts as tournament chairman was, though correct, misleading. It would be like describing Ivan the Terrible as presiding officer at the Council of Boyars. It's right, but it doesn't catch the atmosphere.

Mr. Salant was now asked to rule on whether we should accept the ukase, and came up with a memo suggesting that we do whatever we wanted, including going to Augusta if we felt like it.

The canned nostalgia idea was at once put away and preparations put in train to spill a little prune juice on the brightly burnished golf shoes of Augusta's bureaucracy.

Credentials were secured for a camera crew and producer to work with some acceptable man from a local station. I arrived, unaccredited and unrecognizable in a disguise consisting of a deerstalker hat, dark glasses, a drab raincoat that reached my heels, and a pair of binoculars. I looked like a German expressionist's idea of Sherlock Holmes.

The cameraman was Laurence Pierce, a courtly, unflappable man, now best known for pictures of the shooting of Governor Wallace. Laurence is the possessor of a Byzantine mind, and nothing delights him more than a really complex conspiracy. Clarence Gibbons and Leroy Rollins, the members of his crew, were, like Laurence, full of old Southern politeness until pushed, at which point they made Jeb Stuart look like a good ol' boy sunnin' hisself in high cotton.

We shot the on-camera opening sequence outside the walls of the course, and I got things going with a preliminary compliment.

"The Masters Golf Tournament," I said, "played on the beautiful dogwood-dotted course inside this gate, breathes tradition and prestige."

Warming to my work I continued, "Of course, like many venerable institutions it sometimes has a little trouble with its breathing and becomes as red-faced and rigid as a Coldstream colonel. In its rigidity it has never invited a black golfer. In its fear of irreverence it has barred this correspondent whose mild laughter is perhaps presumed to wilt dogwood.

"An unaccredited correspondent is as forlorn as a notary public whose seal has expired," I concluded, "but he can at least buy his way in to see the course."

Here the genius of Pierce and Lamoreaux was to be tested, because from the moment I entered onto the course, it was necessary for us to work unobserved by either Roberts's security people or the legions of CBS Sports, who owed no allegiance to Salant of CBS News and who, upon seeing me and realizing my capacity to inflame the choleric Roberts, would have immediately called the highest levels of the network and had me withdrawn.

When I went to buy my ticket for the par three tournament, Pierce seemed to be photographing a laughing group of young matrons who were preening themselves in preparation for the envy friends would feel when they showed up on the tube. Apparently panning to pick up their background, cameraman Laurence caught me at the critical moment as I paid for the ticket. Gibbons, apparently on his way to get a new magazine of film, did not pause as he gave me the message, "Stall till Laurence gets back of the turnstile."

Obeying, I approached the ticket taker to find Laurence gallantly bringing his covey of belles through ahead of me, and the dark figure following them through seemed no more than an interesting contrast to their bright gaiety.

Here Lamoreaux, operating behind a pair of sunglasses as big as a duck blind, told me in passing that the next rendezvous point was a magnolia bush at the third green. He and his crew then followed the girls toward the club.

This general pattern was followed all day, and I was caught peering between bushes with mock stealth or picking up the action with my binoculars while nesting in a tree.

Highlights of the genially mocking script were a picture of me walking behind a trash truck "Suitably camouflaged behind a wall of armor into unfriendly territory," and a shot of two fat members looking like prize-winning zucchini, which led to the awed remark that the winner was awarded a jacket "Very like those actually worn by Augusta National members themselves," a phrase swamped with italics.

To Mr. Roberts, who awarded these green membership jackets to Masters winners as if they were the red robes of the cardinalate, this may have been the most unforgiveable jeer of all.

Another highlight was an interview in which CBS correspondent Phil Jones, after a little polite stalling, went up against Roberts with questions about the exclusivity of the tournament and finally why I had been barred. Some of what was said was so obviously the product of bad temper that we considerately left it on the cutting room floor, leaving on the air only a polite hope that blacks might someday play, the expression that I had not been denied credentials, and that, exasperatedly, "I'm certainly not a fan of his."

After a little more fun I closed politely with the thought that "Those deemed worthy of covering the course with the players, saw this week, as they always do, a tough test in a setting that adds to the watcher's pleasure."

We had expected, indeed had rather looked forward to, a protest or two, but none of us foresaw that before it was all over there would be more documents handed around than fuddled the world in Dickens's *"Plainstanes v. Plainstanes,"* and that the video tape of that piece would be run back and forth till its electronic dots were threadbare in the hope of finding a libel suit, or that there would be a serious claim from some of Roberts's associates that the later race riots in Augusta were triggered by my flippancy on the subject of a sacred and stabilizing event.

Caught in the middle of all this was CBS chairman William S. Paley, who was hit with the first hot shock of Roberts's rage together with a demand that I be dismissed instantly. Mr. Paley was very proud of the fact that CBS did the Masters, and at the same time was proud of his news division and had no wish to see it truckle to petulance, even the petulance of the powerful.

He did, therefore, what great executives do at such moments of crisis—nothing. He reassured Roberts that a study was being made and proved it from time to time with mounds of mimeograph paper, which seemed to indicate that the study was as exhaustive as a year's work by a federal commission. Film editors got used to the little groups with briefcases that came again and again to see those fatal few minutes that were said to combine the worst elements of spitting on the flag, sneering at motherhood, and beating small children with candy canes wrenched from their chubby fists.

In eleven months or so Cliff Roberts got busy getting ready for another Masters, and interest in my punishment fell off. Interest in what I was going to do about this year's event grew among my fellow correspondents and a great many golfers, who, taking me aside with nervous whispers, told me that they were glad someone had at last cocked a snook at the Colossus of Augusta.

I had turned down an offer from a golf magazine to describe the whole business, explaining that the feud was all on the other side and that I thought it more comic than cosmic (I describe it now because poor Mr. Roberts, proud and inflexible to his tragic end, is gone, and I doubt anybody's going to be disturbed at this late date—even though I never expect to return to Augusta National).

Bud and Paul and I decided that we would try for the amusement of opposites so, once again with Pierce and his merry men, we set off for Mississippi, to the satellite tournament that gave the lesser golfers something to do while the panjandrums were in Georgia.

It was called the Magnolia Open because a rather stunted little tree produced an occasional blossom outside the pro shop window.

As a symbolic handle to our choice of this little-known event, we picked as our central figure a lame, cross-handed, black golfer named Charles Owens. Despite a stiff knee caused by a bad landing in his paratroop days and an over-and-under grip he had picked up as an uninstructed kid golfer, Owens played a pretty good game and was an articulate spokesman for the fringe players on the tour.

At the end I appeared covered with badges, which admitted me to everything but the Daughters of the Confederacy clubhouse. I announced with a happy smile that it was nice to be welcome, and thus finished my very small contribution to the fire of controversy. The gasoline was flung on the flames in the next few seconds when Mike Wallace, anchoring the program that week, had a post piece comment that ran "Charles Owens, the golfer interviewed by Heywood Hale Broun, finished in a tie for forty-third place and won $28.50. In today's *other* golf tournament, the Masters, the winner was Charles Coody."

It appears that Mr. Roberts had been monitoring the news and at the word *other* had emitted a cry of world-class rage. The exchange of memoranda between Augusta and New York began all over again.

That was, however, the end of the affair as far as Bud and I were concerned. The whistling wind of a teapot tempest becomes, if prolonged, as irritating as the whistling whine of a strong-minded mosquito, and the following year, while the golfing greats were striving for the green coat, we were off in Nebraska looking at unlikely heavyweight challenger Ron Stander, and covering the National Badminton Championships. At this event I demonstrated the sensational serve that had won me the captaincy of the Swarthmore College Badminton Team, and marvelously, just as I did it, there was a burst of applause from the nearby center court. We decided that using it was not really distorting the news.

As far from the austerities of the Masters as Alex Karras is from an Augusta businessman, was the tournament that the former Detroit tackle used to organize each year for the benefit of the Cystic Fibrosis Research Fund.

Assisted by a hyperactive graveyard proprietor named Pete Buterakis, Karras corraled golfers who would pay $50 to be subjected to something between the bright lights and loud shouts of a police grilling and a trip through an old-time funhouse. Coming to the first tee, serious contestants would begin to run through the steps of preparation only to be caught in mid-swing by sharp cries from a PA system apparently firing up through the tee. Golfers who shudder at the whisper of two dimes in a pocket are likely to lose a certain smoothness of arc when they are yelled at, and some of the more sensitive looked like tarantella dancers, as bugle calls joined the amplified advice and crop duster planes sprayed the players with pink liquid from a few feet overhead.

Llamas and cows foraged on the fairway and a giant tortoise made his way patiently across the course, leaving rather attractive claw patterns in the traps.

Karras and Buterakis, accompanied by a somewhat stunned George Plimpton, whom even the highjinks of Harvard had not prepared for the antics of these Lords of Misrule, toured the course in search of golfers who were, despite the siren songs of happy madness, endeavoring to play the game as its dour inventors had planned it in a long-ago world of seaside loneliness. Such spoilsports would send the Karras cart off like an artillery spotter plane, to find a large truck on whose bed a noisy band was playing under the riding crop baton of a midget in a field marshal's uniform. When the truck came blaring over a hill, the coordinated swing would suffer a fatal jiggle and the ball would act accordingly.

"Laugh it up, guys!" Karras would cry in a voice like a faulty fire siren and the eldritch laughter of Buterakis would underscore the command as they bounced off to bother some determined foursome that had organized itself like a British square attacked by 4,000 Zulu freedom fighters.

Despite the considerable battering to which probability was subjected all day, most of the contestants who managed to finish at all, showed up for an evening banquet at which rich prizes had been promised, things like four automobiles and bonanzas of golf equipment.

"You should see the guys' faces," shrieked Karras, who, as a football tackle, had perforce to believe that pain was hilarious. "I mean, you promise them a car and they get all lit up like a kid at Christmas, and we pull the curtain and there it is, something that went over a cliff about ten years ago. The big job is getting those wrecks to the prize tent."

The golf equipment turned out to be bijoulike boxes of used sweat sox, but the evenings usually ended with a lot of beer-fueled fellowship and an announcement from the suddenly serious Buterakis about the amount taken in for the charity.

I appreciated the handicaps of the contestants when, with no more noise than the whisper of the camera, I attempted to sink a five-foot putt, which, when I looked up for my closing lines, would be thrown back out by a device inside the cup. All I can say is that if the best players make, of their five-foot putts, only two out of three then I don't feel too bad at two out of thirty.

Perhaps Mr. Roberts was right when he said that I was basically irreverent. Certainly few of our many golf stories had much to do with the serious business of achieving perfection.

One of our trips down the less-traveled roads of the game was our coverage of the National Left-Handers Tournament. Although some of the players were first rate, the entrance requirements were based on sinistral persuasion rather than general excellence. Indeed, alertness was the big requirement, the first two hundred members of the Left-Handed Golfers Association who applied, making up the field.

It was at this competition in Galesburg, Illinois, that I met a golfer with a proper appreciation of fortune. He was a little old bow-legged man who popped an approach shot onto the eighteenth green of the Soangeteha Club course and then walked up to discover that this green was the size of Monaco and that his putt was about from the border to the last slot machine in the casino. Undaunted, he walked up to the ball, engaged in no tricks of looking through the club shaft, and gave it a hearty unscientific whack. It caromed off worm casts, ran up little slopes and down little slopes and at last, after one hundred fifty feet of a trip as erratic as the path of an Uncle Wiggily board, dropped into the cup.

Rushing over with my wireless microphone I asked, "How do you feel after this whirlwind finish to your round?"

Beaming like a man looking into a vista of endorsements and free golf gear, he cried, "Wonderful! This gives me my hundred!"

I don't know if he ever achieved that miraculous level again or even moved into the rarefied air of double figures, but he was, at that moment, the happiest golfer I ever saw—a man crackling with tumultuous merriment—and a lesson to all those grumpies who snarl in frustration because buying a new golf book has not made them its author's equal.

The only golfer I knew who was that old duffer's equal in the happy acceptance of mediocrity was the deservedly little-known professional, Paul Tomita. Seven years ago when I met him, the sixty-three-year-old Mr. Tomita was the home pro at a nine-hole course in Bucharest, Rumania—the only course in the country. Mr. Tomita had lived through royalty, democracy, iron guard fascism, and communism, without, apparently, getting involved in anything more than an occasional problem with moles on the greens. In the World Cup competition where I met him, he placidly shot four rounds in the low eighties, easily outstripping only his teammate, Dimitru Monteanu, whose regular function, I suspect, was sweeping up around the clubhouse in Bucharest. The fact that such as Gary Player and Jack Nicklaus were leading him by forty-odd strokes for individual honors disturbed him no more than the fact that he had never managed to get his home course stretched to regulation eighteen-hole length. The bulk of players at Bucharest CC appear to have been diplomats, a group united in nothing save a common pursuit of par. Perhaps it was the polyglot nature of his clientele that saved Tomita from the troubles of most who engaged in bourgeois trades like his.

Where would all of them, exponents of left, right, or center, get another pro if anything happened to Tomita? It was clear that Monteanu, be he ever so ideologically correct, and no matter how healthy and searching his self-criticism, was not ready for the job.

It occurred to me that, despite having lived through one of the most violent half centuries in his country's violent history, Tomita probably could tell you nothing about those years save such morsels as that King Carol topped his approaches, and that the German ambassador was late for his tee-off time the day World War II broke out.

As befits a man who has extended an instructional hand to every political persuasion, Tomita teed off with a ball given him by a Rumanian sportswriter, a ball stamped with the name of Richard Nixon, who had passed through ceremonially the year before.

When he smote the ball in a precise, cheerful fashion, the air was thick with the symbolism of international amity, but unfortunately few statesmen are precise and cheerful, or they would be as flexible and as durable as Mr. Tomita.

Golf is not, on the whole, a game for realists. By its exactitudes of measurement it invites the attention of perfectionists. You are not measured against anything so exact as an opponent. There are, for instance, people who make me feel like a good tennis player and others who show that I cannot play the game at all. Golf measures you instead against yourself and against the calculated acceptable number of strokes.

Anything involving something so unforgiving is inclined to employ the soothing arts of superstition, and golf is as rife with it as a textbook on primitive anthropology. Golfers have chuckled in a superior way as their college professors describe the Pacific islanders who try to acquire skill and courage by getting possession of a brave enemy's feather headdress, his war club, or a taste of his heart after it had been prepared according to the proper magic recipe.

When the laughter dies, such sophisticates go out and buy a Johnny Miller hat, a set of Ben Hogan war clubs, and balked, so far, of a chance at that roasted heart, settle for the mythic power that may rise from a pair of Arnold Palmer shoes.

Often, in making my way through golf crowds at tournaments, I have noticed that spectators will be carrying clubs, presumably bearing the signatures of the heroes they are following, and I see them trying to edge close to the great man as he leaves the green and moves to the next tee. Everyone knows, after all, that proximity, in the absence of a fingernail or lock of hair, is essential to good magic, and if the club were actually to touch so much as the mohair fuzz of the royal sweater, who knows what virtue might flow into its head!

Perhaps it is because I became convinced that the gods were personally displeased with me that I early gave up the game myself. The golf I played when young was of an exacting but peculiar kind. My father, who had been an excellent player in college, had shortly thereafter developed the bulk and accompanying foot miseries which, until the arrival of the cart, kept such hefty has-beens off the course.

Heywood then devised a short but fiendish test which ran around the house and permitted frequent rests and refreshment as we pitched over the telephone wires, took penalties for going into the lilies, went up the stony driveway and around the stone wall, etc. There were only three small sand greens but there were nine tees and the master of this be-careful-of-the-windows layout was given possession of a large gold-type cup which had originally been won in a *Daily News* Chorus Girls Long Driving Competition by the dancers of *Shoot the Works,* a show my father had produced.

When a full seventy-two-hole championship match was played, the cup was always filled with champagne, and since championships were played three times a week, the wine bill at the nineteenth hole ran very high. I drank my share of the champagne but it was always bitter beer to me because I never, in three years of trying, won the cup.

A weekend guest won it once, but as rematches were played and the guest continued to win them, the weekend also stretched, with mysterious car troubles and cries about never seeing enough of the guest, until about Wednesday of the following week when the hint was taken and the cup lost to the home pro.

I was always close but, remembering the fate of Oedipus, lost my killer instinct when I faced the big test. My tee shot would loft up, and then come tumbling out of the phone wires like Daedalus, whose melting wings forever proved that father knows best.

The last match, all even at sixty-seven holes, ended in a three up and two to go victory for Heywood and the end of my regular competitive golf.

Occasionally since then I have been persuaded to go around with friends and, after coming up the fairways with a series of gains like those of Marshal Haig on the Somme, have enjoyed myself in the familiar circle of forty yards from the pin.

The gold-type cup is now mine, but only, alas, through inheritance, and my only real golf trophy is a ball mounted on a piece of wood, commemorative of my victory over Paul Greenberg on a par three course at Disneyland.

We had watched the astronauts take off from Florida and broadcast the views of the Common Man on the beach (I aired the views of the Common Woman because she had been nice enough to towel off my face while we all perspired and waited at Cape Kennedy). Then, as the future *Life* writers and motel proprietors sped toward the moon, we flew to California to get the views of the Common Person around a big screen at Mickey's place when the moment of landing occurred.

It took the astronauts longer to arrive, although they naturally didn't have the stackup problems we did, and the golf game filled the gap. Greenberg is a fierce competitor, and although he did not imagine that his intense crash-course year of golf instruction had brought him close to a silver cup, it seemed humiliating to lose to a senior softy like me who proclaimed his nonparticipation. I explained about the dehydrated St. Andrews in Connecticut, but Paul was inconsolable.

"You rich kids," he growled. "You forget more than we have time to learn." Then putting all his frustration into a fiery spear of sneers he cried, "I'll bet you played polo!"

The riches were long gone owing to my father's belief that there was something not quite nice about money, which required its removal in a spendthrifty equivalent of the Saturday night bath, but the egalitarian accusation deserved a truthful answer.

"Yes I did, Paul, but quite badly. I never even made the junior varsity at school."

The astronauts haven't been back to the moon and I haven't been back to play another round. If Cliff Roberts had known that I was ignoring the rituals of my peer group, he would have known what it was that roused his sense of something alien and unclean impinging on his orbit.

Getting to the moon is easier, however, than for "rabbits," as the unfortunate fringe players are called, to make a go of the golf tour. As befits a businessman's game, the sport is organized in a businesslike way, and eligibility for the weekly whacks at the money melon is determined by a number of mathematical criteria, among them last year's earnings (top sixty to qualify), by tournament victories (all winners to qualify), by high finishes in certain prestige tournaments, and lastly by having made the cut to the group leaders who played the final thirty-six holes the week before. The remaining places are filled from among the horde whose motel bills are just as pressing as those of the successful players. In order to pay those bills, members of the horde must first play thirty-six holes on Monday, top finishers to be allowed into the real tournament, then succeed in making the cut, if they are to win any money or get into the following event without another nail-biting Monday.

As there are too many actors, photographers, artists, and young film makers, so there are too many golfers. Like Hefflinger, the baseball player, we all want to put off the furniture moving job or its equivalent, moving paper in an office, but few of the above aspirants have the unavoidable expenses the golfers do.

Eating the expensive clubhouse lunches, the staggering restaurant dinners, and their own hearts, they are so close to the river of money that they can hear its golden flow chinking and chuckling as it runs on to other pockets. They know that a good putt here, a long drive there, are all that are needed to divert its rush their way, but the knowledge is shared by so many that the number of good putts needed seems always to rise—to be one more than the ever-improving rabbit has accomplished.

One of the saddest scenes in our Saturday stories was that of two young, well-dressed, almost first-rate golfers slamming their clubs into a car trunk and setting out in the rain for the next town, a couple of good putts short of making money, the cut, and a chance to sleep late on Monday.

I would like to report that one of them was Johnny Miller or Tom Weiskopf or some other seventies luminary, but I suspect that they are now eating well as club pros but sleeping a sleep disturbed by dreams of what might have happened with a good putt here and a long drive there.

Far from the iron yardstick of the scorecard is the teaching turf of Homer Snead, elder brother of the eternal Sam, and a man who began his teaching career by placing a relatively straight hickory branch in his sibling's hands.

It is Homer's belief that the pupil should learn away from the course, so that thoughts of score can be subordinated to thoughts of skill. Snead used a driving range as his classroom, making the pupils hit out into the nowhere, undistracted by the beckoning pennon of a flagstick. As I watched him patiently and constantly correcting the swing of a man whose coordination was breaking up on the reef of aggression, I realized that the old Virginian in the family-trademark straw hat was, of course, the Zen archery master stopping for a time at a dusty Florida roadside.

It is the essence, you will remember, of the Zen anti-Robin Hood philosophy that one concerns oneself with the technique of drawing the bow and pays no attention to the target. The doing is all. Listening to Snead I realized that his entire pedagogical conversation had to do with the mechanics of the stroke. What it might accomplish would transpire when the student had left him for the lists of competition.

Listening to the endless number of muscular sophistications required to be the Baryshnikov of the seven iron, I thought of a Japanese friend, a Zen devotee far above the American week-end-with-a-paperback level, a 112-pound man in his middle fifties who shot an occasional 79. He was discontented despite my admiration because he felt he was not "playing gracefully." A few weeks later he told me with a happy smile that he had greatly improved his style of play and was approaching grace.

"And your score?" I asked. He shrugged as one does when asked for secondary information. "About ninety," he said.

Of course, there is a level where one may play gracefully, *and* play successfully, a level where making the cut is not enough, where four 69s are not enough—if someone has three of them with a 68. This is the level of such as Jack Nicklaus, for whom perfectionism is a constant spur toward a substantially unreachable goal—I say unreachable because no one has yet reported a score of 18.

Jack, although he has taught himself to be totally polite (It is, in his mind, one of the requirements of champions as it once was of Arthur's knights), is a rather remote man, and I was startled one day when lightning had driven everyone off the course at a National Open to be summoned to his locker.

"Heywood," he said, "did you see that race, Secretariat in the Belmont?"

I had been on the finish line I assured him, as he went on to tell me, "I watched that race in my living room all alone. There was just me and the TV screen but as that horse came down the stretch widening that lead further and further with no urging, I applauded and I cried."

I told him that I thought I knew why he had cried and, invited to explain, I said I thought perfectionism is painful.

"You, Jack," I said, "of all the athletes I have met, are the most concentrated, the most driven, the most conscious of the demands of perfection. In my days as an actor I had not a tithe of your dedication, and yet when I saw Sir Ralph Richardson give what seemed to me a perfect comedy performance in *The School for Scandal* I had a look at the reality of my cloudy daydreams and I wept because I knew I would never achieve them. That horse, flying over the ground like a big wingless bird, was a kind of perfection, too. The race was won but there was something more to do, show the speed and power that was in his blood like lightning. I cried too, Jack."

Secretariat has now the worries of a parent (Did you see Sonny's workout times? Where did we go wrong?), but Jack is still pursuing perfection. He has defined it as winning the four big titles—U.S. and British Opens, PGA and Masters—in a single year. If he does it, I, the man who couldn't win the *Daily News* Chorus Girls Long Driving Cup, will weep.

7

"I NEVER THINK
I HAVE HIT HARD
UNLESS
IT REBOUNDS"

In his brilliant essay "The Indian Jugglers," William Hazlitt describes the skills of his subjects as "the utmost stretch of human ingenuity, which nothing but the bending the faculties of body and mind to it from the tenderest infancy with incessant, ever anxious application up to manhood can accomplish or make even a slight approach to."

This is pretty much how, in my youth, I felt about hockey, and even though the grace of the game has since been badly marred by the thick fist of brutality, it still has moments when, as Hazlitt would put it, "Extraordinary dexterity distracts the imagination and makes admiration breathless."

As a teenager I stood on the iron-pipe railing behind the last balcony row of the old Fiftieth-Street Garden with my hands against the ceiling of the smoky old building, leaning out over the heads of luckier patrons to see such a part of the ice as was visible from my perch, while the New York Rangers and the New York Americans battled through the longest play-off game in the history of hockey.

When my team was defeated in the early hours of the morning and I removed my near-gangrenous feet from a resting place uncomfortable for anything but a turkey buzzard, I solaced myself with the thought that I had seen a concentration of human physical skill which a convocation of jugglers with rings, plates, oranges, and Indian clubs would have been hard-put to match.

In the years between my doing sports for newspapers and doing sports for television, years in which I lived largely on the go and stop bounty of the theater, I spent many hours in the cheap seats of the Garden's end arena, watching the attacking team swarm toward me with the swooping skill that "incessant, ever anxious application" can sometimes produce.

Later in his essay Hazlitt made the point that the admirable jugglers lacked, perforce, the imaginative sweep of the artist, and, as an interviewer, I was to discover that the hockey player, withdrawn since early childhood into intense concentration on this most difficult of games, is unlikely to be articulate and open when he skates over to the microphone.

Still, by odd chance, some of the most memorable quotes of nearly two decades of hopeful listening have come from hockey players, appearing out of seas of silence like sailboats of beautiful design.

At thirty-nine, Jacques Plante, whose face was so seamed with scars that he looked like a man who had been pressed through a screen door, said to me with a sad smile and a musical French-Canadian accent, "When you are young and make a mistake, you think to yourself, it is all right, I am learning and I will not make that mistake again, but when you are old and make a mistake, you think to yourself, how many more will I be allowed to make before I am finished?"

There is a precise and unsparing vision of life's progress and penalties in those words, which is as inexorable and graceful as Plante's moves in his great days as a goaltender, and as he spoke I saw in my mind's eye one of the most terrifying of his mistakes. In a game against the Rangers in New York he failed to see a flying puck, and when its frozen rubber edge sliced his forehead, his face was, in an instant, uniformly scarlet under a cascade of blood. A trainer rushed onto the ice with a towel and for a moment we were comforted as the soft sterile whiteness hid from us the horrid sight, but before he could skate off the absorbency of the towel had drawn the red tide to its surface.

Yet, half an hour later Plante was again in the nets for the Canadiens, his only concession one of the new masks which he had previously disdained. A realist, as his quote revealed, he continued to wear the mask for the remainder of his career, so I suppose the scar I saw inflicted completed the cruel pattern his profession had printed on his face.

The rejection of masks by goaltenders long after efficient hard plastics had replaced such clumsy and vision-obscuring devices as spaceman bubbles and variations on the baseball catcher's mask, was not simply a matter of macho, although that debatable virtue plays a very large part in the philosophy of the game, but, according to old goalies, a necessary spur against boredom.

After all, while the rest of the team races up and down ice, the goalie leads a life not unlike that of a soldier, an existence made up of large portions of tedium and small portions of terror.

Eddie Giacomin, one-time New York Ranger goalie, once said to me, "You may find it hard to believe, but I have to fight from going to sleep when the action is at the other end of the ice. I have found that it helps to sing to myself."

It is, at first, hard to believe, but when you think of the intense concentration that goaltenders must have when the wave of attack approaches them, it is not hard to understand the letdown, with its invitation to somnolence, which follows with the ebb.

Ever ingenious, Lamoreaux once devised a scheme to mount a small camera inside an unbreakable plastic box at the back of a hockey net. An electric wire frozen under the ice would serve to activate it and we were to have a hundred-foot magazine for each of three periods, a stretch of about eight minutes of the action in total.

The view of the rush as seen through this machine's eye had the bloodchilling menace of the advance of the Teutonic knights in *Alexander Nevsky,* and there was no breaking of ice to stem the advance. In most cases our film showed either defense men or the netminder himself turning aside the thrust, but we did have one perfect shot take between the padded calves of Boston's Eddie Johnston, a view of the puck leaving the stick, growing as it flew toward the lense, and popping between the pads as Johnston, too late, tried to snap them together. The speed of the puck and the desperate convulsions of the goaltender made the brief scene look almost like what must be a victim's-eye view of a firing squad.

To play the game at an acceptable level of excellence, one must skate as naturally as one breathes, and show a dancer's rapid reactions and incredible suppleness while balanced on a couple of knife blades.

Like the juggler one finds that "tenderest infancy" is almost too late to start, and Canadian kids who are to make it in the national game are already neglecting their studies and their comfort as, at five and six, they wobble over the town pond, forgetting frostbite in the excitement of the fray.

Lately rinks where artificial ice is always available have sprung up everywhere, and we once did a TV piece about a Minneapolis indoor facility that was so heavily booked that bright-eyed children practiced hockey at four o'clock in the morning while their heavy-eyed parents dozed in the little grandstand. Every hour a new bunch took over and the new popularity of the game was thereby illustrated along with the difficulty of learning it. An American boy, restricted to an hour or two a week, has as little chance of catching up with a young Canadian who has spent the daylight hours cutting school and the surface of a frozen lake, as a weekend golfer has of beating Jack Nicklaus, or a Sunday painter of getting past the agreeable looseness of the inept.

Of course, all this dedication and neglect of the sensible, well-rounded life are supposed to lead, as all daydreams do in a dynamic society, to success, wealth, and recognition. To play for Montreal is, in French Canada, a distinction that will bring you that ultimate accolade, lifetime recognition and respect. Here is none of the lightning-flash fame of the rock singer who is forgotten almost before the thunder of his press campaign dies. Here is a warmth worth all the work and pain that hockey players and Indian jugglers undergo on the way to the easy elegance of mastery.

What, however, of those who have expended the same effort, suffered the same bruises, lost as many teeth as the immortals, all to the end of playing for the Long Island Ducks? This team in the old Eastern League gave its all in a cavernous hall set down in the featureless expanses of Commack, Long Island, a place where directions are given in terms of the fast food emporia that are the only landmarks among the rows of houses—"It's four blocks beyond Carvel." Players at the Ducks' level made, in the early 1970s, about $250 a week and were usually too old or too battered to dream of upward mobility. Still, when they crashed against each other or onto the ice, their bones were as brittle and their pain communication systems as alive and aching as if they were the highly paid darlings of the top-ranked National Hockey League.

Talking to the Ducks I found that in these Gorkian depths of sport there was a whole new set of motivations, far from the "you can do it" cant of the coach's creed. Years of striving had made it clear to the Ducks that they could do it as well as anyone in terms of dedication and ability to withstand the wear and tear of a violent game.

"We play as well as they do in the NHL," said one old Duck, "but we get there just a step or two slower than the boys upstairs."

What, then, keeps men going back for bumps that are not buttered with money and fame? The answer seems to be that dispensing bumps is a prime anodyne for frustration. In our onward and upward world where every child is an almost inevitable disappointment to Dad and Mom ("We want to be proud of you, dear") unless the bent twig has been inclined toward brain surgery, corporate or political power, a seat on the judicial bench, or the highly visible stardom of sport, there are millions who must wear the metaphorical hair shirt that says "Mediocrity" across the front and, in hairy letters in the lining, "Guilt."

Our society has few outlets for the rage that burns on the fuel of bitterness. If you break people, or worse still, things, you are likely to be arrested. Barroom brawlers are banned from the oasis and made to wander in deserts of loneliness, while in the serried ranks of business, sarcasm is likely to cost you several serries.

"I find I play my best game after a fight with the wife," said a scarred old Duck with a nose so bent and rebent that he looked as if he breathed through his ears. A defenseman, he moved on the ice with the ponderous tread of an old policeman, a not surprising state of affairs since he was, when not playing hockey, an old policeman in Toronto.

A colleague whose knees sounded like boxes of breakfast food was, in the off-season, a carpenter.

"The people you work for are always changing their minds," he said, "and after days of pulling out nails you've just driven in, you dream about getting on the ice and bashing a few guys. It's very relaxing. I know I've gone as far as I can in hockey, but I'll miss it. Who can I bash then?"

Brutality has become, I believe, an excessive part of modern professional hockey, but the inner-inspired roughness of the

147

Ducks seems to me, at least, more human than the cold nastiness of the "enforcers" who do their goon squad work as part of the routine of their jobs.

Of course, bashers get bashed, but there is a tradition of stoicism in hockey, perhaps a legacy from the American Indians, who invented the game and to whom calm in the face of pain was a cardinal virtue.

The one word a hockey player is forbidden to use is *Ouch!* whether he be Jacques Plante bathed in blood or a Long Island Duck whose between-periods therapy for a broken cheekbone was a Bandaid.

One of my first assignments with CBS News was a story on Bernie Geoffrion, a hockey player who had been given the nickname Boom Boom as a tribute to his aggressive style. After great years in Montreal he had at last brought his much-patched body to New York for his swan-song season. After the game he waited patiently for the camera crew to set up lights in a spare, cramped room we had been allotted. Sitting on a backless box he sipped beer and answered my questions patiently if monosyllabically. When we were done he wished us good night and walked several blocks to a hospital where he submitted to treatment for muscles torn during that evening's play. No Comanche smiling scornfully as knotted thongs were pulled through his shoulder muscles could have topped the performance.

Drawing words from hockey players is harder than getting them to say "Ouch!" and one of the highest professional compliments I received was one magazine writer's report that admiring colleagues had told him that I could stimulate a moderate amount of volubility among these muscular Trappists.

The years spent in the bleak weather that makes the game possible, in the countryside where school is always secondary to either harvesting or hockey, do not make for much skill in the persiflage that is prized in drawing rooms, and for a further silencer there is the fact that a very large percentage of the players speak English both ineptly and resentfully and are only likely to open up for fellow speakers of French.

I first met Guy La Fleur when he was a shy young man from a working-class background, who was going to leave all that behind because his future hockey stardom was obvious even when he played in Junior A, a Canadian farm league that was called amateur because it had a salary limit of $20,000 a year. La Fleur was the star of the Quebec City Ramparts and skimmed the rink with the grace of a hunting sea bird and a shot as accurate as the sword with which Cyrano de Bergerac cut buttons from a tormentor's tunic.

Off the ice he was the shy adolescent in excelsis, murmuring, stammering, and blushing as he wished me and my camera in hell, a place he probably presumed as eternity in the company of English-speaking interviewers. I won't say that my French reminds anyone of the liquid tones of Charles Boyer, but then neither does the French spoken anywhere in Canada. What I did find when I offered to conduct the on-camera interview in his language was that he displayed an understandable improvement in ease and volubility as I blushed and stammered through the questions. American viewers unable to manage the accents of either Quebec or the Horace Mann School for Boys, were treated to English titles.

Four years later, when La Fleur was a star with the Canadiens, he had managed to speak English about as well as did the late M. Boyer and he had given up blushing and stammering, but even then and thereafter he had the small-town, family-oriented person's discomfort at the trappings of fame. If he keeps on as he is going he can probably end up as the premier of the province, but he will probably decline on the grounds that he wouldn't care for the making of speeches.

La Fleur's teammate and temperamental opposite is Ken Dryden, perhaps the NHL's best goaltender and a man who does not fit any of the game's clichés or definitions. At six feet four he was considered too big for a job that is usually done by squat and agile men not much taller than the net they protect. On a team which represents the nationalist aspirations of French Canada, his name betrays him as one of the enemy, and he is a practicing attorney and an Ivy League graduate playing a game where high-school diplomas are as rare as full sets of teeth.

He managed to get along with his teammates by being as sparing with words as he was with enemy goals, aware as he was that the first time someone called him Monsieur Le Professeur, he would be set off from his comrades in a way that can be fatal in this simulacrum of war where the unthinking closeness of medieval mercenaries, the cold comradeship of the condottieri, is essential to success.

In 1973, however, Dryden had a salary quarrel with the Montreal organization and became one of those rarities, a holdout who actually held out, spending a whole season as a law clerk at about a twelfth of his hockey salary.

During the year of his absence from the NHL Dryden realized a goalie's dream by getting out of the net and becoming an attacker, joining the eternal boys, the almost-wases and the never-weres of the industrial leagues. He played for the Vulcan Packagers. I asked him why he did not continue his specialty in this off-year, and he said with the reasonableness that in one less qualified would be arrogance, that obviously opponents would never score.

For his unfamiliar new position he had to learn to skate again, since the twenty-pound protective pads no longer encumbered his legs, dictating a modified waddle over the ice. One can relearn physical habits but mental attitudes present, as those who have groaned on the analytic couch can tell you, a much more difficult problem.

When Dryden scored a goal for the Packagers, all his reflexes signaled disaster. He had done the unforgiveable and put the puck in the net, a place he had been dedicated to protect. It was, in symbolic terms, the commission of an unthinkable rape.

"I didn't know what to do, actually," he said later. "If I had been able to think about it, I probably would have gone after the puck and I would have thrown my arms in the air and everything, but I didn't know what to do and so I just ended up lining up again."

Also during that year he felt the wrenching loneliness that actors and old athletes feel when they meet the "family," the cast, the team, from which, for whatever reason, they have been separated.

Visiting the Canadiens in Toronto he found it "a very difficult experience. I didn't really enjoy the game very much, and I went down to the dressing room afterward, and it was like you were sort of thrown back into something that you knew very well and you felt very much a part of, and then, all of a sudden, everybody was dressed and going out for the bus to go the airport to play in Boston the next night, and you were going out to the car to go home to go to the office the next day. And it was—that was—the most difficult time that I've had since I've stopped playing."

Subsequently Dryden settled his differences with the Montreal organization and returned with distinction to his job with the Canadiens, so that the law will have to wait until Ken, like Jacques Plante, makes that last mistake which convinces the front office that when everybody goes to the next town, he must stay behind.

I first saw Dryden play for Cornell when, investigating the college hockey scene for CBS, I discovered to my surprise that the game as played under intercollegiate rules is faster than the professional variety.

The reason is that body checking, the head-on crash form of defense, is severely limited by the rules, so that instead of looking like a Dodgem arena where the little round cars are always colliding, the rink resembles the surface of a lake where waterbugs fly past each other in ever-changing patterns.

One of the motives that sent us to watch the college game was to go into the question of helmets, mandatory at the school level, but proudly eschewed by most of the pros.

Since skulls are soft and rinks are hard, not to mention the edges of carelessly or maliciously wielded sticks, it had always seemed rather foolhardy of the pros to avoid a protection which even the wildest old berserk Viking never went without.

There was not even the excuse, advanced by the goalies, that the mask might induce carelessness and encourage inattention. The helmets did have one disadvantage, however, which few had considered. They were a bar to easy identification.

Hockey players go on and off the ice in endless waves, since all-out skating is quickly exhausting even to the most well conditioned, and although the devoted fan has memorized the numbers on the program, the constant change and the speedy scurry often makes the reading of numbers difficult. In modern arenas hockey is largely viewed from above, the only place from which the pattern of play has much coherence, and the tops of heads are therefore valuable clues to who's who. From the Dagwood pompadour of Bobby Orr to the flax-girdled bald spot of Bobby Hull to the gleaming skull of old Ching Johnson, follicular identification proved very valuable to the hockey devotee and soothing to the player who is as anxious for recognition as any of us. Moments of greatness lose their savor when ascribed to another.

The college players perform for the most part before crowds of modest size and seem comfortable enough in the white leather hats that protect one's longevity at the expense of one's identity.

It is interesting to note that helmets have recently blossomed among the pros like mushrooms in a damp meadow, and I suspect that TV's increasing role in the game may have something to do with this. In a live situation the fan must follow the action himself, but curled up in front of the glass eye he can be sure that skilled commentators will name and rename everybody he is seeing, and describe and redescribe, with the aid of replay, everything that takes place. Distinctive plays are not only rerun, but rerun in slow motion and freeze frame so that no moment of glory passes by on the wings of confusion and excitement before it can be totally understood, and its heroes and villains placed in exact perspective.

In its constant search for sporting novelty, TV, which has immortalized just about everything you can do with an automobile and celebrated the sporting ineptitudes of the famous, might consider giving the viewer a glimpse of college hockey. It admittedly lacks the popular violence but there is something exhilarating about its speed. Watching it makes me think of an assignment I once had to cover 150-pound football. The agile little men raced about so rapidly that viewers were convinced that trick effects had been achieved by controlling the film's rate through the projector.

Even though a certain amount of crunch has always been part of hockey at the NHL level, I suspect that the game as played in the seventies is rougher than ever before, not because of television, that popular whipping boy for every sign of decline in our lives, but because massive expansion drew ineptitude to the top and filled the league with players who, like the bullies in boys' books, substitute clumsy brutality for deft maneuvering.

At the height of the craze for the Flyers in Philadelphia, a team that was rather pleased with being called the Broad Street Bullies, it seemed that skill was passé, rather like using a fencing foil against a tank.

The Flyers were not, however, full-time fiends, but rather like the characters in Gothic ghost fiction, who, at stated phases of the moon or at the command of properly spoken incantations, turned for brief periods into things that weakened the sanity and whitened the hair of the narrator.

Coach Fred Shero was the man who spoke the incantations to the team and as he put it, "We have a great, big, strong group of young hockey players and they've got to use their muscle." As a tactful description of healthy incompetence that is fairly succinct, but a further extension of the idea came from Dave Schultz, a young man of considerable charm—if you approach him holding a microphone instead of a hockey stick.

"It's something that just happens on the ice," he said. "It's kind of like a—maybe a split personality. When you get on the ice you kind of change into a different person, and some players have strength and some players have ability to score goals. And I don't have that ability so I have to use my strength more."

One is reminded of the words of Henry Jekyll, stepping onto the rink as Edward Hyde and remarking, "I felt younger, lighter, happier in body; within I was conscious of a heady recklessness, a current of disordered sensual images running like a mill race in my fancy, a solution to the bonds of obligation, an unknown but not an innocent freedom of the soul."

There is, of course, a built-in invitation to violence in hockey, an invitation that arises from the extreme contrasts between free flow and juddering halt that are a part of its pattern. The skilled skater comes as close to negating the laws of friction as anything outside an oiled plate in a laboratory vacuum. The sharp blades, in their minimal contact with the slippery ice, provide the swooping ease that gulls display as they ride the invisible roads in the air. To have this progress painfully interrupted by someone swooping on a collision course, is to change the smoothness of the ice for its hardness and the grace of flight for the clumsiness of the crash. It is no wonder that one gets up feeling like Mr. Hyde, "wicked, tenfold more wicked," and anxious to wreak some terrible vengeance on the person who has broken one's dream of free flight.

Of course, in hockey's long-ago such crashes were less frequent, not simply because Dr. Jekyll had not yet drunk the mixture that makes monsters for an increasingly bloodthirsty audience, but because skating skill made it possible for the first-class hockey player to feint a defender out of position and then skim around him.

In this, the age of sports expansion, we forget that there was, in the thirties, a time of sports contraction when professional leagues packed their records into cardboard boxes and their debts into bankruptcy petitions, and players of promise put aside their hopes and wandered away down the dusty road to factories and offices. Those who survived were, like the cream at the top of old-time milk bottles, rich with golden talent, and in big-league hockey, which, in my childhood, lost a third of its teams—the New York Americans, Montreal Maroons and Ottawa Senators—the six remaining clubs were, perforce, all-star down to the last substitute.

Some sports do not suffer when the level of play sinks to the fireman's-field-day level. Badly played football is in some ways more exciting than the skilled mayhem of the pros. The errors of the gridiron lead to long runs and great arching passes which fall into the arms of unguarded receivers like plums pulling free of their stems.

Games where delicacy of touch is paramount, however, are not at their best when the touch is the sweaty ham-handedness of the inept, and hockey, like billiards or polo, is, when awkwardly performed, only an irritating reminder of how marvelous it is when the masters display their skills.

Certainly the hours I spent in the aforementioned Minneapolis rink watching the small boys were in a class with time spent at dog-show puppy classes, show-business softball games, and lunch-hour volleyball in the financial district, swollen hours as zesty as those spent reading airline magazines in a holding pattern.

Even when the Minneapolis boys fought, which at the behest of their frustrated fathers they occasionally did, they lacked the spontaneous fury of the schoolyard, and you expected that they were waiting for the fight coach to pull them apart and start them again under his guidance.

Perhaps the future of hockey lies in the direction the Russians have been laying out, a direction as rigidly patterned as the Bolshoi's choreography, a style in which one passes to a teammate even in front of an open net because the play, as designed, calls for that pass. The Russians have played on almost even terms with the best of the Canadians, but if the play of the Minneapolis miniatures depresses us by its sloppiness, so, curiously, the precise rigidities of the Soviet Army Six depress us by their mechanical evenness. The Russians play the game as well as rational men can do it, and I suppose what I miss in their game is the divine irrationality that I saw when old Bill Cook of the Rangers would go the full length of the ice passing to himself by bouncing the puck off his own skate blades, or when Maurice "the Rocket" Richard of Montreal proved that sporting nicknames are not always hyperbolic, or, in our own time, watching Bobby Orr of Boston skate at two defensemen waiting to hit him high and low. Classic strategy and the modern Russian blueprint agree that he should pass left or right and try to scramble to a position near the net.

Again and again with the unanswerable arrogance of the virtuoso he would skate at the two defensemen, appear for a moment to have vanished into a gold-brown blur, and then reappear on the other side of the baffled enemy, who, like comedy villains, would have knocked each other down.

No one would even plan such a play, and if hockey becomes the drawing board drudgery that the Soviet success threatens, no one will be allowed to try it. Hockey will then join many other sports in the joyless devotion to the "team play" concept that is so popular with the coaches and administrators who think of sport in terms of "training for life." Obviously Soviet sport is an arm of the government's propaganda machine. Less obviously, sport in the western world is both part of the propaganda machine and part of society's tool chest for providing itself with people who will leave decisions and the rightness thereof to assorted managers, father figures, and political leaders.

Of course, any game played by more than two people requires a good deal of skilled interaction, but there is no accident in the fact that the military and the modern sporting establishment have exchanged vocabularies and are eager to exchange philosophies and techniques. Team play as the stimulating and aesthetically satisfying interaction of a group of willing participants is the essence of sport. Team play of the "hup, two, three, four" sort, as practiced by those who think of games as athletics to the end of a more efficient anthill, is gaining ground very fast. The burgeoning bureaucracy of sport uses the athlete to a variety of manipulative purposes in the same way that the educational bureaucracy has given up teaching in the interests of expanding its new purpose, the profitable proliferation of administrative functions.

It is odd to think of Canadian hockey players, wrapped in their provincial, anti-intellectual macho, as spokesmen for freedom, but their neck-or-nothing style of play, their swagger, and their constant defiance of common sense in matters of medicine, motion, and the limitations of the human body, make them the natural opponents of the sport-as-useful-discipline school.

Hazlitt denied his Indian jugglers status as artists because once they had achieved their level of sensational competence, thought ceased and "the muscles ply instinctively to the dictates of habit . . . the limbs require little more than to be put in motion for them to follow a regular track with ease and certainty."

Here, at least, the hockey player surpasses the juggler, since the ease and certainty of the regular track is denied him even though his muscles must ply instinctively to the dictates of habit. The choices that he must make are immensely varied, even though he must, in dealing with them, show all the ingrained skill of the man who keeps a Sargasso of objects aloft.

As I write, it is seventeen years since the hockey moment that for me most exemplifies the defiance of uncertainty by skill, the moment when the jugglers' parabola of plates or oranges becomes a net of lightning bolts.

One of the participants in the moment was the man considered to be the all-time number one player, Gordie Howe, then of the Detroit Red Wings. The other was a man who made the cover of every national magazine, but couldn't make it as a regular in big-league hockey, Jack MacCartan, goaltender for the victorious American Olympic team of 1960.

American hockey players at that time were considered the equal of English baseball players or Russian golfers, and the victory of the U.S. team sent the media into a frenzy. Because of his spectacular play MacCartan was at the incandescent center of publicity's luminosity, and the then second-rate New York

Rangers decided to try to fill Madison Square Garden with those who had not managed to get to Squaw Valley to see MacCartan do Horatius at the Bridge against the Red Tide. It would be a big jump from the Olympics to the pros, but the Ranger management, used to losing, decided that whether the young hero was ready or not, there were dollars to be made in finding out.

The only voice I heard raised in opposition to this plan was that of the cab driver who took me to the Garden.

"Aren't you ashamed?" he said when I gave him the address. "What do you think is going to happen to that kid? I'll tell you what's going to happen. He's going to get slaughtered while you and a bunch of other ghouls get your kicks out of his humiliation. He did something for his country and now he's going to suffer for it."

The driver stopped short of ordering me onto the subway, however, and I arrived at the full Garden in time to see MacCartan take the ice to what seemed to me surprisingly encouraging cheers from putative ghouls.

Twelve years later MacCartan told me that he had considered not going to the Garden at all that afternoon.

"I didn't know if I belonged there or what. I didn't know what to expect, not having seen much of the National Hockey League, and I just didn't know how I was going to do."

He was the juggler just going from four oranges to five and in the course of what turned out to be a great performance, he faced Howe, the master, coming in on him all alone with lots of time to pick the spot for his shot. What drove MacCartan that night he was unable to remember, near the end of his career as he talked to me in a little house too small for his souvenirs, but he simply dove at Howe's sharp-pointed skates, flinging himself like some G. A. Henty hero going for a sputtering shell, and with greater risks, since Henty's heroes were never hurt. Risky as it was, the dive had been perfectly timed and perfectly aimed and it was the only move that could succeed.

The Rangers won that game 3–1 but the road turned rocky for MacCartan after that and he spent years in towns where media coverage is no more than a line score. From the Olympics to the Rangers to the Kitchener Beavers to the Minnesota Fighting Saints, he kept trying for that ease and certainty that practice is supposed to produce. Obviously ease and certainty were not "cemented into closer and closer union" and MacCartan was left at last regretting "that I could not have done a better job, been a great one, because I admire those fellows so much."

Still, and this is a thing that keeps us all looking at sport, he had a moment under tremendous pressure when he transcended what mere skill is supposed to achieve, when he went across Hazlitt's dividing line between craftsmen and artists. It was "that which is seen but for a moment, but dwells in the heart always."

Of course a game is no more than a diversion, as is the spectacle of the juggler, but the tremendous dedication that even the lesser hockey players bring to their practice and play pushes them as close to the arts as sport is ever likely to get, and at moments like the confrontation between Howe and MacCartan there is a picture, frozen thereafter in the mind, of perfections coming together like sparking flints.

Common sense confesses that it was less than art, but the glow of memory insists that it was more than muscles plying instinctively to the dictates of habit.

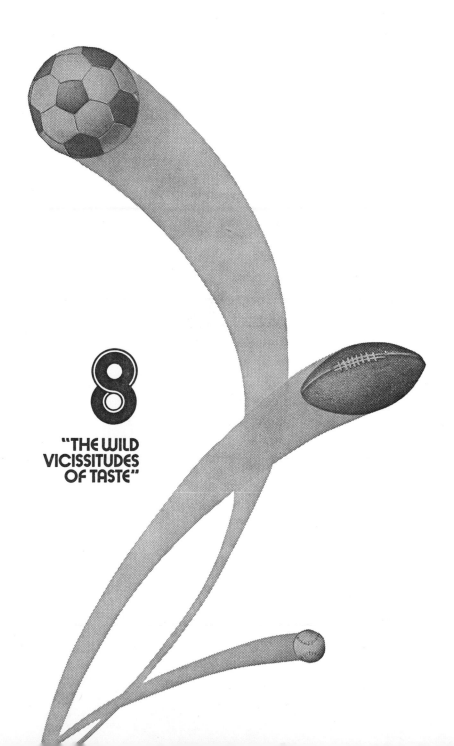

8

**"THE WILD
VICISSITUDES
OF TASTE"**

In no other sport are there so many close scores and dramatic final minutes, as in basketball. Those who don't like the game have suggested that it might be a good idea to announce a score of 100–100 at the outset, play for five minutes, and arrive at the 118–117 or 116–114 figures that the full-length games so often produce.

Those who love the game point out that the variety of play is such that there is no danger of satiation, and the ghetto children endlessly shooting baskets through the night shadows of an ill-lit playground are as tirelessly eager as they were when play had begun under the red sun of early morning.

I am somewhere between columnist Red Smith, who invented and urged the five-minute game, and the zealots who will sit happily through a high-school tripleheader, and with the detachment of the neutral, I point out that the see-saw quality of the game has a philosophical equivalent when one judges the virtues and vices of its effect on many of those who play it.

Every year thousands of high school and college players give up the idea of education in any field off the basketball floor in order to pursue the dream of professional success. After all, no other game is so richly rewarded, and the constant announcements of six-figure salaries for substitute players are powerful incentives to kids who run on a diet of starch and gravy.

What happens to most of them? Let me quote to you the principal of Boys' High School in Brooklyn, a school whose basketball team could probably beat a good many college fives.

"During my time here," he told me in 1969, "I have sent thirty-five boys to college on basketball scholarships. Only two of them received degrees, not because the boys were stupid or ill-prepared, but because the colleges they attended would not let them take enough courses to be graduated. If they had wished a degree they would have had to return for a fifth year at their own expense. The two exceptions went to black colleges that went on the basis that a diligent player should be rewarded with a diploma even though education may or may not have gone with it."

How many of those who spend four years educationally undernourished on the thin gruel of pop culture courses and seminars on driver education are going to move on to professional ball? Twenty-odd will make it in the National Basketball Association and perhaps another hundred or so will settle for the four- and five-figure salaries of minor league and industrial basketball, or go to Europe and play for people whose cheers they can't understand.

The rest have been prepared for nothing but discontent. Like the teams they played for, they seemed to have come so close. A missed basket in a post-season game, a sprained ankle the night the scout was there, inferior teammates who didn't give one a chance—were it not for these accidents, think the rejects, they might be fulfilling the dreams that outshone the lights of the playground.

In the year I saw Boys' High play, the team was forced, by a New York Board of Education decision, to play most of its games in tiny gyms. Some disturbances at school games in Madison Square Garden were responsible for the decision, which, fair or not, doomed these athletic virtuosi to perform their magic in low-roofed rooms where the pillars outnumbered the spectators.

As a relief from this claustrophobic routine, Boys' High had a single trip that year, going to New Haven to play Still House High in the unaccustomed light and luxury of the vast Yale University arena. A further excitement was provided by us, the CBS News crew, which would, for a moment, open the window of immortality and let the world see Boys' High at the end of a brilliant season in which, maddeningly, no one had seen them.

The game proved another of those close ones and, convinced that they were getting the worst of the officiating, the visitors retreated into a set shot game to cut down on the foul calls. With six seconds to go Boys led by three points, and as New

Haven came down the floor in a last attack, Coach Jones shouted to his team to let Still House have the basket lest a vigorous defense lead to a foul call and the possibility of a tie and overtime. So, in the moment of their TV triumph, the Brooklynites were as stock-still as the support posts in their home gymnasium, then, as the gun sounded, celebrated their one-point victory with the traditional leaps and cries. I am sure that at that moment all of them saw a future of Cadillacs and penthouses, the goals the sports pages promise as they report the financial triumphs of the player agents shooting baskets at the bank.

In fact, to my knowledge, one member of that Boys' High team, Mel Davis, had a so-so career in the pros, and the rest, whatever they got from college, probably didn't get an education.

They played the game with an insouciant grace that all those playground hours had polished, and, not having been inside their heads, I can't say that they were all full of unrealistic dreams—although circumstance certainly encouraged them. I think back on that game not as the triumphant end to a happy story, but as probably the first act of a rather grim one, a one-point win to be followed by an awful lot of the might-have-beens, which seem like one-point losses.

The role of the basketball foundry colleges is obviously indefensible but the world is full of indefensible enterprises that are thriving, and the players would probably be the first to cry out against any reform that might close to them the carousel and its tantalizing brass rings.

A civil rights zealot might have been pleased with some film we had from the University of Texas at El Paso. Here in the deep South was an all-black starting five. If you looked closely at the film, however, you realized that there were no black faces in the watching crowd and none on the bench. The mercenaries were limited to the minimum necessary for success, and I suspect that their classroom schedules were the minimum necessary to maintain the fiction of their student status.

On his way to professional success Calvin Murphy, considered too short by most college scouts, accepted a scholarship at Niagara University. Fascinated by a five-foot nine-inch phenomenon in a giants' game, Lamoreaux and I braved a Buffalo area winter to do a feature on Calvin, who proved to have a wit as quick as the reflexes that permitted him to triumph among the tall.

Wit tends to wither, however, without the nourishment of laughter, and it soon became clear that the only time Calvin heard the comforting sound of approbation was when he sank a shot. When the camera followed him across the campus to lunch, we noticed that he went substantially ungreeted and sat alone in the cafeteria. Asked if he had no friends to join for the meal he said with a bleak smile, "What friends? I'm here to play basketball."

Calvin is now at the top, but the path from the playground to the pros was paved with slippery blocks of culture shock.

Several years after he had left school, while he was a successful professional with a happy marriage and a splendid home, he still kept on his wall a group picture of the Niagara basketball team from which the coach's face had been inked out as a reminder that as far as Calvin was concerned the bitterness about his college years had not subsided.

I remember in that connection a remarkable speech from a Columbia University recruiter who was urging New York high-school boys not to leave behind the camaraderie of the ghetto. I never thought to hear the ruins of Harlem described as a superior social club, but there was a strange logic to the recruiter's spiel about what life would be like in a white American college town where producing an Afro-pick comb might get one arrested for carrying a weapon.

The carefree existence of Joe College long ago disappeared for the scholarship athlete, but for the black scholarship athlete there is often a special loneliness that makes his passage through the youthfully buoyant collegiate ambience as detached from the fun as the life of a banquet waiter. The voluntary segregation of the black colleges resonates an alarm in the minds of liberals who hope for a color-blind America, and yet I am aware that athletes at Grambling, a black school with a big-time sports program, are obviously and joyously a part of the student body in a way I rarely saw in colleges where the black athlete, already a little separate as a mercenary, was more separate still because he was a black mercenary.

Still, there are those multi-year multi-million-dollar contracts being signed each year and in a society where lottery tickets, slot machines, and numbers games are among the devices that will finally Make It Come True, the basketball players are going to be under the streetlights and in the school and college gyms hoping for that One Big Break.

For Pete Maravich basketball was less a lottery than a legacy. His father, Coach Press Maravich early began turning his son's steps to the court with the dedication that is admiringly reported when great musicians pay tribute to their hard-pushing parents.

Pictures of Pete in childhood action—and there are plenty of them in 8x10 glossy finish suitable for newspaper reproduction—show the eerie perfection of the talented zealot, and by the time Pete was ready for college the elder Maravich was able to sell a package to Louisiana State consisting of freshman Pete and head coach Press.

Almost immediately Pete began setting college scoring records, although his nickname, Pistol Pete, suggested that some thought he was more concerned with points than team play.

I interviewed the father and son when it became clear that Pete was within easy reach of the all-time collegiate scoring record, and found that success was a paramount emollient for the inevitable abrasions of their athletic Oedipian relationship.

Press admitted that he had decided that the boy would be a basketball player almost as soon as he found out that his son had ten fingers on two hands but, as he tells it, the early approach was an "Isn't this fun?" introduction in which Dad set up a backyard basket and took shots until the toddler asked to try what seemed a fascinating pastime. Pete missed and Press scored, and, at last "He said why didn't mine go in and I said, 'Well, you can't beat the old man [Are you listening, Sigmund?] and I've got to teach you,' and he said, 'well, then, teach me,' and from that day it became competitive with us in basketball." The word competitive implies an equality that seems inevitably to have been lacking, however.

Talking to whatever millions watched the CBS Saturday News on January 17, 1970, Pete calmly told how, in a game in his sophomore year, he had questioned his father's judgment in a time-out conference. "He jumped up and whipped me across the head and said, 'I'm the coach, you're the player, so listen to me.' I was so embarrassed."

Embarrassed seems a word of almost incredible mildness, but after fifteen years of "You can't beat the old man," it has a wonderfully understandable servility.

The elder Maravich's words on that occasion are also curious in the assumption that the coach-player relationship permits the teacher to wallop a student who asks questions. Still, whatever resentments may have burned in the boy who, since early childhood, had been, in a sense, imprisoned in a hardwood square, careful camaraderie was the public face of the relationship.

There were rumors that the Maraviches might go to the pros in a continuing team relationship, with Press taking over the club with which his son would sign. When I brought up this prospect in our interview, Pete showed his only sign that his ears might still be ringing from the assorted knocks of his education and, with an anxiously deferential look at his father, said he thought it was time he began thinking about going it alone.

The following year Pete went to the Atlanta Hawks with the traditional fuss about the huge sum he was paid, and Press was left to fill a new, Maravich-inspired 15,000-seat gym with a fairly ordinary team.

Like the root masses, which gardeners divide for the health of the plant, both Maraviches seemed to wither a bit at first. Press failed to win with his Peteless leftovers, and a year later was let out at LSU. Pete failed to get along with his new teammates and lived alone in an apartment as elegant and warm as the conference room of a Swedish conglomerate. When I visited him there he told me with some pride that though the best decorators had done up the place, he had picked the pictures. They were cool abstractions, which, I suspect, reminded him of those in-and-out-round-about paths to success that his father used to draw with his fingers on the sidelines. Pete had questioned one of those paths and had been humiliated for his temerity, but after all, those drawings had led him to unquestionable success, a home where every glistening, unused accessory to the good life shouted Money.

In the following years Coach Press kept moving and Pete kept improving until he was acknowledged as one of the game's greats, but I often wonder if anything after those triumphant LSU years had the same fierce fullness.

I was reminded of them again when I was sent to one of those little Midwest towns that, for the good of everyone, have been left off the road maps. There we were to film a high-school phenomenon whose father was hoping to coach him into the right scholarship which would at last lead him through the prosperous portals of professional basketball.

In a sense, our visit was a great opportunity to show the athletic wares but it was also obviously a cruel pressure on a teenager who doesn't want to make mistakes in front of millions and who, thinking of the possibility, tightens up until failure has become reality. Although the evening was not an unrelieved disaster, the cyclopean eye of CBS seemed to stare the young star out of countenance and sometimes even out of competence, and at one point, as he came miserably to the bench and picked up a water bottle to irrigate his tension-dried mouth, his father snatched the water away and, virtually into our microphone, shouted, "Do you have to be so bad on national TV?" It occurred to me then that though we have a vast literature on how difficult it is to be a son, we don't have much on how hard it is to be a father.

It's nice to report that at game's end the hopeful pair went off arm in arm, making prospects out of odd pieces of consolation.

Shortly afterward I left TV news and I can only hope that someone gave Mickey Crowe a drink of water and a scholarship.

One who got a scholarship at twice the age of the schoolboy was a remarkable man named Ed Butler, who turned out to be one of the best spokesmen for the value of sport in general and basketball in particular that I ever met.

At the age of fifteen Butler, with several companions, had taken part in a grocery holdup. One of his friends had a gun and killed the grocer, and all of them were sentenced to life imprisonment. Although a juvenile, Butler went to an adult penitentiary where he was continually saying, "You can't do that to me!" and then serving time in solitary confinement because the essence of imprisonment is that they can do it because the state has asked them to do it.

One of the purposes of prison is, of course, to break men so that they will not be troublesome to those who have the job of watching them. Whether they are of any use to society after their release is society's lookout and not that of the prison bureaucracy.

The task of the prisoner who wishes to remain a whole person

167

against the time when being a whole person will have a value, is to pretend to be broken while maintaining a lamp just big enough to light the soul. Since, as Max Beerbohm pointed out to us in "The Happy Hypocrite," masks have at last a tendency to dictate the shape of the faces beneath them, many prisoners masquerade as robots so successfully that they become them, but Butler, with a minimal hope of ever being released, achieved the balance of administrative pliancy and inner independence through the outlet of exercise yard basketball. In the course of play he became so adept that the Baltimore Bullets, after an exhibition game inside the walls, told him that they would give him a tryout if he ever got out.

Basketball gave him a permissible safety valve for the inevitable aggressions of cage life. It gave him as well a goal—perfecting his skills within the confines of a game that gave him that freedom of which Sartre spoke, the security of taking part in an activity whose rules are logical and understandable. Fortified by this experience Butler "Didn't ever give up hope. I don't know—something inside me just kept saying, 'You're going to get out one day.' I didn't think like a convict. Didn't think like an inmate, that is. I just constantly kept in touch with the street through magazines and books. And I tried to live in here like I would in the street."

The "street," a revealingly wistful prison word for the whole outside world, opened to Butler after fifteen years. During those years he had perfected himself at a game and, more importantly though relatedly, had achieved maturity.

The act that had much to do with bringing about his release was characteristic of that maturity. He talked his fellow cons out of a rebellion by hammering into desperate minds the thought that a brand-new warden ought to be given a chance to redress old grievances and that burnt mattresses just led to hard beds.

He had then to make the choice between the long-held daydream of pro ball and the solid achievement of a college education. Wisely he decided that though age erodes skills, it can't steal knowledge, and he became a student and basketball captain at Baltimore's Loyola University.

He was a thirty-two-year-old undergraduate when he went back to the Maryland State Correctional Institution with me to be photographed and interviewed pacing between the narrow cells that once had housed him.

The constant clangor of gates opening and closing punctuated our talk, and as we walked, he stopping occasionally for an encouraging word with a friend, he pointed out to me the pattern of colored floor tiles, on some of which, as part of their conditioning to meaningless obedience, prisoners are not allowed to step.

He told me of men so perfectly "conditioned" that upon their release to civilian life they wept helplessly at the task of choosing between two different-colored shirts after years in the unalterable drabness that offers no choice. He told me again that basketball had kept him from becoming one of those who, faced with the choices of freedom, commit the meaningless crimes that lead them back into the bleak safety of a steel-webbed cell.

Later we went out into the yard and watched the prisoners surging up and down the basketball court. Watching them, Butler told me that he wanted to make a career as a psychologist in the hope that he might guide a few old and new comrades into a life they could handle. Head fakes and hook shots don't have much to do with wisdom or a wider view of the world, but if Butler is right, his game provided a valuable way station, an oasis of logic, where the ego could mend its cracks with measurable accomplishment.

Covering sports over a stretch of years one discovers a startlingly varied series of motivations and satisfactions within any single sport.

If basketball means fortune to some, and salvation to Ed Butler, it meant, to Tom Meschery, the poet of the game, a chance to earn a few scars and bruises as proof of his dedication.

"I need a good floor burn or a heavy fall to get me going," Meschery told me. "I think there's a little bit of the masochist in me."

The pain perhaps excuses the violence that, in his playing days, used to swirl around Meschery like twigs around a whirlpool.

"I don't go seeking after it. I don't go looking for a fight on the court. But it seems that every time there is one, Tom Meschery is involved."

More objective than Dave Meggysey, the football player, who seemed to strike blindly and indiscriminately in an effort to cut loose from the dragging pack of pain he had carried since childhood, Meschery was quite clinical in his approach to the need for violence, which sends some into crime, some into sport, and some into the military service. He saw it, on occasion, as a dark mirror image of the Puritan ethic, a chance, through the obvious effort of physical fight and its concomitant physical pain, to achieve the peace that is supposed to be the reward of accomplishment.

It was Meschery who developed for me the theory that happiness in sport is only possible to those of limited accomplishment, those, that is, who have a clear idea of the dimensions of their potential and can give a sigh of satisfaction when those dimensions are filled.

Obviously such satisfactions are not available to the great, whose limitations are out somewhere in a shadow area beyond the well-defined boundaries of probability. They are like Sisyphus, who, you may remember, tricked Zeus and for this crime was condemned endlessly to push large rocks uphill. So the great, who make the rest of us look depressingly ordinary, are, for that crime, condemned to push the rock of accomplishment uphill without ever being able to say, "This is far enough."

Tom put it a good deal less flossily.

"After nine years in the National Basketball Association," he said, "I have a scoring average of 9.2 points a game. Any time the tenth point drops in, a little spring unwinds inside me and I say to myself, 'Congratulations, Tom, you have done your best.' But what is the best for a Wilt Chamberlain? Wilt once scored a hundred points in a game. What was his potential? He was never sure and therefore never content.

"I'm not a pastoral or philosophical poet," said Meschery. "I kind of think of myself as more of a hard-nosed poet."

Oddly he treated his writing as he treated the game, making a struggle of it, putting together his excellent verses while staring at the deplorable decor of depressing motels and sweating.

"I love sports where I have to sweat, where the whole feeling of the sport is vigorous. I could never play golf, for instance. An old buddy of mine told me that I could never play golf because I could never foul anybody. It's not just the violence, I like the feeling of sweating. When I write, the same thing occurs in a way. I become tense and I write—and I usually find that I write in big spurts—and then once I've finished writing, I know right away that I'm through and then I can go to sleep."

So even poets, even athletes, are as driven as the struggling businessman who says, "Boy, I'd love to be paid for playing a game," or "I know you write, but what is your real job?"

All of us, poets, players, and executives are apparently hearing the gentle voices of our elders, filled with kindly and relentless admonition, as they ask the child returning from the day's adventures "What did you accomplish today?"

For Denise Long, the marvelous star of the Union-Whitten team in the Iowa State girls tournament, basketball was the fun of instant fame.

"I miss basketball," she said years later at a teaching clinic in Massachusetts, "but I miss basketball like in high school. There was more glamor in it then, more prestige. We had large crowds watching me play and I—that's what motivated me more than anything—playing in front of crowds."

Unhappily Denise was like a coloratura at a rock concert, since women's basketball in the sixties had not developed as had golf or tennis to a point where there was a full-time future for a first-rate practitioner.

Denise can only hand on her skills and hope that some lineal descendant will arrive at a fame more enduring than that which ends when one is a teenager in Des Moines.

"I feel like I've been bottled up," she said, looking back on a five year post-high-school career that included a few girls league games, which were no more than halftime entertainment in the NBA, and a brief tour of the Orient. "I've been bottled up and suppressed. I had something to offer and it was suppressed. And it lasted for a while, and then, you know, there's nothing I can do about it, really."

While we were at the Sam Jones Camp the eye of our camera became for Denise that long lost crowd, and she reached for the icy excitement of competition in a shooting contest with NBA star Jones. She was barely defeated and the sudden fire of her chagrin showed how much she missed the simple thing she had asked of the game, the sound of cheering crowds.

Moving to the basket and making the shot is as instinctively built into the player as the drive of a salmon on the way to the breeding grounds, and I was bemused, therefore, to visit a college that made a fetish of staying away from the basket. Ohio's Ashland Purple Eagles gloried for a time in leading the nation in defense, or as sportscasters have taught us to call it, DEEfense. In order to do this the Eagles spread their wings and stood in a bouncing line in front of their basket, defying the enemy to break through without committing a foul. Naturally this moat-and-portcullis style does not produce high scoring, and the figures in the papers sometimes looked more like the outcome of a loosely played baseball game, but it produced that precious by-product of prowess, fame.

Ashland will forgive me if I say that it is not in the first flight of American universities. No one has written a book called *Stover at Ashland,* no one has complained that there are too many Ashland men around the President or on the Supreme Court, and its red brick buildings, created, it appears, from that single architectural all-purpose cube drawing that is the backbone of our educational configuration, do not suggest the dreaming spires of Oxford.

Still, for years, wherever sports statistics are read, Ashland's name and defensive figures led the list.

At its games, egged on by cheerleaders and a selfless student smothering in that taxidermical oddity, a purple eagle suit, the packed stands rocked with excitement because *nothing was happening* while they chanted DEEfense DEEfense. Ten thousand extras charging a British square in a Kipling film couldn't have matched the noise.

It occurred to me then how fitting is the definition of sport as a shared delusion. The participants, once they agree on the delusion, can be excited by the most unlikely of circumstances.

It is said that in great public squares in Moscow crowds watching big electric chessboards go wild when, in a match some miles away, a player moves P-QB6.

I do not know if Ashland still pursues eminence through specialization, but its players, driven by their curiously negative motivation, remain in my mind as wonderful examples of the variety of approach that sport allows.

There is no nonsense about DEEfense in Harlem's Rucker League, where basketball at the highest level is to be seen on the pitted asphalt of city playgrounds. Pros, ex-pros, those who hope to be pros, and local legends in the game of one-on-one play in the Rucker League, and from my observation I would guess that the motivation here is the purest in sports. It is the simple wish to test one's skill against the best—not for money, not for headlines, not for any tangible reward except a team T-shirt and the intangible reward of the approval of a unique crowd. Unique is a much misused word, but in all the games I have seen there has never been a crowd so knowledgeable and so expert as that which watches the Rucker games. It appears that everyone in the rickety stands, in the branches of nearby trees, or perched atop streetlights has spent a large part of his life playing the game, and the players who win the nod from this bunch have a distinction to which more meaning is given than the trophies for which athletic press agents fight.

The league was named for Holcombe Rucker, a teacher and coach who realized, as Ed Butler had, that the structure of games can be a kind of lifeboat in an existence that seems to have no structure at all.

Before his early death, Rucker tirelessly organized teams, taught players, and refereed, drawing the young away from the life of the street corner and the anger that grows in the sour soil of boredom.

It soon became a tradition that many of those who play in the high-level games of the league spend a good deal of time teaching so that their contributions will not be simply an isolated moment of once-a-week glamor.

When we went with our camera crew to film a hot summer Sunday of Rucker action, I noticed at once that the crowd, while pleased with the attention of TV, gave us no further heed once the action began. No matter where our lenses turned there was none of the witless waving and grimacing that is such a boring part of baseball broadcasts. If there was a "break in the action" the spectators turned to each other for learned discussion. To look at a camera would be to waste time better spent in appreciation or criticism.

There was also a good deal of the humor that is created by striking sparks off the adamantine grimness of ghetto life.

At one point Charley Scott, a college star at North Carolina who had just signed a big contract with Washington's professional team, flew into the air and landed elbow-down on the asphalt. A man sitting next to me roared with laughter, subsided into gulping chuckles, and then wiping away tears of pleasure, told me that he had been picturing the face of Charley's wealthy new employer if he could see his precious toy being bounced off the pavement.

When Scott got up he was laughing too, perhaps in relief at the discovery that he could lift his arm.

Even as that Sunday's tripleheader rolled along, lubricated by the sweat steaming out of a city summer day, there, on a playground behind the grandstand, kids who might have been watching had chosen the sincerest form of admiration, imitation, and were plugging away to improve themselves to a point where they might move from behind the seats to in front of them.

One professional team that could have used some time behind the grandstand was the ragged regiment that represented Cleveland in its first NBA year. Called the Cavaliers, perhaps after the Royalist army that lost to Oliver Cromwell, they were assembled by one of those professional drafts in which a city is allowed to pay for the players who would otherwise be released by the stronger teams. When I arrived to immortalize their ineptitude they had won two of their first thirty-five games and were achieving a kind of unhappy eminence as experts debated the weighty absolute of whether they were the worst team ever to play in the big leagues.

I expected to find a somber group given to locker kicking and wall pounding, and was surprised to discover that in the great tradition of brokenhearted clowns, they were hiding their tears behind laughter. There was, indeed, a good deal of material for mordant humor. Things had gone wrong even before the season began. Owner Nick Mileti had decided, for instance, that his team, however bad, would start things off with a flourish worthy of their dashing name, and to this end was ready with ten-thousand-odd glasses bearing a plumed swordsman, and the requisite amount of wine. The idea was that as the team took the floor for the first time, the audience would rise and toast them in the best seventeenth-century manner, although Mileti hoped that the wish for a souvenir would overcome the impulse to smash the glasses at the end of the toast.

Unfortunately the twentieth century is rather fuddy-duddy and the Ohio Board of Alcoholic Beverage Control began grumping about serving drinks without the appropriate licenses, and the end result was a routine start for what soon became a repeated routine exercise, a Cavalier loss.

The unhappy Mileti was left with a lifetime supply of one of those vaguely identified pink California wines that do not improve with age.

He took to pressing it on visitors at every hour of the day, even those who, like myself, arrived at nine in the morning more in the mood for coffee than for an imprinted glass of what appeared to be a mixture of Kool-Aid and after-shave.

As loss followed loss, Mileti and his coach, Bill Fitch, fresh from college triumphs at Minnesota, must often have thought of carrying the wine about in brown paper bags as a sugary shield against the hard edge of humiliation.

Fitch developed a splendid comic routine for use in the weekly fan luncheons at which he had to talk about the weekly defeats. High point of the act was a piece of game film which showed the Cavs executing a dazzling pass play that ended with the ball dropping through the Cleveland basket. Like a man who can't keep his tongue away from an aching tooth, Fitch would run the film backward and forward, indicating with Pagliaccian laughter that only when the film was reversed did his team run in the right direction. Bob Lewis, the player whose confusion after winning the center jump started the whole rush into the ridiculous, was identified and re-identified to the lunch guests while he stared into his melting ice cream. John Warren, who dropped in the naturally unopposed lay-up, was then metaphorically beaten with bean-filled bladders and the whirlwind of fun ended as Fitch, like some comic penitent, would wield the lash on himself and his coaching and then go home to sit in the cellar of his home and stare at his college trophies.

What was it like to own such a team?

"It's dreadfully—it's—it's incredibly—it's unbelievably—it's indescribably painful," said Mileti, sipping from his wine glass and wondering where was the joyous freedom from care that Bacchus is always promising us through his press agents, the poets.

Five years later when the team had achieved respectability, I reminded Fitch of his unfailing good spirits as the statistics of that terrible season tightened the rack.

"I was supporting myself with humor," he said. "Have done it all my life, but I needed a little bit more, a couple of crutches during those years. If you recall, we didn't win too many in a row; in fact we didn't win too many." Then, letting the red-rimmed eye of truth open for a moment, "I would rather paint this house with a toothbrush than go through again what we went through five years ago."

In a moment, however, he was back dancing on his phantom crutches as I asked him whether, as the losses mounted in that first season, he had ever thought of giving up.

"Aw, I don't know," he said, setting up his defenses more skillfully than his players used to. "Giving up life maybe, rather than coaching."

There are many more losers than there are those who can laugh through losses, and much as Fitch and his lost battalion suffered, it must be said that if they were the worst of teams, they were not the dullest of teams, an honor for which there are far too many contenders.

One of the problems of those old Cavaliers was that the rest of the league had foisted on them too many tinies, that is, little fellows only a few inches over six feet tall.

As the game progresses and the heights increase I think back to my college days when every team wanted a six-foot center, though some had to settle for five eleven, and as I do, I realize that the world as a whole has not grown so much since then. Old chairs, old beds, and old rooms contain us comfortably. At five feet eight and a fraction I look the average American straight in the eye, because statistics say he and I are as alike as tin soldiers on parade. Whence then these mighty figures who must duck their heads beneath sequoia branches? The reasons are for geneticists and nutritionists to discover, but the time has not yet come when this new breed is comfortable anywhere but on a basketball floor.

Ours was the first camera crew to accompany a pro basketball team on an air trip and the sight of these men occupying spaces designed to be within a sixteenth of an inch of discomfort for me and the millions of my mid-sized fellows, was as pathetic as watching a father trying to manage his little daughter's miniature tea set during a make-believe meal. Playing cards had to laid out in the aisle since there was not room for knees and drop tables both, and naps were as impossible as conversation at a discotheque. At the end of the trip there was a brief stretching of legs and then the constrictions of the motel, where beds require geometric thinking in the search for the comfortable position.

All this sometimes make me wonder if the sport is not on the edge of that dangerous ground where we will be alienated from it through failure to identify with the players as our fellows.

If, for example, space travel revealed a race of fifteen-foot people with six tentacular arms per person, if person is the right word, we would probably not thrill at their athletic accomplishments as we would have no way of evaluating them. This is admittedly an example both extreme and unlikely, but when I heard about the eight-foot Chinese basketball center, I wondered if we were not beginning to reach the neighborhood of that dilemma.

Constricted in a world made for smaller people, exhausted by travel schedules of astronautical proportions, forced to play an increasingly physical game in costumes created in the days when the pattern was of quick little men avoiding each other, competing with hungry thousands for each of the lucrative jobs in the NBA, the stars of big-time basketball seem to me the least enviable of sporting luminaries. Their one great moment is at the pay table.

Admittedly this is the best-rewarded of games, but what is forgotten is the hacking hand of the Internal Revenue Service (Huge salaries, like sweepstakes winnings, are always unrealistically announced at their original figure), and the fact that almost any athletic contract will self-destruct like a secret agent's orders if the player receives serious injuries. On the other hand, the player who performs cautiously in order to avoid injuries finds his contract assigned to one of those collections of minor league hopefuls who travel in buses to towns that destroy hope.

Al McGuire, the soundest and best basketball coach I ever met, was one of those who deny the validity of Leo Durocher's oft-quoted and obviously inaccurate remark, "Nice guys finish last." A highly irritable man, Leo endeavored to make a virtue of his harshness, and a macho-minded sports establishment seized on his self-justification as if this intellectual burp was a valuable piece of wisdom.

McGuire approached his game, first as player, then as teacher, with the rare mixture of dedication and objectivity— qualities that seem to preclude each other but that are magnificent when coaxed into harness—that keeps the human spirit out of culs-de-sac.

His playing career was fierce but short, and as soon as he realized that his quickness of mind was more important than his slowness of foot, he turned to coaching and, in his years at Marquette, produced a number of first-rate teams, ending with a national champion.

He knows the rewards and the price that must be paid for them, and looked for those to whom the rewards, educational and/or athletic, would mean the most.

"I think I am a tenement recruiter. I do much better recruiting in big cities and in kind of middle- to low-income brackets. For some reason or other when I go into suburbia, where there is grass in front of the houses, I don't feel too comfortable. I feel I lose some blue-chip high-school players because I don't cater to them. I can't cater to you in June and drive you in October."

He was realistic about the pain of pressure on his players.

"I think they do enjoy it personally—they enjoy it when it's all over. At the present time," he said in 1971, "we run a major league operation here at Marquette University, in that the pressures are passed on from year to year, and it's a tremendous amount of pressure on a young student athlete coming to college. In the town he left as a hero they wait for him to do it again, and I think it is one of the saddest things in sport to see a boy, particularly a minority boy, come to school, not get a contract or a degree, and then go home to put on his shades and shape up on the corner. His life has just been thrown away. I'm a firm believer in degrees. I do not run a plantation at Marquette. My ball players get degrees."

It is easy to see why his fellow coaches often called McGuire "controversial," a word often used nowadays to denote uncomfortable honesty.

He eschews the aggressive passion which often sends teams onto the floor more ready to charge a redoubt than to set up the precise timing of effective play.

"There is no way you can kid young kids today. I can't walk in and all of a sudden I'm going to put my game face on and give them the Rockne talk and kick two lockers, so they'll run through the door and knock it down."

The realist is further in evidence when he explains that part of his plan was always to showcase those seniors who have professional prospects. I once saw him remove a hot-shooting sophomore from a game and lecture the youth about passing to the product, a senior, and saving his shots for two years thence.

Though he is among the few coaches with enough long-range vision to drive his players to that job ticket, the degree, he regarded it as a tool rather than a talisman.

When Jim Chones, a sophomore at Marquette, made application for a hardship exception so that he could join a professional team that season rather than, as the rules demand, serve out his college eligibility, McGuire aided him, making himself even more "controversial." Most college coaches will, in order to hang onto their cheap labor, give such impassioned speeches about the Amateur Ideal and the Joys of Learning (such of it as they permit their players to have), that you would think the traitor would be swept by finer feeling and make a barefoot pilgrimage to prexy's house to kneel in the snow and beg forgiveness.

"I have looked inside Jim Chones' icebox," said McGuire, "and think this is a case where the risk of injury in the next two years with me is enough to make it best for him to take the bonus and leave now."

This flexibility on the question of the degree and the occasional inefficiency that may result from showcasing individual players are a long way from the series of ringing absolutes with which sport likes to raise itself to a point where the smell of incense almost drowns the reek of liniment and sweat.

Absolutes are not found in the streets where Al McGuire grew up, however, and his unwillingness to go along with the cruel cant that comes, without cost to themselves, from the lips of the collegiate priesthood made him seem vulgarly commercial to some, destructive of the romance of sport to others.

Yet, when in his last collegiate game, his team won for him a national title, he knew the magnitude of the gift and the sharp calculating face he had so long presented to the world was suddenly cracked apart. Almost unbearable emotion pressed against his lifelong hard-guy pose, and in a moment the cracks were filled with tears, and he walked blindly from the floor into retirement. It hadn't, he had said, been fun, but I doubt he knew till it was over, how much it had held of fulfillment.

Sitting through what sometimes seems to me to have been aching aeons of basketball, I have often wished myself somewhere else—the racetrack, the ball park, or even the dryer room of a laundromat, but then I think about Ed Butler and Tom Meschery and Al McGuire, and I realize that whatever I think of the play, I have found rich and rewarding variety among the players.

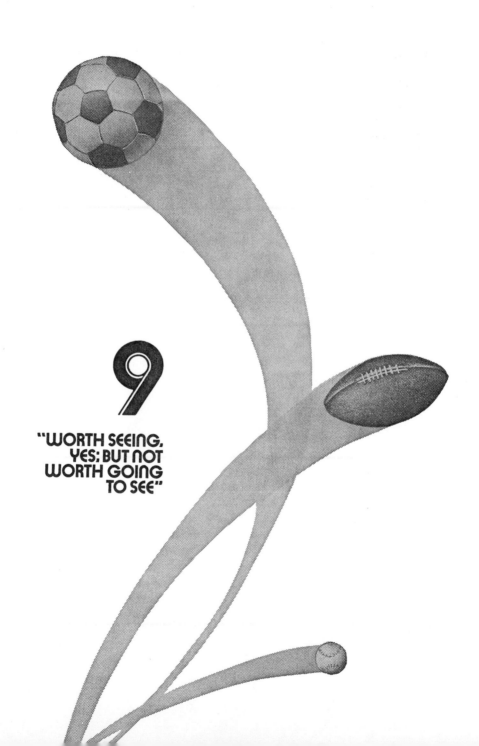

9

"WORTH SEEING, YES; BUT NOT WORTH GOING TO SEE"

When Bud Lamoreaux and I arrived in Mexico City in October 1968 to cover the Olympic Games, we represented the most prestigious, widely-viewed news operation in the world, CBS at the peak of its dominance of the field. Such a position seemed to call for a certain amount of bowing and scraping and the scattering of a rose or two along our imperial path.

A few days before the games, however, the most widely viewed news operation in the world had shown films, taken by a courageous CBS team, of federal troops firing into the retreating backs of Mexican students who were endeavoring to leave the Square of the Two Cultures after a peaceful demonstration.

Despite threats to their lives, the newsmen had photographed the whole methodical slaughter and gotten the films out of the country with the only record of a tragedy as senseless as the one which was to scar the Munich Games four years later.

I was proud of CBS News for showing the films despite obvious political pressures about rocking the boat on the eve of an international event, but I rather wished I could have expressed my pride from a position with NBC or ABC because Lamoreaux and I were welcomed like leprous paparazzi.

"CBS, CBS," murmured a credential official to Lamoreaux. "I have heard the name somewhere but I don't think I have anything here for you. Why don't you try again in four years?"

Appeals to the CBS foreign editors in New York would have been fruitless. Two years later they were to send us to the World Cup Soccer matches in Mexico without basic permits to film, and a lively possibility of arrest for the lack thereof, and on that occasion, as on this, we knew that vague "Do Your Best" adjurations were all that could be elicited. Such communications have the same effect as Marshal Haig's morale messages to the mud-caked troops on the Somme.

I don't know how Bud achieved it, but armed with nothing more than a belief in the rightness of our presence, in a midnight meeting with an Olympic official was finally able to get over the idea that with credentials being showered on the representatives of Bulgarian literary magazines and crossroads radio stations, it would seem odd and damagingly prejudicial to deny CBS on the grounds that it purveyed embarrassing truth.

Provided with little plastic passports to the fun, we started our coverage with the welcoming ceremonies in the giant Zocolo Square in front of the National Assembly building, an edifice whose top we reached by flourishing our New York City Police cards ("Is entitled to pass police and fire lines wherever formed—Not for parking purposes"), whose shield shape is a symbol of authority as powerful as a general's pennon on the front of a limousine. Using our two equipment-laden cab driver-porters as blockers, cameraman Herb Schwartz wedged a space among the dignitaries along the roof rim, among them the nearby President of Mexico, scattering the reluctant with sharp cries of *"muchas machinas,"* a claim to mechanical plethora that always seemed to win a respectfully open path in a culture that is cripplingly short of *machinas.*

From our vantage point we filmed a spectacle that seemed to be made up of equal parts of beauty and terror, thousands of people moving in awesome unison, a unison achieved through the subjection of individuality to the rasped wishes of the drillmaster. At the climax five thousand gymnasts in white moved through angular patterns that made the whole square look like a *danse macabre* by fish skeletons.

Equally chilling to me are Olympic opening ceremonies, although here I am in the minority, since at almost every set of games more people seem anxious to watch the athletes march than to see them play the games.

Each nation is in some sort of uniform for these parades and the choice is extremely revealing about cultural gulfs. The Americans, North and South, and the Europeans set great store by a kind of no-nonsense neatness, with the women dressed in the kind of military nurse outfits that airline stewardesses quit wearing in about 1949, and the men in blazers and slacks with cheerless hats of varying ugliness.

The Asian and African nations, on the other hand, see no reason for getting themselves up like a column of movie ushers, and they move through the stadium in swirls of glittering fabric, in turbans, in elaborate headdresses wound out of the same cloth from which the costumes are made, in odd-shaped caps that have nothing in common save a beauty that reduces the repellent American salesman's skimmers to just the thing for a Sauk Center Saturday night.

Although a good deal of kapok is distributed over the world about the nonpolitical nature of the games, they are about as free of politics as the cloakroom of a crooked legislature.

In 1968 the Russian team arrived before the thundering echoes of the Soviet tanks in Prague had rumbled into silence. Aware that the Mexicans were going to give them a full-throated booing they decided, inexplicably, that powerful grace-lessness was the proper answer.

With a tact that would have made Genghis Khan stamp his foot with envy, the Russians entrusted their banner to weight-lifter Leonid Zhabotinsky, who held the heavy flag parallel before him, an act of immense strength which he maintained all the way around the arena while the fans, to whom his size, muscular might, and arrogant display were an almost perfect analog of his country's least attractive traits, jeered ecstatically.

Parenthetically, the Americans, who can divide into parties of left and right over the question of where to hold a Sunday School picnic, four years later had a tremendous preparade brouhaha as to whether our flag should be carried by a peace advocate or by one who supported our efforts in Vietnam. The peace party won and the flag was carried by Olga Fikotova Connolly, the most beautiful two-hundred-pound woman I've ever met.

The entry of the Czech team in Mexico City was the occasion of a burst of approval suitable to the arrival of Dolores Del Rio, Cantinflas, and the shade of Benito Juárez. While the Czechs were bathing in the love we always give to people we're not going to help, I was already on my way to try to pluck out of the parade people we were later going to interview. Since ABC had

185

a firm grip on the mainstream of the games, having paid some millions for the privilege, we outsiders were left to search for crumbs like sparrows on the porch of the poorhouse, and our eye had been caught by a team that had no debate about who would carry the banner because the team *was* the banner carrier, Edward Monsel, a sprinter from Surinam.

I wanted further to find Mrs. Lorna Johnston, a British equestrienne who, at sixty-eight, was the oldest competitor in the games. Zigzagging through a procession that was dissolving under the stands, I was held up by the Outer Mongolian team, stocky men in double-breasted suits made for men even more stocky than they. The Mongolians were smiling cheerfully and distributing large cards that contained, inside an attractive design, a message that was either political propaganda, greetings from Ulan Bator, the capital, or an offer to teach the recipient the Kazak language at a fee of ten tugriks per hour. At a souvenir-happy event like the Olympics the cards were going like wildfire, and getting through the wildfire proved a difficult task.

I found my subjects, however, and arranged the interviews, having time to note, while talking to the British ladies, that some national stereotypes are true. Though the French and British women's teams wore equally characterless uniforms, you had only to look at the latter's hats to know that the English Channel is metaphorically ten thousand miles across and that no milliner has ever crossed it.

It was the issue of souvenirs that had drawn our attention to Mr. Monsel. One of the principal pastimes of all contestants was the trading of little national buttons, about forty of which had been issued to every athlete. Each day in the Olympic Village there was a bazaar as some handed buttons around for friendship and some haggled fiercely in an effort to set up some scale of values based on the classic economic concept of rarity.

There were thousands of Russian and American buttons, argued the athletic economists, and it was obviously unfair to trade them button for button for such prizes as were held by little nations that had sent four athletes from the three atolls that were the whole country. In my script I likened Monsel to Button Gwinnet, the Declaration of Independence signer whose autograph is rarer than Surinamese Olympic souvenirs, but his odd first name in a piece about buttons and the fact that nobody had ever heard of him made my narration as puzzling as a jock's jargonical explanation of a football play. In any case, we had planned to follow Monsel about the village as he doled out his tiny and correspondingly precious supply of trinkets.

Alas, poor lonely man without a friend to cheer him on or a coach to guide his steps, he had arrived in Mexico City on a microscopic budget raised by businessmen in former Dutch Guiana, a budget that did not allow any expenditures for buttons. Perhaps if he had had time he might have found an alert entrepreneur who would have produced a little metal Surinamese flag (red, white, and green with a gold star in the middle) for a cut of the harvest, but a serious young man, Monsel spent all his time running and at last ran out of the money in a qualifying heat and disappeared from our ken.

I had been tempted to give him a Detroit Tiger emblem I had brought from the World Series, but I realized that the Tigers were probably not a big thing in Paramaribo, Monsel's home town, and I can only hope that he at least got one of those Outer Mongolian Olympic cards.

Mrs. Johnston turned out to be an agile Margaret Rutherford. I had asked her a delicately phrased question: "What's an old lady doing playing games with a bunch of kids?" was the burden of it, but I think I put it as "Do you find it difficult to be at a gathering where there are so few people who share your mature attitudes?"

Taking my meaning at once, Mrs. Johnston laughed heartily and said it wasn't her advanced years that she worried about, but those of El Guapo, her horse. At twelve he was only middle-aged for a dressage mount, but he had had a heart attack and Mrs. Johnston did not know whether the high altitude was going to affect him adversely. She herself was so busy buying souvenirs that she had not really had time to consider her position as senior athlete, and although she doubted that she would be trying again in Munich, she was by no means ready to quit and said she would go as far as El Guapo would take her.

She indeed did show up again in '72, this time bringing her husband, daughter, and a new horse. They seemed to step out of one of those golden English film comedies of the fifties, the husband a retired army officer with pale blue eyes, a little white moustache, and a tweed coat of great age and elegance, while the daughter was a hearty sort in a twin set, whose large hands and feet belied the delicacy that had won her the ladies' fly-casting championship of England.

Despite the dotty, character actress look, Mrs. Johnston was a first-rate performer and in both Olympic years, though failing to win a medal, finished well up among the competitors.

To find eccentric amateurs of the high-hearted, low-skilled sort, it was necessary to visit with the American frontenis team. There must be a pause here, because so many hands have been raised by those who want to know what frontenis is. Well, each host nation is allowed to choose a sport that will be competed in on a nonmedal basis by such nations as choose to try, and the Mexicans love a game played by teams of four armed with paddles in the high cement-walled fronton that is used for jai alai. It is a kind of open-faced squash with chili sauce, and since no one north of Nogales had ever heard of it, the United States had made no plans to send up a team until a group of Wall Street athletes who normally eased their financial frustrations by playing the multitude of indoor racquet games which make the Ivy League old grad community such a boon to heart specialists, decided that they would fill the gap.

Led by printing executive Dick Squires and broker Bill Tully and accompanied by cheering wives, the American frontenistas were the closest thing to the original Olympic ideal that I saw at the two sets of games I attended. They were truly amateur, had indeed paid their own expenses, and they had come to learn, to teach, and to meet fellow enthusiasts for the games of the artificially extended arm.

This was what Baron de Coubertin had been thinking about in 1896 when he saw the games as an international get-together, a fresh-air festival celebrating simple-minded ideals of health and fellowship. The frontenistas were in the great tradition of that English competitor who entered the first modern Olympiad because it was the only way he could get time on the Athenian tennis courts in the summer of 1896.

To ice their cake, the Americans upset a complacent overconfident Mexican team before losing to Uruguay in front of our cameras. There were no medals for them to take away, nor did they play well enough to win them, but they epitomized Dr.

Johnson's tumultuous merriment much more than the driven competitors of the first confrontation between Czechoslovakia and Russia, the Ladies' Volleyball tournament. Volleyball is, under normal circumstances, a game played on the beach with a lot of laughing and falling over the beer cans that were emptied along the way, but the match we covered and ABC inexplicably ignored, had all the fun of trench warfare and was played before a packed house that shouted approval at every Czech success as if the six Soviet girls had all driven tanks into Prague. This partisanship was a triumph of ideological thinking over the Mexican macho, which dictates for many that feminine beauty shall win immediate and audible approval. Confusingly, the Czech girls, representing free choice and sunlit democracy, were, whatever their true personalities, a fearsome-looking bunch of short-haired, overmuscled, slab-faced stockies such as Central Casting might have assembled to audition for *Cruella, Woman Warrior.*

The Russians, meanwhile, stung by criticism that some of their previous feminine athletes, like Tamara and Irina Press, had been so masculine-looking as to raise doubts as to their sex, had added a beautician to their sports bureaucracy and the Soviet volleyball team was all hair ribbons and lipstick, and came bounding onto the court as if, having finished swim suit and evening gown, they were now ready for the talent competition.

Abandoning their traditional sexism, the Mexican men booed and the Mexican women, with no irrelevancies to cloud their sense of right and wrong, added the full throat of their disapproval.

Despite the novelty of being outnumbered, the Russians plowed steadily ahead to victory, and at the end the baffled crowd gathered its energies for a final frenzy of moral protest, only to be balked by a politician as shrewd as the cosmetician. A Russian official barked a sudden order as the teams were about to leave the floor, and each departing loser found herself accompanied by a smiling winner so that Good and Evil were so mixed that they could not properly be adulated or anathematized, leaving nothing to do but mutter.

This story was one of our hurry-up specials and I had to write the script in the cab returning to the hotel. This was difficult to do since the exhausted flashlight could manage no more than five seconds at a time of "Look, I'm a glowworm!" and the matches were burning my wife's fingers before she could turn off the stopwatch, whose figures dictated the shape of our piece.

Perhaps because we brought off a pretty good script and achieved exclusive coverage of a dramatic event, I never, until sitting down to write these lines, realized the full ugliness of the whole silly business of loading the weight of a war on the shoulders of twelve young women. Because of this grotesque displacement of emotion the thing was played under a tension that suggested a Czech victory would lead to the withdrawal of the Russian troops while the actual outcome meant that the Soviet grip would be strengthened.

There had not been, could not have been under the circumstances, any enjoyment of the odd breaks of this fast-moving and fluid game, and the laughter, so normal a part of the sport, appeared only rarely and was distorted into ugly derision at occasional errors. I suppose hindsight plays a part as well. There is still a certain absurdity about making the course of a white leather ball the path of destiny, but fewer and fewer people seemed to see the absurdity, so that the joke at last falls flat enough to be inserted easily into one's dossier of treasonable activities.

Perhaps the fun began to drain out of the Soviet-Czech absurdity when the United States, in the matter of John Carlos and Tommy John, proved that commissars of sports thinking can come out of the door on the right as well as the door on the left.

John and Carlos, if memory doesn't serve you, were the American sprinters who gave a black-power salute on the victory stand, an act interpreted by the U.S. Olympic Committee as a profanation of everything America holds dear. We are supposed to hold freedom of expression very dear, but freedom to express what, has never been clearly defined, and there seems much one may not express.

The two men were hustled out of Olympic Village on the very day of their gesture with a haste that suggested that the committee thought they might either molest children or talk to the press.

I was present when Douglas Robey of the committee assembled the newspapermen and TV correspondents milling around the U.S. living quarters and gave us a brief and arrogant statement on the matter. He treated our requests for a few answers to questions as if we were tradesmen importuning a duke, and departed in a protective dudgeon.

It seemed to me wise of Mr. Robey to avoid questions because someone would certainly have asked why the Olympic Committee had not vigorously denied all the rumors that had circulated during the previous summer that the black boycott organized by Professor Harry Edwards of San Jose State and other black leaders had been abandoned because of informal promises that if the black athletes came though for the U.S. a few symbolic gestures would be condoned. No more than anyone else who has not the handy adhesive feet of that famous fly on the wall, in private councils on the matter, do I know what was said but I certainly know what everyone was permitted to believe and when the black-gloved fists were raised, another fist, that of Establishment power, broke the deception as if it had never existed.

Of course, even what is actually said is often subject to interpretation, which can run all the way to denial.

Four years later at Munich, for example, black American runners Vince Matthews and Wayne Collett were deemed to have been irreverent on the victory stand because they chatted during the playing of "The Star-Spangled Banner."

I happened to catch Mathews before the rest of the press did when the announcement was made that the men would be punished by dismissal from the team, and I advised him that his best bet would be to go into hiding until the hysteria cooled, advice he took by moving as only a well-conditioned quarter miler can.

Clifford Buck, president of the USOC, held a press conference later in the morning in which he spoke soothingly about the situation, leaving it a little unclear about whether the impetus for the suspensions had come from the American Committee or the grand panjandrums of the International Committee, but stating that he didn't think the men involved were aware that their actions would arouse such a furor, and indicated sympathy for their plight and the hope that they would be permitted to run again, that they could, in fact, be made eligible for the 1600-meter relay that week.

The only question he avoided was an impertinent one from

me as to whether setting standards of behavior during the playing of anthems was not in itself one of those political acts that seemed to be so universally deplored.

Buck's actions did, however, soothe the black runners who were to engage in the 400-meter relay who went out and won it after talking for a while of boycott.

Matthews and Collett were not restored to eligibility but after the 400-meter results were in, Mr. Buck gave an interview to my CBS colleague Tom Fenton on the subject of Olympic finances and asked during the course of the interview if he might address himself to a subject Fenton had not brought up. There seemed, he said, to have been some misinterpretation of his remarks a few days earlier about the errant Americans. He had never, he told Fenton, had the least sympathy for their unforgiveable behavior and the only question in his mind was whether they might, at some future—very future—date, be restored to amateur eligibility. He hoped he was now clear.

That the black athletes had performed for the United States after his first set of remarks may or may not have had anything to do with the misunderstanding of his views, and everyone, including CBS in New York to whom I suggested that it would be amusing to run the two sets of remarks seriatim, decided that the whole matter was best forgotten.

Talking to Jack Laurence of CBS in Munich, Maurice Peoples, a black runner who lost a chance to compete in the relays after the suspensions, put the whole matter in a perspective that obviously never occurred to the barons and businessmen whose thinking shapes Olympic philosophy.

Peoples didn't think Collett and Matthews had done anything so terrible, "It was just that they, at that time, felt like this medal really didn't mean much for a black man. An athlete who isn't black can win a medal and the next thing you know, he's doing some authoritative job, but if a black athlete wins a gold medal, he doesn't have much of it, you don't see him on TV much, so what went through their minds was, 'Wow, big deal, I win a medal now, but then I'll go home and do my same old regular job.'"

The old boys in the oak libraries would tell him that he's not to think of anything beyond the honor to himself and his country, but if you've seen Bruce Jenner hawking dry cereal, you'll know he wasn't chosen as a nutritional expert, and you'll doubt that he won the decathlon just by adding sugar and cream and some sort of fruit.

A great truth that impressed itself on me at both Mexico City and Munich is that there are two kinds of power, the power of performance, which is the power of youth, the power of specific accomplishment, the power of the brave who overcome great odds; and the power of control, the power of the old, the power of those who dictate what the accomplishments will be, the power of choosing which of the brave will be sent against the odds.

We give the medals, sporting and military, to those with the power of performance, and we give them a moment to stand in the light, but the controllers have their power for as long as they want it. They don't have to win it, and if they do not stand in the light, they at least enjoy the warmth that always makes it toasty cozy for the boys in the back room and the staff officers at the chateau.

The thought first came to me in Olympic terms when the CBS crew, in its relentless search for interesting and obscure events, turned its attention to the 1968 kayak races, held in a ditch on the outskirts of the city, which had been built at great expense with the idea of using it later to train Mexican Navy cadets in whatever kayak work they might need.

While awaiting the first dig of the paddles I pored over the program which I had managed to pry from one of those uniformed upper-class girls who, at every set of Olympics, have been trained to say "I don't know" in a multitude of languages so that they can be understood in their ignorance by visitors from around the world.

A delay in the start gave me a chance to count the list of officials, which turned out to number eighty-two. This seemed an amazing total for a fairly simple event. After all, how does one cheat in a kayak race? What rules can there be other than get there first and don't run into your opponent?

There is an old saying among financiers and economists that there is no free lunch, but when I noted that for the 1980 Winter Olympics at Lake Placid a man had been hired at a hundred thousand dollars to try to reduce administrative costs of these games below thirty-three million dollars, it seemed to me that the economists have not considered that hundred-million-dollar track meets must at least be providing some sandwiches out of such staggering sums. It certainly doesn't cost that much for tape, chalk, and starter gun blanks.

Later in the day at the Mexico City ditch, a local free-lance camera crew complained about our presence to the navy, and while we were holding off a lieutenant and a group of armed sailors with the threat that we would make them carry us and all our gear to the parking lot, the championships got under way. I wasn't able to check, therefore, if a great number of officials were necessary at the very beginning, but as the day wore on I didn't note the need for much work, particularly since you could only get two kayaks at a time into the ditch, a circumstance that made it unnecessary to have an official who decided who finished third.

Later in the same set of games I learned a second great truth, which is that one is not an official in a satisfying sense unless one officiates, or, to put it in another way, interferes with the outcome of the contest.

This was demonstrated during some bicycle races, the kind that go on for long periods and involve four-man teams. I forget the number of kilometers the young men had to cover, although on a hot day it seemed equivalent to New York to Chicago, but only one rider at a time was straining every nerve. Cyclist A, that is, represented his nation until he got a leg cramp, at which point he touched cyclist B, who took over until sick to his stomach, at which point he tapped cyclist C, and so forth. Those who were resting slowly circled the top of the velodrome and recovered while waiting for the next tap. One of the big rules of this sport was that the cyclistic apostolic touch was to be no more than a symbolic pressure. One was not allowed to hurl a friend into the fray with any sort of shove.

As the race wore on the Danes established a considerable lead and the West Germans seemed comfortably ahead of Italy so that there was little suspense as the whirling group entered the last lap. At the final turn a German competitor, apparently delighted at the prospect of a silver medal, gave a teammate a congratulatory slap on the back, and there was an immediate stir among a group of judges who, up to then, had appeared as bored as we were.

The public-address system harrumphed and grumphed and at

last it was made clear to us that, with a captiousness worthy of the original Olympic gods, who spent a lot of time tormenting innocent mortals, the judges had decided that the Germans must be disqualified for pushing. It was in vain that the heartbroken Teutons pointed out the simple high spirits of the gesture and the fact that no one could imagine that at that point it was intended in any way to be propulsive.

They got no further than Orpheus did with Zeus after his impulsive touch of the eyes with Eurydice.

One thing, of course, was achieved. A crowd, which all day had been paying attention to young men in the fullness of the power of accomplishment, was forced to give its full attention to old men who wielded the power of control. From time to time the young must be reminded that though theirs be the auto-kinetic joys of the dance, they didn't write the score and they don't get to conduct it.

One of the most rule-ridden of sports is yachting, especially, of course, Olympic yachting, but when we went down to Acapulco to do a story on it, it turned out that the infractions of rules were cameraman Schwartz's assaults on the complex structure of royal protocol.

As was noted earlier, the fight for network time is a bitter one, with a host of skilled correspondents offering a long list of interesting pieces to be shoehorned into two daily network shows, and Lamoreaux and I, not just shooting for our Saturday spot, figured we had a sure winner in Crown Prince Harald of Norway sailing a Dragon Class boat.

To begin with, the iron structure of Walter Cronkite's news judgment has a soft place. Show Walter a heeled-over sloop and he is instant John Masefield, anxious to go down to the seas again and ready to throw out some budget-balancing stuff from Washington so blue water may fill the screen.

Add to that the fact that many of Walter's colleagues are as childishly excited by the idea of royalty as their children are by the idea of rock stars, and all we needed was that Harald not be disqualified to be assured of two minutes of the nation's time.

The Norse heir had been having a rather up and down time of it that year. After being at last permitted by his royal father to marry a commoner with whom he had had a romance of many years standing, he had brought her to Mexico, where he had, for a time, lost track of her, because the hotel personnel at the place where the yachtsmen were immured were under the delusion that his name was Mr. Crown and kept paging this mysterious gentleman to no avail.

Given the modern predilection for reversing names it is certainly reasonable to read a register entry of "Crown Prince Harald" as "Crown, Prince Harald."

After reestablishing contact with the princess, the royal sailor then lost contact with the rhythm of the winds and, to our horror, had just gone on the wrong tack when the gun sounded to start his race. Subsequent maneuvers of a complexity I could neither understand nor describe proved the value of the Viking strain, but at the finish the prince was well behind the prizewinners, and no one wanted much to approach him for the interview that was to be the heart of the piece.

A social mayfly who had buzzed about us all day with offers to introduce us to anyone from the prince to Merle Oberon, then the local ruler of fashion, simply said, "There he is," and spread his wings in flight.

My knowledge of protocol comes entirely from romantic fiction and as I approached the royal mariner, then democratically engaged in hosing down his boat, I was groping not only for the tactful approach to a loser but also for the appropriate form of address to a prospective king.

A passage from *A Prince of Graustark,* by George Barr McCutcheon, supplied the form of address and I took my bow from a remembered production of *The Prince of Pilsen.*

"Your Royal Highness," I said as I recovered from my bow, "I represent American television, and we would be honored if you would consent to be interviewed."

"What do you want with me, I've just finished eleventh of fourteen boats," he replied with incontrovertible logic and no trace of the "yumpin' yiminy" accent I had expected.

At this moment the ghost of Talleyrand whispered in my ear, and taking his cue I said, "We all regret Your Highness's misfortune, but it is well known that you are devoted to the cause of sailing, and if a person of Your Highness's distinction would do the interview it would guarantee its appearance on American TV and would be of material assistance in publicizing the sport."

Prince Harald gave a sad smile—the amount of oil poured over him in any given year would fuel a navy—and indicated that he would be ready when we were.

Schwartz, who like all cameramen, is as devoted to the sun as an Egyptian high priest, decreed at first that the prince should climb a nearby hill to get the full effect of the waning rays. Sharp and urgent words convinced Schwartz that personages only climb hills if they think of it themselves or are provided with a litter or sedan chair, but nothing stops the artist in his pursuit of perfection, and I froze with horror when Herbie stepped briskly up to the modern Fortinbras and, seizing his chin, gave it a sharp, almost chiropractic twist toward the light.

"You'll look a lot better that way, prince," said Schwartz cheerfully, apparently unaware that a berserker blaze had for a moment given a red tinge to the potential monarch's mild blue eye.

I thought of saying, "Herbie, you don't touch princes," but I knew that there is no weapon against fanaticism short of forcible restraint and that I should be grateful that my egalitarian associate had not told H.R.H. to tuck in his shirt or take off his hat. *Lèse-majesté* on top of a whomping loss does not produce much in the way of garrulity but the heir of Norway, like his brothers and sisters in the dynasty business, spent his childhood in the grip of governesses and tutors who chockablocked him with good manners, and he said enough to achieve two minutes on the Cronkite News.

I don't think anyone in the royal family saw the show, but Schwartz is convinced that they would have thought that Harald looked very nice.

I came away from the Mexican Games aware that they had, whatever their idiocies or excesses, succeeded in their major, if unspoken purpose, which was to put Mexico City on the map. As the Tokyo Games had eliminated the old image of warrior Japan and replaced it with a picture of smiling and helpful bustle, so an Olympiad later Mexico City, fourth largest city in the world, shed the stereotype of a collection of *campesinos* in big hats sleeping against adobe walls. The architectural splendors of the town were widely displayed and the political problems that were hinted at by the demonstration CBS had filmed were forgotten. Mexico City was, and still is, more than a big star in an Atlas, more than a place to buy colorful crafts and get diarrhea, although both are still readily available there.

Munich obviously had hopes that it would cease to be principally identified as the garden where the Nazis grew. It was around, after all, many centuries before the Beer-hall Putsch and had fought the tyrannies of Bonaparte, the Corsican Corporal, before it hatched the tyrannies of Hitler, the Austrian Corporal.

When we arrived for the '72 Games we decided to take care of the credentials first and then get a good rest to ease the problems of the time change, but in a world where simple identification for a hotel reservation is a complex business involving a lot of glowing computer screens, credentials are never going to be simple again.

The little booklets of Mexico had now given way to a huge humming machine, which, given a photograph and a mass of documentation, whirred and flickered and spat out at you your picture forever laminated to a card which admitted you to the wrong places.

In our case, Lamoreaux and myself were allowed to go everywhere but Avery "Olympic Czar" Brundage's bathroom, but our cameramen were limited to the press box. We tried to explain that the restrictions should be reversed but were firmly informed that once you were laminated you were as inevitably frozen to the destiny indicated on the shiny card as a fly laminated inside an amber glob is destined to an existence in a necklace.

Our problem was eventually solved in a wonderfully German way by Frau Schultz, an elderly lady, who was the factotum of the CBS Bonn bureau and as adept at the chessboard maneuvers of bureaucratic precedence as anyone I ever met.

She took on the problem and very shortly informed us that a new overriding priority had been put into effect. Really important cameramen would be identified by a blue and green armband and, since somebody high in the credentials staff had been best man at her wedding, the task of distributing these armbands had been given to Frau Schultz.

Until the tragedy of the assassinations made the whole business seem sad and pointless, we pursued the same plan we had used in Mexico, going to the odd corners in search of the odd story, hoping that its human interest would make up for the fact that the world was not waiting on the score or the outcome of the event.

It seemed to us of whimsical interest that spectators who could not get tickets for the events in the central Olympic complex were enabled to have at least a partial view of the goings-on by perching on top of an artificial mountain which the city authorities had created out of the rubble of the city's smashup by Allied bombers and artillery. The green hill seemed a hint that man's ingenuity might yet turn some of our coming disaster to some good account.

It seemed to us grotesque enough to be newsworthy that the United States soccer team should celebrate with World Series fervor the moral victory of a 0–0 tie with Morocco, and we were there for the glorious nonscoring, which proved that America was making a little progress in the game that all the rest of the world was playing.

We talked to heavyweight boxer Duane Bobick, not about his prospects of victory, but about his embarrassment at being a putative "White Hope" in the professional ranks, which he expected to join later in the year.

We watched and photographed Americans engaging in another sport of which they knew relatively little, a European favorite called team handball, a hybrid that might be described as hockey played with a volleyball by seven men using modified basketball techniques.

The Americans, used to looking to an overhead goal in the form of a basket, seemed confused by the idea that they were to throw the ball past a guardian who ranged in front of a ground-level goal. The odd thing, from a sports culture point of view, was to watch the sureness of the passing suddenly dissolve into awkwardness at the sight of what appeared to be a hockey netminder who hadn't dressed yet.

This confusion resulted in a thorough drubbing by the Hungarians, a defeat so thorough that those who affect to believe that sporting excellence is an earnest of a nation's success, a profoundly silly idea that is the major notion behind the Olympics, should have been packing to go to Budapest that very day.

We watched black American runners, male and female,

perform with such dash that those bound for Budapest might stop and consider moving to Harlem, and on the eve of the Munich tragedy we achieved the greatest professional triumph of the Lamoreaux-Broun team—two appearances on the same Walter Cronkite show.

A few days before this mighty moment we had shoehorned ourselves into Kiel, on the Baltic, to await the coming of the tall ships that were going to add the majesty of their presence to the Olympic yachting events.

Owing to crowds of sailors in town for this sailing landmark of the twentieth century we were only able to get rooms in a small waterfront hotel, where, from the sounds coming through the walls, the jack-ashore pastimes of the nineteenth century were in full swing.

Jurg Wieland, our brilliant German cameraman, a Berliner who had dismissed the Bavarians of Munich as "a combination of Austrian efficiency and Prussian charm," explained to us that so many nations mingled in the ports of the old Hanseatic League that no one people should be blamed for the Hogarthian riot that raged around our little island of sleepless innocence.

The next morning, in a small cabin cruiser whose rent for the day still causes eyes to roll back in their sockets in the warrens where the business affairs of CBS are transacted, we set out to sea accompanied by what appeared to be the entire population of Schleswig-Holstein mounted on anything that would float. Fishing boats contained more people than they had herrings, outboard motorboats tugged manfully at strings of rowboats and rubber rafts, hulks with juryrigged sails sagged along in a waterlogged way, and well outside the harbor, two ocean liners made a corridor down which their four-masted predecessors would pass in review before passing through our sargasso of spectators.

Those who saw the beautifully symmetrical rigging of the line of antique argosies come up the Hudson River in 1976 were struck dumb by the geometric poetry of cord and canvas, but the best way to see such ships is to watch the first white wing fly up over the horizon to be followed by a Jacob's ladder whose rungs were rows of curved white sails. As the ship grows closer one can see that the ladder is festooned not with Jacob's angels, but with cadets arranged along the spars like well-disciplined birds.

When the vessel from Colombia sailed past the liner that served as a reviewing stand, the cadets saluted with three hurrahs, shouted with a precision which indicated the power of drill, a power that had even persuaded several cadets to stand at parade rest on little circles of wood atop the masts, swaying hundreds of feet above the deck and producing stark terror in a middle-aged TV correspondent seated safely on a deck.

As the ships rose and fell in the gentle swell, and the carpet of spectators undulated around them, Jurg Wieland, like some genuflecting stork, bent his knees and rose to his toes to keep the ships centered in his lens. The beauty of his pictures, simply presenting the sight of man's last great accomplishment before the Machine Age brought about the divorce of ingenuity and beauty, made clear the price we paid for our age of convenience.

Returned from Kiel, we had the good fortune to locate, through CBS Bonn correspondent John Sheehan, the parents of Mark Spitz, the American swimmer. Filling them with beer, sausage, and sight-seeing, we kept them happy and out of sight, awaiting the moment when their brilliant, moody son, voted the most unpopular American at Mexico City, would win his seventh gold medal and set a new Olympic standard for achievement.

As Mark stood dripping on the stand after the requisite victory, I stood below with four security guards, and as his feet hit the poolside tiles I said firmly, "We have your mother and father, Mark," and then realizing that the words and the no-nonsense look of my boys in belts and buttons might have sinister connotations, I added hastily, "In a studio down the hall."

Bud and I had met Mark in the mid-period between Mexico and Munich, when he was restoring his ego and rebuilding his skills under the tutelage of Doc Counsilman, Indiana University's remarkable swimming coach. Doc managed to push his pupils through the pain barrier with a mixture of cajolery, psychology, and treats of hard candy, which he dropped into the mouths of his charges as if he were keeper of the seal house.

Trusting a familiar face, therefore, Mark marched away between my guards while the world press clamored and protested. Bud had instructed me that when we entered the studio I was not to plunge into questions, but should permit the camera to pick up the affecting meeting between proud parents and successful son, so I remained silent as the three came together at the moment for which they had all worked and waited. Unhappily they remained silent also, except for some quick and calm hellos.

After a minute or two Mark asked if I didn't have any questions and, in view of the odd muted nature of the reactions, I inquired as to whether in his long, single-minded pursuit of aqueous fame, he had considered quitting and letting someone else put up with the gritty mixture of boredom and hurt that is the price of those medals, which are not, in fact, even gold beneath a thin and shiny plating.

"The last time I thought of quitting was two weeks ago," was his surprising answer, and then with an ease and directness that is sometimes weariness's gift to the guarded and repressed personality, he surveyed a life that had had no room for anything but competition, and decided that on this particular night it seemed worth it, but that he would not be inclined to let any child of his go through it. He denied the Zenlike notion promulgated by coaches that the doing is in and of itself of great value. There are sports where this might be true but the essential monotony of the fifty-lap practice sessions made this a game too much like work. He thought he might go to dental school, but when I pointed out that a machine tuned to endless physical effort might find it difficult to sit listening to a lecture on the structure of the incisor, he admitted that the future was indeed cloudy as to direction.

In the years since the great Munich effort, his has been a career that has always seemed to me marked with a curious listlessness, and I would guess that he suffers more than most from the loss of that cocktail which mixes fear, anger, anticipation, and determination, and which is the addictive tipple of athletes, soldiers, circus performers, and actors of the better sort.

Its symptom is the aforementioned rusty iron taste in the mouth, the taste of immediacy, and it does not well up at seminars, sales conferences, or in the presence of any of the well-structured certainties of mature and responsible existence.

At the time the taste is detected there is often a strong wish for escape into the unsurprising safety of m. and r. existence, but the tang has its seductions, and deprivation leads to restlessness and in later years, endless reminiscence, as any who have been caught in a corner by an old striver, warrior, or busker can tell you.

After our interview Mark went off to join friends, and his parents accompanied us to the studio to see how we would cut the interview in different ways for the CBS Morning News and Evening News.

The day after our double-barreled appearance on the Evening News with Spitz and the ships, a day for us to savor our success, was, instead, a day of disaster and tragedy for a whole world that was made to realize that the terrorism of the times, armored against argument by its hard shell of idealism, was not going to be limited anymore to attacks on the sites of its supposed grievances. Now it was going to reach out to any festive occasion it chose and drown the fun in blood.

I was awakened early in the morning by a call from CBS Radio in New York reaching across thousands of miles to tell me what had happened around the corner while I slept, and shortly Lamoreaux, Sheehan, Frau Schultz, and I were trying to learn more than the bare fact of the kidnapping of members of the Israeli team.

Weirdly and unforgiveably, the Olympic Committee decreed that the Games should continue, and TV watchers in Munich were treated to long stretches of what now seemed agonizingly irrelevant competition, with an occasional chilling insertion of a shot taken over the wall of the Olympic Village, a shot that frightened us by telling us nothing. An apparently empty building filled the screen and we could only guess at what was happening inside.

After a time the local television stations switched to a Mozart concert, and if you wanted to speculate about man's progress, you could listen for a while to the ordered beauty of eighteenth-century music, then hear a bulletin about the witless ugliness of twentieth-century "kill for freedom" politics.

During the day rumors of increasing hopefulness rippled over the city. Some of the Israeli hostages had been saved, it was believed; then that all of them had been saved, it was believed; then it was certain that all of them had been saved; and then late that night a press conference began, and, slowed by the need for multilingual announcement, a narration began: "At five o'clock this morning; a cinq heures du matin . . ." Listening, I felt sure that if there were bad news it would come first, instead of this chronological narration, and I became more and more convinced as the babel droned on. Suddenly, though, the weary voices were saying, "And so all are dead; tous sont mort—"

I wept and watched Jim McKay weep on an ABC monitor, and heard McKay say spontaneously what I thought all of us felt at that moment, that the games should stop at once, that they were over for anyone of sensibility, be that person competitor or spectator.

All of us did not include the advertisers or their network representatives in Munich, however, and a moment later I saw in fascinated horror that the ear button that links us talking heads to our masters had sprung into action. A colleague of McKay's managed a ghastly smile and said that Jim shouldn't forget that some pretty exciting competition was coming up in the next few days that viewers wouldn't want to miss. I omit his name since he has always seemed to me a decent sort of man, and because, after you wear that button long enough, you make Pavlov's dogs look like anarchists.

The same spirit of don't-forget-the-swell-competition-still-to-come, activated the authorities the next day when their public-address systems gracelessly "regretted" any inconvenience to ticket holders caused by the decisions to suspend the games for one day so that a memorial service might be held.

At the service, Olympic chief Avery Brundage said that there had been two great tragedies in Munich, the assassination of the Israeli athletes, and the banning of the Rhodesian team. Later he apologized for giving equal weight to the two happenings, thereby setting an Olympic record for apologies by Avery Brundage.

New York asked us that day to round up some American athletes and send a live hour of discussion of the competitors' viewpoints that afternoon. Lamoreaux and Sheehan, waiting in the studio, were understandably nervous when, sixty seconds before airtime, they were the only persons present, but in the best traditions of Tom Mix, Errol Flynn, and John Wayne, a rescuer was at hand. The doors flew open at that moment and a disheveled correspondent arrived with three athletes in tow.

Rounding up the guests had not been easy, but we had arrived at the building with ten minutes to spare, only to be denied entrance by a guard on grounds of general panic and uneasiness. We had rushed around to another door, only to find that it was inexplicably being nailed up by a group of workmen. My hysterical efforts to pry the plywood earned me a broken fingernail, derisive laughter, and the sudden ugly wish that I wanted to be an armed and order-giving sergeant as I had been in 1944.

Circling back to our original door we confronted the adamant guard again and I murmured to quarter-miler Lee Evans, who was on my heels, "Push me." He did this with such a will that the guard was knocked aside and we were all down the hall and into the studio before my ringing sesame, "Stop being silly!" had ceased echoing in the hall.

The subsequent broadcast produced the same consensus I got from the majority of athletes of many nations to whom I subsequently spoke: that it was time to go home even if one had not yet competed. Going home was, of course, put off till the last medal had been awarded, the last ticket collected, and the last commercial aired.

My ultimate memory of those games is one that comes back to haunt me now and then. The closing ceremonies, like the opening ones, were highlighted by a parade. The numbers were reduced for the farewell but the banners and bands were there, and the martial spirit of the organizers was given one more oompah as the uniformed platoons swung by.

This time though, as the serried lines came down the well-lit running track, there was a sudden indecision in the normally single-minded mass, and then groups broke out of line and ran into the shadowed center of the arena, where they joined hands and defied the minatory rhythms of the drums and danced in circles like children.

It was a ceremony of innocence, an act of joyous rebellion, a reminder that games had once belonged to children, had given to them the pleasure of order— "Count to a hundred . . . Take a giant step . . . London Bridge is falling down . . . That tree is out-of-bounds . . . This stone is home plate . . . One, two, three, alevio"—in a world of chaos.

It was a condemnation of the adults who had let their games be invaded by merchandising and murder; who riddled the rules with everything from nationalism to psyching to steroids; who had decreed that joy had no place in sport, that sport was instead, service to one's country.

Well, all the nations had been served, the show was over, the receipts banked, and for just a few minutes there bloomed in the dark the spirit of play, diversion, and tumultuous merriment, all the more heartbreaking because the dancers knew how brief were to be the measures of their pleasure.

In the dawn of games, when the Olympics were awarding no more than olive-leaf hats, Pindar of Thebes became the laureate of the Games, so a few words of his seem a fitting finish.

"The bright actions of the just," he wrote, "survive unburied in the kindred dust."

Let the memory of the dance, then, survive, and let a cloud of merciful but thick dust obscure the deeds of those who tried to choreograph it as a march.

10

"LIFE IS VERY SHORT
AND VERY
UNCERTAIN. LET US
SPEND IT THE BEST
WAY WE CAN"

In 1931 my father took me to Agua Caliente racetrack in Mexico, which was then part of a luxury complex with a casino and hotel attached. In the gardens of the hotel beautiful tropical birds moved as far out on the branches of exotic trees as their leg chains allowed, and at some point in that splendid week I somehow found myself chained to the racetrack.

I will spare you a description of my first winner, of whom I remember nothing except his name, the price he paid, and his margin of victory, and it was not the traditional lucky start that forged my shackles. In the ensuing forty-odd years I have won and lost inconsiderable sums of money without much affecting my station in economic life, so that I seem to be neither the traditional self-destructive gambler nor, God knows, the disciplined mathematical wizard who makes a living out of chance.

I just like to be there when the charge begins, whether the horses emerge from a starting gate, walk up to a tape as they used to when I was a boy, or come bursting out of a clump of trees at Auteuil steeplechase course in Paris.

Writing in 1646, a Lincolnshire chronicler noted that in the town of Stamford "A concourse of noblemen and gentlemen meet together in mirth, peace, and amity for the exercise of their swift running horses, every Thursday in March. The prize they run for is a silver and gilt cup, with a cover, to the value of seven or eight pounds."

A good deal has changed since 1646. The prizes have grown, the racing season has been extended, and noblemen are few in number on winter weekdays at Aqueduct, but Mr. Butcher, the Stamford sportswriter, has put my feelings in a phrase and I must say that mirth, peace, and amity are what I have found at a variety of tracks from that old Agua Caliente, where, in the glory days, beautiful girls came to your clubhouse table to take your money and returned it appropriately augmented when you won, to the old Empire City racetrack in Yonkers, whose bucolic air belied its urban setting, to countryside racing of farmers' horses in Opelousas, Louisiana.

There are a number of absolutely fascinating psychological reasons for my devotion to horse racing, but in long conversations with my friends I have discovered that one's psychological complexities are fascinating only to oneself, so I'll spare you mine and simply say that every odd closet in my head is bulging with racing lore and racing memories.

When I went to work for CBS News I began at once to beat the drum for lots of horse pieces on the Saturday News, but after my early encounter with Buckpasser, months seemed to pass in the dreary rounds of football, basketball, and baseball while somewhere bugles were blowing, mutuel machines clicking, and hooves drumming—all beyond my reach.

In the fall of my first year at the network there came to hand a story combining racing with glamor in acceptable proportions, and our team was off to Far Hills, New Jersey, a place where people keep hunters, peacocks, and packs of hounds and where the belief is widespread that things have never been the same since good King George's day.

Far Hills races, a one-day country meeting, doesn't differ much from those jolly Lincolnshire Thursdays of long ago. The races, mostly over jumps, are run around the countryside and the crowd perches where it will and devotes the time between races to eating and drinking since there is no form to study and no machinery for the acceptance of bets. The prizes run more to silver nut dishes than money. Tailgate picnics are an accepted accessory to American sport but only at Far Hills is the provender handed round by liveried footmen, and certainly the chicken soup spiked with bourbon that I was once offered outside the icy purlieus of the Minnesota Vikings would hardly be served from the silver trays that further brightened a flaming October day.

Watching the varicolored silks of the gentlemen jockeys against green meadows I felt that somewhere all around us was a huge cardboard mat and a gold frame. We were part of a John Leech print called *A Rousing Finish,* or *Neck or Nothing*.

There didn't seem to be any noblemen present but I did run into a gentleman I knew who bade us home to tea at a weathered old brick house of that faded pink that two hundred years of drenching rain and drying sun achieves. There, his wife, late in arriving to preside over the heavy silver service, apologized that the delay had been caused by the need to feed the peacocks, and a day in the nineteenth-century was finished with a flourish.

Nothing epitomizes the vast variety of the racing world than our next track assignment, a trip, a few months later, to the Charlestown course in West Virginia.

In the romantic fiction of my youth, failed vaudeville performers often ended their professional days in the smoky dives of Singapore and the more raffish port cities of the Malay States. The horses equivalent to those broken buskers are to be found creaking around ovals like Charlestown, where the races are run at night for the benefit of the working man and where exotic bets of every kind abound. These combinations, which involve sustaining one's good fortune over a longish stretch, offer to the desperate the prospect that one good break is going to change the course of a so-far drab life. Just let 3, 6, 1, and 8 or 7, 9, 6, and 2, or whatever, come in, and it's good-bye to the gang at the plant and ho for the bright lights, the champagne, and the sunshine. It may seem silly to hope for such an unlikely concatenation of circumstances but every night somebody gets several thousand dollars for two. Why not you?

If the hopes of the bettors are high, the expectations of the horses are low. Bud had the cameraman squat down and take a picture of knees along a line of stalls. Much is made of the slenderness of the racehorse's leg but after enough running the knee begins to look like something between a large orange and a small grapefruit, and these old warriors have more mileage on them than a New York City cab. State law in West Virginia forbids more than ninety-nine successive days at one racetrack so just before the hundredth day the trainers come out of the trailers in which they live and instead of turning left to Charlestown, they turn right to Shenandoah Downs, which happens to be across the road. The horses, possibly dreaming of a few weeks resting up in a meadow, discover that the pressing nature of feed bills means that the only change in their lives is a different route to the starting line, and the knees get a little bigger before ninety-nine more days turn them back again toward Charlestown.

Still, here in the racing equivalent of those Kuala Lumpur nighteries where old singers drop notes and old jugglers drop plates, I found the romance and high-heartedness that is as characteristic a part of the game to me as the shrill cries of the touts at the gate who promise that here, at last, is the day of fortune.

I discovered this quality in the person of a septuagenarian owner-trainer named John Wright, who had two horses and about three teeth. As most Charlestown trainers did, Mr. Wright wore a string of safety pins down his leg, which made his jeans look like Charro pants, the pins being proof of the unsoundness of his horses, whose scarred old legs were constantly being bandaged in assorted supportive and analgesic ways. Should his two fragile meal tickets give way altogether, Mr. Wright seemed a likely candidate for the poorhouse, but his manner on the day I met him, and apparently on every other day of his life for many decades, had been that of a man with full pockets, a full heart, and an overflowing supply of genial self-respect.

Since I was, at the time, suffering the middle-aged depression that is the lot of those who think they disappointed their parents, I looked on Mr. Wright with considerable wonder. He seemed to me to have every reason for anxiety short of an imminently fatal disease, but regal good cheer shone around him like an aura as he discussed the possibility of upgrading his stable if he could pick off a few Charlestown purses.

Much later, after I had extracted his story, it occurred to me that much of our attitude toward life is geared to our early expectations. I was one of those who was expected to be a violin-playing lawyer who wrote a brilliant newspaper column and won prizes for his nasturtiums when he wasn't displaying a beautiful seat on a horse or dancing divinely.

Mr. Wright, as a ten-year-old black boy, had been tossed up into a truckload of horses to try to keep them calm on their way to a railhead. He never saw his parents again, having somehow ended up on the train with the horses, and must, somewhere in the fearful stretch among the rearing monsters, have made survival his goal. Sixty-odd years later after enough desperate times to fill a Russian novel, he had beaten the odds and, as indomitable as a gnarled cypress tree on a mountain top, could say that he had fulfilled his highest expectations with honor. I envied him and poured more acid into my cup of self-pity.

Toward the end of our brief stay in Charlestown Bud and I interviewed a trainer at the other end of the scale from Mr. Wright, a busy conditioner with the largest string on the grounds. He had no champions, of course, but he was making do on sheer volume and advised us to back three of his charges that night. The first two won for us, and as we counted our winnings and prepared for the grand finale I suggested to Bud that maybe we were wasting our time at CBS. If we won the third one, perhaps we should join the trailer colony and take up gambling in a serious way. The horse then finished out of the money and we went on working, but I often think, when people speak scornfully of the "leaky roof" circuit of cheap tracks, that the detractors don't know what vast schemes and impossible dreams are hatched as the geriatric cavalry circles under the lights.

Certainly dreams of fortune animated the indomitable horseplayers of New York who, when the local tracks closed down for the winter, used to take a daily two-hundred-mile ride to Bowie, in Maryland, in search of the magic numbers that meant a new life.

One February morning at an hour when the insomniac perceives futility in stereo and full color, when the very ill decide to relax the convulsive grip, Lamoreaux and I were standing on one of Manhattan's grimier side streets, pointing a sleepy camera crew at the door of a bus that was filling up with men who expected, against all probability, to become rich at the end of the ride. Indeed, when they had become wakeful enough to be interviewed, several told us that once their fortunes had been made they would give up going to the races.

"Let me win forty, fifty thousand dollars and definitely I would quit," said a man whose immediate need, it seemed to me, was a couple of dollars' worth of repairs to his zip jacket. The fact that two dollars would purchase a daily double ticket had long postponed those repairs.

One old gentleman who had spent forty years trying for the forty thousand and had not, as he put it, "Even got a tie with them," was asked if, looking back, there was anything he would change. We waited for some homely philosophy about the winds of chance or a little elegiac regret about a wasted life. What we got was the pragmatic thought, "Well, if I had it to do again, I wun't have got married."

Racing dreams come in all sizes, and we were a long way from flat caps and flat wallets when we turned up at the Saratoga yearling sales a few months after our trip to Bowie. (All the dreamers returned on the bus that day as no one had won limousine money and no one had been able to sell the latter half of his round-trip ticket to make a last bet.)

At Saratoga, as at Keeneland, in Kentucky, and the other big sales, the ambience is such as to make the expenditure of large sums of money on inexperienced young animals seem a rational, indeed even shrewd, way of acquiring that fortune that eluded the travelers to Bowie.

To hear Humphrey Finney, the Robert Morley of horse auctioneers, expressing agonized surprise that no one present has the simple common sense to bid more than two hundred thousand for a daughter of Whozis out of Whatzis or one of the few sons of Howzat to be sold this season, is to see artistry of a high order, and when you hear someone say, "Two ten!" you are seeing credulity of a high order. And yet, my own hand has been pulled down, admittedly at a lower level, by a sensible man who pointed out that fortunes are made by selling dreams and not by buying them. It's just that buying them has always seemed to me a good thing to do with whatever fortune one has.

At the evening sales the auctioneers and their keen-eyed assistants, who seek out the imperceptible nods, pencil semaphores, and catalogue codes that mean yes to more money, are all in dinner jackets, and the young horses are triumphs of the cosmetic art. As they are led into the sales ring they fling back the dazzle of the lights as if they had inner light instead of careful brushing with equine brilliantine. A little judicious hoof trimming can widen knock knees or take a bit of the depressing curve out of bowlegs. The eyes glow with fright and as the auctioneer's assistant begins to intone the scroll of ancestral accomplishment that has culminated in the big baby bouncing around in front of the crowd, one has the feeling that something magical is here for no more than a moment and that if we do not catch it in the folds of a check, it will disappear forever.

Sometimes this is true.

George Swinebroad, who for years genially bullied the rich in Lexington, Kentucky, predicted in the early seventies that someone would soon pay a million for a yearling, and two years after his death his successor, looking down at a Secretariat colt, intoned the magic number and then looked up to say to a presumably seraphic Swinebroad, "How'm I doing, George?" Half a million further on, a groom at last led away a beautiful nine hundred pounds of hope, which might end up in anything from the winner's circle, to the breeding shed, to the anonymity of distribution through dog food cans.

Such sums lead to fulminations about better uses to which such sums might be put, the same fulminations that erupt when an actress buys a diamond necklace or a person signs a million-dollar contract to play a game.

I would stay and debate this great issue with you but the daily double window closes soon and I must hurry away.

Dr. Johnson, a realist, as gloomy people often are, remarked dourly that "The bowl of pleasure is poisoned by reflection on the cost," and it is the task of those who sell horses, old masters, and precious stones to make the bowl so sparklingly delicious that it will not occur to the brain above the nose in the wine that a reckoning must be met.

Hope is the fuel that keeps people running through the world of chance, and it seems a mercifully inexhaustible fuel. I'm sure that somewhere my zip-jacketed friend from Bowie is still living on stale sandwiches with undimmed expectations of his fifty thousand dollars, while the expensive nods of the auction bidders are affirmations that ignore the warning whispers of dull old common sense.

Sometimes, just for a few minutes, the tank is empty, and there are few sights sadder than the spectacle of an optimist whose eye has been distracted from the sky above to the dust below.

Somewhere in the archives of CBS is a piece of film that shows a Bahamian jockey named Alfred Gibbs, just after he had received a piece of indigestible bad news. If you think Charlie Chaplin wrung your heart at the end of *City Lights,* you should see Alfred.

Gibbs, whom we chose to interview at an odd and pretty little track in Nassau, was a seventy-three-pound apprentice whose riding career at Hobby Horse Hall had, in a year, netted him ninety dollars for his single winner and another seventy-five dollars for his twenty-five losers. The rest of a less-than-living-wage had been earned with a stable fork and a water bucket.

We picked him because he wasn't really living on his income but on *joie de vivre,* of which at fourteen he had an overwhelming supply. We photographed him riding a horse into the sea, which is where the Hall's half-bred ponies got most of their exercise, and as he and the little horse sported in the turquoise tropical waves, the brightness of their delight shone out of the camera frame. Later we photographed him sitting proudly on the same horse in a post parade, his narrow shoulders squaring to fill the silks and his skinny legs trying to find more than the bottoms of a cavernous pair of boots.

As the field came around the final turn it was obvious that Alfred was not going to win, but it was also clear that unless he fell off, always a possibility at Hobby Horse Hall, he was going to be third, in the money for the second time in his career. So sure was he of this happy eventuality that he steered his mount to the outside rail where we were filming so he could smile right into the lens as he rushed by.

Dismounting he was all smiles still, and carried his big hunting saddle as if it were the postage stamp that heavier men use at bigger tracks, but when he stepped on the bathroom scales that served to check weights, there was a good deal of murmuring and calculation followed by the announcement that he had been disqualified because of something beyond his control. A five-pound lead weight had fallen through a rotting place in the saddlecloth and there was no choice but to place him last. Suddenly the saddle weighed more than all the lead blocks at the track, and suddenly the narrow shoulders seemed unable to fill even the collar of his jacket. Down the suddenly endless walk from the track to the jockeys' quarters Alfred

Gibbs was that most desolate of sights, a racing man shorn of his last shred of optimism.

I like to hope that the next day's sun and surf washed away his cares and relit the fire of his small ambitions, and that better still, he finally had another winner, but I remember him as one who reminded me of the fullness of emotion to be found in what Nimrod, the old Regency turf writer, so grandly called "the passion for equestrian distinction."

Certainly a passion of some unrealistic sort animated me on the day in 1939 when I accepted an invitation to attend the Kentucky Derby. I was a college student at the time and a friend who was a reporter on the *Chester Times* ("What Chester Makes, Makes Chester") announced that he had two passes to the big race and wondered if I'd like to go. It didn't occur to either of us that the Churchill Downs press box was unlikely to set aside space for two representatives of a small-town Pennsylvania newspaper, nor did it deter us that we faced a twenty-nine-hour bus ride and no prospect of accommodation when we arrived.

It was enough that we were going to the Derby, and Alfred Gibbs, coming down the stretch, was no happier than we, rolling through a long day and a longer night, firing our boiling blood on a diet of gray hamburgers and pink hot dogs, which, even in memory, brings a reminiscent burn to the heart.

The disaster that struck Alfred at the scales struck us at the gate when we discovered that the passes entitled us to no more than entry to the julep and tulip area, a garden behind the grandstand where one could drink and listen to the cheering. The bus trip, which had seemed a heroic search for the golden fleece, now seemed a tiresome trip to a leaden fleecing, but with a resolution on which I look back with wistful wonder, we prowled the premises until we found a high wire fence at the first turn, which, with hands wrapped in torn pieces of shirttail, we climbed to hang pressed against the wire like electrocuted insects until we saw Johnstown make history and defeat our choices. It had been, after all, a day in which we had triumphed over unfriendly circumstance, if not the mutuel machines, and the long bus ride home was softened by memories of our ingenuity.

I didn't get to the Derby again for thirty years, and when I returned it was with all the cachet attendant upon being a member of the CBS Sports broadcast team.

I was a replacement for the late Bryan Field, that wonderful and irreplaceable man who rose from the sidewalks of West New York, New Jersey, to create in himself a perfect image of a sporting country gentleman. As Jimmy Cannon, who had known Field during a rugged boyhood, used to remark enviously, "Bryan even knows that real aristocrats always need a haircut and wear shirts that are just starting to fray."

Not since George Meredith, tailor's son, great novelist, and a man who dressed like a poacher and looked like a duke, had there been such a work of art as Bryan, and I felt very uneasy standing in his place, particularly since the role he had played, and I was about to assume, was the production of a kind of verbal fluff intended to fill some of the corners on a one-hour broadcast that enclosed a two-minute race.

To others went the task of speculating about the odds and being learned about workout times, while the largest part of my job consisted in being, like Bryan, a country gentleman full of enough tallyho musings to fill a stretch of time without visible gasping or making the ten thousandth reference to Aristides, winner of the first Derby, always subtitled "the little red horse," and by now a subject so tedious that people might tune away until race time.

I had two further tasks at that 1969 Derby and before they were accomplished I wished that I were back hanging on the first turn fence, safe from steel heels and the Secret Service. My troubles began at the dress rehearsal of the broadcast when we timed all our moves, and I discovered that there was one move that I was not going to be allowed to make. According to the plan I was to make my way across the tulip garden as the horses went out onto the track and take the press elevator to the roof, whence, as the winner cantered back to the ceremonies, I was to fill a little time with something high-flown in the manner of Nimrod, the Druid, and the other laureates of the sporting print period in racing history.

The first check was at the elevator, which I was told was out of order. This seemed so unlikely that I questioned its guardian, who said uncomfortably, "Well, Heywood, the President is here today and I was told to say that right now it's out of order." The thought of all those bourbon-hobbled sportswriters huffing up and down the stairs amused me momentarily, and then I was struck with the thought that I was going to have to huff up them at a dead run. Amusement gave way to panic as I began my ordeal and then gave way to exasperation as a man stepped in my path and said in the low, even voice of the enforcer who is too deadly to bother with bluster, "Not this way, Jack." My explanation of myself and my errand was not very clear because it was necessary for me to take two breaths between every syllable. I could type it out here and it would be mildly funny but we don't have time, we must get to the roof before post time. There was no thought of trying to evade the presidential protector. Like all reporters I have run past my share of policemen, but this was no good-natured bluecoat. It was clear to me that any dodging on my part would impel him to push some nerve behind my ear and drop me paralyzed at his feet. I did at last manage to make clear that though I had not voted for Mr. Nixon, I meant him no bodily harm and really was required to go past the presidential box at which I promised I would not even look.

Either my story or the fact that assassins are usually in better condition than I, softened the man's mood for a moment. "Okay," he said grudgingly, "but just this once."

My explanation that this was merely the dress rehearsal failed to move him and when we assembled to compare notes I told the vice-president of CBS Sports that he had about half an hour to get me a security clearance, which might be difficult because of such dossier entries as that my father had run for Congress on the Socialist ticket and I had contributed to Yugoslav War Relief.

Rather loweringly the Secret Service identified me with cheerful condescension as "the one with the funny coats" and perhaps on the assumption that one who dressed so conspicuously could not be bent on mischief, I was given clearance to run upstairs again.

The next problem was one that arose because of the nature of time, which, contrary to popular belief, does not move at a measured pace but maddeningly stretches or tightens up so as to make sure that plans are revealed as ramshackle pretensions.

Despite a good deal of cooperation from the Churchill Downs authorities, the schedule of events is never right on the nose, since distances and crowds are great and horses are often intractable.

It devolved, therefore, that an interview between myself and Paul Mellon, the owner of Arts and Letters, which was planned for an empty saddling paddock, took place in a paddock crowded with people, on the dangerous edge of which crowd stood the master of Rokeby Stable and myself, while horses skittered past within easy hoof range. Mr. Mellon was game and I was anxious to appear so until an exceptionally mean-looking animal rolled his eyes at us and swished a tail into which had been braided a red ribbon, traditional racetrack warning of a malicious nature.

"Look out, Heywood, this next one is a kicker," murmured Bull Hancock of Claiborne Farm, and before I could say, "thanks, Bull," I had Mr. Mellon by the arm and we and our mikes were out of camera range while my voice was heard telling the audience that they could look at the horses while I continued the interview.

Thinking it over later, I realized that it really wasn't myself I was worried about, but Mr. Mellon, and for the wrong reason. It was reverence for money that made me pull him away. I had not realized how deeply ingrained I was with the bourgeois virtues of generations of dull Scottish Brouns who were better at percentages than at poetry.

"It's wrong to kick millionaires," was, I suppose, the verbal translation of the overpowering impulse that took the talking heads off the screen at that moment.

Leaving an unscathed Mr. Mellon as the horses went out on the track, they to cover a mile and a quarter in a little over two minutes, I to cover half a mile, most of it vertical, to my roof perch. On the way I gave a small respectful wave to my Cerberean acquaintance on the stairs and got the small smile of the preoccupied in return, preferable, certainly, to the slight but punishing pressure on the mastoid.

Mr. Mellon had survived the paddock but his horse, Arts and Letters, did not survive the stretch drive of Majestic Prince, the favorite, who won by a neck. I did my road company Pindar routine and subsequently reflected that thirty years after I had picked a horse that finished second in the Derby, I had advanced to picking one, Dike, that finished third. The President, always a favorite player had, we were told, purchased a ticket on the winner.

Those of us who have gone racing (A word here to would-be snobs. Outsiders and cads "go to the races." The illuminati, the cognoscenti, and the rich "go racing.") for a good many years have a tendency to gabble on like old golfers about triumphs that mean nothing to anyone but us, and if you were thinking of skipping here to avoid a stride-by-stride account of a series of Derbies you need not, since there is one alone which leaps to my mind when I think of Louisville in May, and it would to yours had you been there and may even do so if you spent that day underwater or in a cave, if I can convey to you any of what a hundred-thousand-odd people felt.

The Derby I think of is Secretariat's, in 1973, the ninety-ninth running of the race.

Charging through my memory go races that were more unexpected in outcome or exciting in finish, and many that meant more to me financially or emotionally, but this stands above them all because the horse seemed to me to surpass any reasonable expectation of what equine flesh and bone could do.

The official chart puts it less emotionally than I, and I might as well quote it as a balance against the rodomontade that I am having difficulty keeping reined in.

"Secretariat relaxed nicely and dropped back last leaving the gate as the field broke in good order, moved between horses to begin improving position entering the first turn, but passed rivals from the outside thereafter. Turcotte roused him smartly with the whip in his right hand leaving the far turn and Secretariat strongly raced to the leaders, lost a little momentum racing into the stretch where Turcotte used the whip again, but then switched it to his left hand and merely flashed it as the winner willingly drew away in record-breaking time."

That is a highly professional view but let me tell it my way. To me it seemed the longest sustained effort that a horse has ever made. There is a theory in racing that a horse goes all out for at most three-eighths of a mile, an effort that can be done at the beginning, the middle, or the end of the race. With such as Citation it often occurred going down the backstretch, the race collapsing into a parade as the champion displayed his speed, and then cantered home without much further effort.

Secretariat early displayed a strong-mindedness, which in an animal less distinguished would be called pigheadedness, and when Ron Turcotte endeavored to restrain him in the Wood Memorial prior to the Derby, the three-year-old decided that he knew best and refused to give his best when asked for it. He made it clear that he would manage his own strategy in the Derby and, you will note in the businesslike language of the chart, that shortly after he began "improving his position," he "passed rivals from the outside." Jockeys are supposed to seek the shortest route which is, of course, on the rail, but Secretariat didn't like to see horses in front of him and frequently went to the outside just to have a clear view of his goal, which, with febrile hysteria, I have always taken to be a place in the sky he hoped to reach by achieving a velocity that would make practical a sort of rocket takeoff.

I watched this race from atop a tower over the starting line, which, in this case, was at the head of the stretch, so I was in a perfect position to see the place where he "lost a little momentum" and, with all due respect to the observational powers of the *Daily Racing Form*'s experts, it seemed to me that he did not so much lose momentum as almost throw himself over the fence by the power of his centrifugal force. Horses usually go wide on a turn because they are tiring and yielding to the force, but as he hit the turn Secretariat was almost skidding as his feet slammed into the ground with a sound that John Henry's hammer must have made when he beat the steam drill. As a spectacle of blood-fired power I have never seen the equal of that battle with physics, followed, as he straightened away, by a display of zestful speed— "he willingly drew away"—which made me check to see if he was at last leaving the ground.

On my wall hangs Tony Leonard's photograph of Secretariat's walk back to the stables after the race, and it shows a prancing animal with arched neck and, as sole mark of his effort, a band of sweat where the saddle girth had gripped his mighty barrel. Every line of him says, "If you want another mile and a quarter, give me five minutes and let's go."

Most of those who saw this champion are primarily impressed with his Belmont Stakes, that fantastic mile and a half which he finished thirty-one lengths in front of the second horse. Indeed, Jack Nicklaus, a man whose emotions are usually caged by a discipline as rigid as that of an eremite on a desert pillar, told me that sitting alone in his living room watching the stretch run on television, he had wept. Jack did not demur when I suggested that to a perfectionist—and I don't think Jack will be content until he can hand in a scorecard that says eighteen—the sight of perfection achieved by another is painful.

As I, an old actor, wept as I laughed at Sir Ralph Richardson in *The School for Scandal,* so Nicklaus wept at the awesome physical perfection of the big chestnut horse tearing down the stretch. The race was incontrovertibly won, the jockey sitting still, and the horse was running simply out of the fierce joy, the "tumultuous merriment" if you will, of feeling his own physical balance and power.

When I last saw Secretariat he had retired to the stud at Claiborne Farm in Lexington, Kentucky. It was seven o'clock of an autumn morning and we were filming him in a pasture previously occupied by his father, the great runner and sire Bold Ruler.

The light was red at that hour and so were the leaves, dappled with snow, which the big red horse was spurning under his hooves. The sky framed and contained all that red with its intense deep blue, and in the middle of this perfect setting the horse suddenly lifted his head and tail and went diagonally across his domain at an odd gait, a majestic extended trot of the kind it takes a long time to teach in the show ring.

Perhaps with such a gait Nicklaus will run to the clubhouse after he has turned in the card with its series of holes in one.

When I saw the film we took in Kentucky I had a frame of it enlarged and the perfect horse, frozen by the lens, trots forever across a piece of paper in my wallet, where it is one of two souvenirs of the racing world.

The other, a considerable contrast, but perhaps not so much as it first appears, is the plastic-enclosed chart of an obscure race at Belmont Park in 1968. If you will read the small type you will discover that a ten-year-old gelding named Try Cash, entered to be claimed by any owner who wished to put up thirty-five hundred dollars, had won a mile-and-a-half race by a head after leading all the way except at the top of the stretch where he had been passed by another cheap horse named Colonel Bay.

As is the case with most statistics, the real story drops through the wide mesh that mere numbers makes.

Wandering around the paddock that day at Belmont I had

stopped to look at Try Cash because he had a foreleg so enlarged at its lower end as to look deformed. The tendon and the bone were obviously long since estranged. At that moment a racing man I knew came up and told me that he always came to look at the old horse whom he much admired. It appears that in his younger days Try Cash had displayed a good deal of quality and now in his sere and yellow did quite well at a lower level where no one ever claimed him for fear that each race would be his last. He was, said my friend, as honest and willing a runner as any champion who carried away trophies at the highest level of competition, and a half hour later I saw what he meant as the three-legged veteran, against all strategic thinking for long races, went right to the front. He never managed to draw off to the comfortable sort of lead that gives a horse a chance to relax, and with the competition constantly at his jockey's stirrup iron, a collapse seemed imminent, so that when Colonel Bay pulled past him coming out of the last turn, it was the triumph of the inevitable. Of course, in racing there is no inevitable, and to my amazement Try Cash began inching back up the leader's withers. For a moment he surged ahead, then fell behind again, then produced a final effort that nodded his head in front at the wire.

This titanic effort meant $3,250 to H. Jacobson, the owner, $21 to me, and another day's work to Try Cash. His time for the race would have placed him approximately fifty-one lengths behind Secretariat, but his effort had been equal to that of the great champion. Each had given all he had, and in that fact is, I suppose, the essence of my fascination with the sport. I am by nature a rather cautious person, aware that if you give all you have and find that it's not nearly enough, you are going to have a considerable ego problem, and I stand in awe of these fierce animals. At the end of the little chart I carry appears the name of a 77–1 shot named Aden G. with the notation "eased." So far behind was he after two-thirds of the race, that the jockey pulled him up, but the very fact that it is necessary to restrain the hopeless has a smack of magnificence to it. Sensible humans step off the track of their own accord when it's clear that another day will be a better day, but Aden G., barely able to see the field ahead of him, was going to keep going till someone said, "Enough."

I'm sorry I wasn't around for a 1753 race reported in a book of horse anecdotes written one hundred fifty years ago (Where do you think I got all that stuff with which I used to help fill up the hour?). Here Captain Thomas Brown reports that "Mr. Quin had a famous racer, who entered into the spirit of the course as much as his master. One day, finding his opponent gradually passing him, he seized him by the legs, and both riders were obliged to dismount, in order to separate the infuriated animals, who were engaged with each other in the most deadly conflict; they were got apart with much difficulty."

It seems a pretty un-English thing to do, and indeed Captain Brown heads the story "Mr. Quin's Wicked Horse," but there is something in the spirit of that disagreeable old thoroughbred that epitomizes the fiery spirit that runs up from Aden G. and down from Secretariat, the willingness to run into the wall of exhaustion and try with what strength is left to knock it down.

Obviously Derbies, Preaknesses, and Belmonts mean more that the race is won by such as Try Cash, but it is only partly because the stakes are higher and the quality of performance appropriately raised. Good horses and big purses alone do not create the special excitement of the great races, for reasons which are hard to shape into logical form because they are made from the impalpabilities of emotion.

Some say the Kentucky Derby is America's most famous race because it is the first big test of the three-year-olds, others because it comes just when we're sure it's spring, some say it's the symbolism of Kentucky, with all its B-movie nonsense about gracious colonels, wilful beauties, and juleps in profusion. The cynical say it's the result of the longest public relations campaign in history, set in motion by Colonel Matt Winn and kept going by a succession of master flacks, and I just say it's because it's the Derby. The fact that at the very first one, the race won by Aristides, you couldn't get a hotel room in Louisville or arrive at the track in time for the first race owing to the crush on the roads indicates that it was always the Derby. If, as I have always maintained, the fascination with sport is a shared delusion, it is likely to follow that the nature of the delusion may be as mysterious as the delusion itself, a set of Chinese boxes, inside the last of which is not an answer but instructions as to how to put the boxes back together again.

The Triple Crown excitement has a more specific base in that Charles Hatton, a racing columnist who was also a playwright, thought up the name for the successive three-year-old tests, the Derby, Preakness, and Belmont, and found eager assistants among the track press agents, who now had a vast multi-wheeled structure to push through the spring and early summer.

Going to the three races for a number of years I was fascinated by the different flavors of Churchill Downs, Pimlico, and Belmont Park, as each approached its big moment of the year.

Louisville in the week before the Derby is a continual series of parties. The wealthy and powerful who stream in to see and be seen are, for seven days, as crowded together at one affair after another as their humble employees riding the subways to the tasks of making the rich richer, except that the subway riders are not holding glasses of whiskey.

Bourbon is the universal fuel for all this gaiety, either in the form of juleps or with tap water, which, during these festivities, must always be referred to as "branch water" as everybody revels in Old South language and custom (hoop-skirted hostesses are everywhere) while cheerfully ignoring the fact that Kentucky was loyal to the Union.

When you consider that the state's principal contribution to the nation's food is franchise fried chicken, you will realize why lots of bourbon is needed to wash away the heartburn of Derby week. Aware as I am that somewhere in a city the size of Louisville somebody must have prepared something palatable in the first week in May over the past decade, I can only say that it has not been my privilege to eat it.

Still, one doesn't consider the stomach much when one's heart is involved, and I must say that the entry onto the track of the Derby field, while a high-school band plays "My Old Kentucky Home" with more fervor than fluency, seems to me to be unmatched for a mixture of excitement and awe since Charles the Bold of Burgundy could make the people tremble and weep with reverence by parading the streets of Flemish towns. The sound of the crowd is not the simple roar that greets the appearance of teams at major events. It is the intense murmur of a single person's inner excitement magnified a hundred and fifty thousand times, and as the murmurers turn to their neighbors, it becomes the sound of some Brobdingnagian beehive. Speculation adds its varied notes to the thrumming chord of the magnified murmur, and the horses, feeling the hysteria as palpable in the air as the aftertaste of lightning, do a certain amount of nervous hopping. This quiets neither the crowd nor the band. No one is quiet until sometime after the last ticket has been cashed on the last race and the roads are as jammed in a townward direction as they had been that morning trackward.

Pimlico, home of the Preakness, has always tended to act toward Louisville like Chicago vis-a-vis New York and occasionally and unfortunately apes some aspect of the Derby. Every few years, for instance, a new drink is devised to rival the julep as a symbol of racing merriment, but since most of them taste like a mixture of French-bottled lemonade and Mexican gin, they fail to make a mark.

Proud claims are made that the race is older than the other two jewels in the crown but since it has moved about both in location and distance, the claim is both hard to substantiate and uninteresting.

What no one seems to make much of, but what has always struck me, is that Preakness day at Pimlico is the largest picnic since the distribution of the loaves and fishes, and infinitely more varied as to available comestibles.

Marylanders have always been noted for their devotion to food, and against the tide of industrial progress they have sacrificed jobs and closed factories to restore health to the Chincoteague oyster beds of Chesapeake Bay, which also houses the marvelous Maryland crab.

Where the Derby infield is largely filled with febrile collegians watching each other climb whatever towers are available, and nerving themselves with beer for imitative feats, the Pimlico infielders have no time for such frivolities. The crowd, which begins to assemble at about eight o'clock in the morning, has the appearance of laden refugees from some city in the path of conquest. Family groups appear carrying tables, chairs, hampers, coolers, radios, shopping bags, cardboard boxes tied with string, and assorted toys for those children who are too young to care what's happening on the circumambient racetrack. I have talked with families who have occupied exactly the same picnic space in the big inner oval for decades, and although they are not as ignorant of the details of the racing as their children, their memories seem more to extend to a wonderful year for crab cakes or the time Uncle Ned forgot the snapper soup, than to the wonders performed by Secretariat or Seattle Slew.

Even in the stands, where gustatory considerations take second place to gambling fever, and where the blunting influence of mass-feeding techniques is obvious, you can still get a very decent crab cake if you'll stand in line for it, and since at Triple Crown events you have to stand in line even to get into the medical aid station, this is no hardship.

The Pimlico picnickers are entertained by the anonymous rock bands that seem to spring into being to work the big racetracks and the weekdays of the lesser country fairs, but they also have an entertainment that is characteristically Maryland, a lacrosse game on the morning of Preakness day.

Fans of this lively Indian game are aware that its two centers are Canada and the Baltimore area and they can probably tell you why this is so; suffice it here to say that as an attraction on the day of a big race, it harks back to the great race meetings of nineteenth-century England when, as long as the crowd had taken the trouble to get there, they were given everything from boxing to a theatrical troupe that spiced up Shakespeare with sword swallowing and juggling. In those days the tumultuous merriment spilled right out onto the track as mounted fans would ride the last half mile with the field, often altering the order of finish with their jovial interference. Modern racing, with its meticulous electronic measurements, is a long way from such hunting field behavior and it's probably a good thing, but one can't help sighing for the lost playfulness.

A lacrosse game may seem a small symbol, but it and the picnics in the midcity "countryside" of a grassy infield remind us of the rural roots of racing outside New York.

If New York was silk hats and big bets, the tracks of Maryland, of which a heartbreaking number are now gone, were always farmers' fun and lots of food.

You don't see many silk hats at Belmont anymore, but the third race in the Triple Crown series has a very different flavor from its two predecessors. The fatigues of battle have usually eliminated a large number of the hopefuls who had begun pouring into Louisville in April, and the mile-and-a-half distance, a rare one in sprint-minded American racing, discourages some of the marginally successful milers. The Belmont is sometimes referred to as a "breeder's race," indicating that those who are seeking an infusion of the mysterious quality called "bottom," a quality whose mundane effect is the ability to display quarter horse speed at pony express distances, will be interested in this winner as a progenitor.

The phrase "breeder's race" has a certain remoteness, however, since the average fan is not much concerned with tomorrow beyond the hope that he will have more winners than he had today, and with a kind of proud perversity New York has never put in the promotional work on this race that the other two places invest in theirs.

The thing one notices at the Belmont that makes it most different from the Derby and Preakness is the very New Yorkness of it, that is, the fact that visitors, of whom there are no doubt many, are swallowed up and lost in a crowd that is very like the one on a rainy Monday, only much larger. At Louisville and Baltimore one is very conscious of a ragout of regional accents, and there seem to be innumerable conversations about hotel difficulties and airplane reservation tangles.

New York, like the old Manchu Empire, can swallow up all the invaders that come and either absorb them or outnumber them so that they are no longer visible.

The great exception at Belmont was the June day in 1971 when Canonero II tried for the Triple Crown and carried the hopes of the entire Latin American world, a startling percentage of which had come to the track to watch him do it.

Track executives in New York have told me that they get a feel for potential crowd size by the volume of VIP requests for boxes in the last few days of the week. When upstate assemblymen begin reminding them of long-ago favors, they know it's going to be a big day, but Canonero's big day caught most people by surprise because it wasn't boxholders who packed the trains and filled the roads, but a great mass of people, many of whom had never been to the races, with nothing in common but their language and a vague sense that today they were going to show the Anglos and have a good time while they did it.

Hundreds of them brought musical instruments and long before the first race bongo drums were echoing in places where nothing was usually heard but the murmur of old horseplayers mumbling inaccurate information to each other.

There was not a great deal of logic in the notion that Canonero represented any particular country. He had been bred in Kentucky, the son of an unfashionable English sire, and because he had a gimpy leg had been sold as a yearling for something in the neighborhood of sixteen hundred dollars. This modest beginning may be the essence of his subsequent appeal. This was a price that poor people could understand, and he seemed thereafter to be an underdog of some sort until his unexpected triumph in Kentucky.

He belonged, in fact, to a wealthy Venezuelan manufacturer and won six races in Caracas before coming to the States to try his luck at Louisville. He arrived there with a jockey and groom who didn't speak English, a trainer who spoke some, and an entourage that included a man ready to interpret for them but finding no interest in what they might have to say.

By the time the Venezuelan champion arrived in New York, while the Derby and Preakness trophies went to Caracas, he was being pushed for sporting sainthood from Tierra del Fuego to the Mexican border. In Caracas the president of Venezuela stood ready to make a speech to the whole world about the connection between a three-year-old horse and his country's eminence, and the drums were rattling all over Belmont Park.

Oddly and sadly Canonero's fourth-place finish that day was one of his bravest races. Subsequent examination showed him to have been suffering from some odd but debilitating illness, and it appeared that he ran through agony and exhaustion of such shattering intensity that he was unable to raise his head for weeks after the race. The drums stopped beating, however, and the crowd straggled home, while the president in Caracas called for his limousine and cursed racing luck, not the first head of state to discover that power ends where chance begins.

In 1976 a Puerto Rican-owned horse, Bold Forbes, won the Belmont under the distinguished Puerto Rican jockey Angel Cordero, and there was a certain amount of olé-ing as he was led into the winner's circle, but I never saw before or since such a rush of passionate ethnic affirmation as was roused by Canonero II.

After nearly half a century I suppose I can claim to have seen as great a variety of racing as anyone. Professional assignments, considerable personal travel, assiduity of interest, and simple longevity have seen me standing around every conceivable sort of course, from a path over the fields to the big places where they run the big races.

It is, of course, an idler's claim, and the time I have spent on the intricacies of the form sheet could have been used to master Greek, to achieve familiarity with celestial navigation, or to find pleasure in playing the unaccompanied violin sonatas of J. S. Bach. What I got instead of these accomplishments is a few old programs, a lot of unshareable memories, and a set of racing colors which I have never seen carried to victory, although they have been seven times in the winner's circle. When the multicolored random blocks are there I am elsewhere, but I contain myself in patience. Unfinished dreams are the best kind and the moving ceremony in my fantasy in which I accept the elaborate cup on behalf of my noble representative, is more wonderful than the more likely reality: someday a silver mug for winning the secondary feature at Oaklawn Park.

I am sorry that I never got anywhere with the sextant, the strings, or the sages of Athens, and unlike the old man at Bowie, I'm glad I got married. But looking back, would I change it? I don't think so. I would miss out on so much mirth, peace, and amity.

11

"SOLEMN CONTESTS EXHIBITED TO THE PEOPLE AS SPECTACLES"

In my first months with CBS, my role as sports "essayist," a name I made up to give dignity, if not meaning, to the odd sort of pieces I was doing, I never seemed to get near the big events, which were covered by network luminaries. My humbler role was to do what was called in TV jargon "situationers," which meant arriving in town before the hotel room shortage had even begun and doing a background piece on what was going to happen next week.

In this role I visited a normal Louisville in April 1966 and wandered though the Derby Museum followed by a camera. The high point of the piece was a shot of me operating a hand-powered mutuel machine whose dials reached some staggering sum like a hundred thousand dollars.

I got to the Augusta National golf course while paunchy members were still spraying it with hooks and slices, and followed Jack Nicklaus through a couple of practice rounds for the following week's Masters.

I was in Indianapolis ahead of the first motor home looking for a good spot to view the 500, and interviewed mechanics and drivers whose coveralls had no marks on them save those bought by the innumerable merchants who peddle products on the bodies and cars that compete in this most commercial of sports carnivals. In between these brushes with the big time I was doing things like interviews with the ninety-year-old groundskeeper at Sportsman's Park, the old home of the St. Louis Cardinal baseball team (when difficulties with the camera forced us to rout out the old gentleman for two repeats of the talk, he became quite irritable and at last hurried away to a burrow in the new Busch Stadium where he hoped we couldn't find him), and a report on the first main event fight for Joe Frazier, a fighter regarded by most experts as too short of arm and too easy to hit. The experts were right, of course, but you would have lost money listening to their wisdom.

The interview with Jack Fleck, which was my first sign that the ice was melting on the upper reaches on the CBS mountain of power, was wrapped up and on the plane with Bud and me before the unhappy Fleck shot the first of the mediocre rounds that were to eliminate him from the Open.

I registered no complaints about this state of affairs. Bud was keeping my technical ignorance hidden from the people at CBS, and I was afraid if we started going to major events I would run into network luminaries from the opposition who would discover they were up against a man who didn't know what *FAX* and *MOS* and *loops* meant (I found out, of course, but I'm still not sure how loops work).

My first brush with the big time since my newspaper days occurred in the fall of '66, when none of CBS's stars seemed available for a World Series game in Baltimore between the Orioles and the Los Angeles Dodgers and it was decided to give me a try. Since I was only hired for Saturdays and this was a weekday game scheduled for the Cronkite News, I had to rush to a phone booth and arrange a piecework rate which later caused a lot of annoyance at Business Affairs. This order-minded group always resented my semiautonomous status, a role that led to my being left out of the CBS phone directory every other year.

My modest compensation settled, I plunged into the job zestfully after discovering that my ignorance of TV terminology was matched by my rival news correspondents' ignorance of baseball.

After the game we fought our way into the dressing room, which contained several hundred newsmen, twenty-five baseball players, and Vice-President Humphrey. As Mr. Humphrey, bubbling with congratulatory words, approached third baseman Brooks Robinson, alert Secret Service men grabbed Bud and shoved him against the wall, but oddly ignored me and the crew. As I pushed the microphone between the two men it occurred to me with a cold shiver that were I an assassin I had the perfect disguise. Either my mike or the camera lens could have been rigged to emit something deadly, and yet the news crew appears so obvious in its purpose that it is somehow ignored as a possible menace. It has a further protection in the fascination that celebrities have with the camera as bestower of immortality. That it may be the enemy, even in its legitimate function, occurs to few.

Despite the distinction of Robinson's performance in that Series and the automatic media importance of Mr. Humphrey, nothing was gathered in by the microphone that was worth sending out to a waiting world, and a brief shot of two smiling faces was all that went into our piece.

Over the years it has seemed to me that the press, as a totality, has steadily shrunk, with newspapers and magazines dying at a terrifying rate, their employees being forced out into the uniform of the newsman's uneasy ally and sometime enemy, the flack, or public relations representative, to give the much preferred title.

Despite this fact, the crowd of news people at any public event has grown immensely. When there were nine newspapers in New York, as there were when I became a member of the Baseball Writers' Association, the press box easily contained, even for critical games, all those representing the People's Right to Know. At World Series time, some few rows of seats around the box were set aside for newspapers outside those of the two cities involved, and, in the evening, the ballroom of some local hotel was just comfortably filled with eaters, drinkers, and tellers of old baseball stories. We were a large family but largely familiar with each other.

One of TV's initial problems, of course, was the cumbersome nature of the electronic communicative process. As noted earlier, in the days before the tape minicam, it took about fifty people to put together a two-minute segment, and about forty-five of these had to be in the park, about twenty of them with seats that permitted them to see the action.

A press association with a similar constituency can do the job with a man to write the lead story, one to do the dressing rooms, and a photographer or two. This is not to say that press associations are all that spartan, since a certain number of executives and other drones must be assigned phantom work which will make them part of the glamorous "working press," but networks have this problem too, on top of the working platoon.

Another phenomenon that has swelled the ranks of media people at big sporting events is the "happening" phenomenon, which draws a cross section of correspondents to everything. In the twenties and thirties one's journalistic bent, early inclined, was rarely changed, and sportswriters went only to games, fashion writers only to couture shows, while food experts were divided into those who read menus and those who read recipes.

When my father went from writing sports to reviewing plays, there were shock waves through two professions, journalism and the theater. Ethel Barrymore announced coldly that she didn't care to have her work judged by a baseball writer, which, considering the time she spent at the Polo Grounds watching the Giants, seemed a bit ungracious. Still, she spoke for a world that believed it took a long time to become an expert about anything, and that there probably wasn't time to become expert about two things.

Today, when the opinions of experts are suspect as smacking of elitism, we are willing to listen to the views of everybody about everything, and it does not, therefore, seem grotesque that a Super Bowl should be covered by rock music papers, magazines devoted to celebrity photographs, and specialty publications of every sort. Under such an assault the simple press pass gives way to a series of varicolored badges like those at the Olympics and a pecking order as complex as that at the court of Louis XIV. Unlike the Sun King's set, which seemed always to sort itself out, the badge wearers seem to end up bitter and confused. A man at Munich told me that *Newsweek* magazine had managed only two photographer's passes, while Japanese free-lancers with no known affiliations had managed to collect over a hundred. I asked him why he was surprised, and told him about the time I had covered the 1969 World Series while crouched on a girder behind a box full of people from *The New York Times* circulation department.

I don't think all this confusion arises out of malice, although occasional examples occur, but simply out of the fact that there really isn't all that much room at the top, and that therefore the accreditation of every desirous VIP in a nation of over two hundred million, plus the accreditation of all those who ought to be there, added on to a bunch of people who, through persistence, have managed to get some sort of badge for *The Poultry Fancier's Gazette and Bee* and Radio San Marino, created inevitable chaos.

Perhaps because the athletes, besieged after the game by the entire horde, never know whether they are talking to the world at large or the world of fancy poultry, they tend to trot out the same impenetrable remarks for all, but it doesn't matter that much because the people on the outer edge of the crowd who are shouting, "What did he say?" have drowned out the speaker and spared the rest of us from being bored by it.

In my career I have been at both ends of the pecking order. Representing the newspaper *PM* in the 1940s did not rank me that far ahead of Radio San Marino, and I have never forgotten the chill that filled the room when I announced my affiliation at a fashionable Newport tennis club. How I wished my request for a seat had been on the letterhead of *Podiatry Review* or *Philately Today*. I was then one of the resentful *sanscullottes* who felt that the powerful press, which monopolized the good things of life, paid for those good things with corruption and toadyism to the Establishment.

When I arrived at CBS with the built-in power of hundreds of TV stations I found myself continually running into young resentful people who assumed me to be gorged with good things, and I was always too busy trying to push my cameraman to a place where he could film the perspiring bore in front of his locker to explain to them that it wasn't true.

On one occasion in my CBS career I covered a major event without even a ticket of the seventh rank (Bearer may park in the press lot but not come inside).

This was that 1970 World Cup soccer series in Mexico which, at the last minute, the network decided should be covered. Unfortunately the Mexican government does not like such things to be decided at the last minute, and as the consul's representative explained to me, I should be prepared to return the following day with three passport-sized photographs of everyone in my party and be prepared, on that day, or the following day if the consul was busy, to submit to a personal interview in which I would be allowed to explain my purpose in taking pictures. Should the explanation hold water, documents would be processed as quickly as possible, in perhaps two or three more days.

By that time, of course, the soccer championship of the world would have been decided and the people of the winning nation would already be recovering from their post-victory hangovers.

I went back to square one, a clerk in the outer office, and with the clear, steady gaze of the dishonest, told him that I had changed my mind about going to Mexico for professional reasons and had decided that Mr. Lamoreaux and myself, never having seen the Pyramid of the Sun, would do well to visit this architectural marvel, to which end I required tourist visas for us. The clerk looked at me with the sad, steady gaze of one who has heard too much fabrication to be shocked and surprised and filled out our papers.

Once in Mexico and needing something more than tickets for the pyramid tour to get into the stadia, we procured from a friend left over from Olympic days a group of laminated pink cards of the highest level (Holder may enter refreshment area at any time). The only trouble with these cards was that under the laminations were photographs of handsome Latins with lots of hair and beautifully groomed moustaches. Cameraman Izzy Bleckman looked Latin and had a neat moustache, but like me, who looks as Latin as Colonel Blimp, he had more hair on his upper lip than he had on his head. Bud had the hairline but nothing else and the sound man had a crew cut, so all of us moved about with our thumbs mashing the noses of the men in the photographs.

The crisis came as we joined the thousands bound for Guadalajara Stadium, where Brazil and Pele were going to play a semifinal match against Uruguay.

The guard at the press gate looked at all those passes held in identical fashion and with surprisingly gentle insistence in the face of obvious fraud indicated that he would like to see what the photographer had made of us. For a moment our moist thumbs began to press at the faces beneath as if a sufficient force might squeeze them beyond recognition, but then Bud said sharply, "We forgot the long lens," and even though we had no long lens, the crispness of his command was such that we wheeled at his word and started back toward the car. The guard, conscientious, but not aching for a confrontation, relaxed, and just as he did, Bud said, "Oh, to hell with the long lens," and we turned and hurried past the gateman before he could rouse himself to alertness again.

Safe inside we went about work that seemed to me to be of not such sensitivity as to require all the documents that we didn't have, but there did at last come the moment when we needed some piece of camera gear that had been left in the car, and it was decided that I, least valuable member of the team at this moment, should take the risk of going outside again.

I chose a different gate and spoke to the attendant on the way out explaining that it was necessary that I telephone my superiors, producing simultaneously the familiar old N.Y. paper police shield. If he got the impression that I was Inspector Broun, in pursuit of evil forces, it was what I hoped he would think, although to be fair, I hadn't said so. In any case, he readmitted me without incident and I was spared an afternoon in the parking lot. Time schedules forbade our trying to crash the Mexico City final, which is why I have never been in jail. From the depths of cuckooing with someone else's credentials, it's many miles up to the occasions when CBS did the Super Bowl telecast. After S.B.I, when Bud and I alone among CBS people had been disrespectful, we were, for a couple of years only, allowed to do news pieces about the game in those alternate years when NBC did the telcast and disrespect at CBS was encouraged, but after a while we were there every year and no one privileged to sit on the corner of the President's Oval Office desk ever had more impressive keys to the kingdom than those that used to hang from me every other year. I would have more labels than a final sale item in a bargain basement, tags for the dressing rooms, the sidelines, the press box, the bar, and the pregame barbecue party; they were anchored to every button including the art metal one in my lapel, which admitted me to the commissioner's press conferences. This display of assorted privilege has always struck me as the most brilliant facet of the beautifully planned campaign by which the PR people of pro football have put across the idea that a game between two exhausted teams in a stadium that is home to neither is the major sports event of the year.

Super Bowl week differs from World Series week in the important matter that, with the exception of the travel day, something happens on a playing field every day in the Series. Writers must bestir themselves and create actual accounts of the game. Evenings around the press bar tables are agreeable, but there is a good deal of work to be done.

Monday to Sunday in the sunny city selected for the Super Bowl, however, is a paid vacation of a luxurious nature. It is true that once a day the men and women of the media are loaded into buses and taken to the site of some light calisthenics, but the uninteresting stories that result practically write or film themselves. Players and coaches express confidence, say that they have been looking forward to the game all year, and hint that there will be surprises in store for the opposition. This can be done every day, using different players. The small chore out of the way, the correspondents are ready to line up for trinkets. No one, in financial terms, could accuse the NFL of bribing or corrupting the press. The total value of the loot carried away by each professional visitor is trifling, but the prestige value back in Littletown, U.S.A., or even Bigtown, U.S.A., is very large. The price of the souvenir wristwatch is not such that it must be reported to the IRS, but the second hand is a little football. So also the tie clasps, club bags, and lunch pails on game day are emblazoned with something that shows that *you were there.* It is little wonder that after being bombarded with attractive toys, the assembled communications industry communicates the news that here is the acmeapexclimax of the sporting year. It must also be said for these communicators that they are honest in their actual game reports, which almost always bring the news that the contest was dull, cautious, and uninspired. The act of heroism that earns them all their decorations is the dressing room rush after the game, which is the most terrifying in sport. Because of the sun, the fun, and the spoils, there are more press people here than there are at any other event in the world of games, and the locker rooms are just that, places for changing one's clothes with the inevitable rows of lockers for that purpose, lockers against which the incautious are crushed with painful results.

Camera crews and newspapermen begin the vigil under the stands at the beginning of the fourth quarter, and in the early stages of the wait everyone is as decorous as the people who wait for standing room at the Metropolitan Opera House, with a discernible line based on earliness of arrival and a certain amount of good humor about efforts to move up a few places.

About one minute before the end of the game, the second wave arrives and washes away order and good humor amid cries of outrage from the earlier arrivals, who are now being brushed aside by the elbows of the new horde. At the final gun the third and largest group arrives and then, as Pope puts it,

> Lo! thy dread empire, Chaos! is restor'd;
> Light dies before thy uncreating word;
> Thy hand, great Anarch! lets the curtain fall,
> And universal darkness buries all.

Or even more pithily, things get completely out of hand. I still remember a year, the last in which I joined the hunt for football's final *mot juste*. By patience and a certain eelyness I was at the very forefront, pressed against the corner of the door. As the pressure from behind increased, as more and more reporters endeavored to emulate the running backs they had just been watching, there seemed a real possibility that my rib cage would be caved in against the unyielding defensive line set up by the door jamb. My cries for surcease were lost in the howls and execrations of the have-nots at the back, some of whom, as they informed us, represented publications and TV powers far more important than those of some of the people unfairly but irrevocably up front. At that moment the door of the dressing room opened, there was a surge and a dangerous further flattening of my ribs because it appeared that the opening of the door was not for admission but simply for the appearance of an angry official to tell us that there would be a delay. The archangel with flaming sword who was denying us admission to Paradise was Harold Rosenthal, press chief for the American Football League, now the American Football Conference. Harold and I had been baseball writers together in the forties and had talked, as young men do, about the great things we would someday accomplish, about the writers we admired, and about the way we would change the world if we had the chance. Just a few days before this confrontation Harold had handed me an embossed tie clasp, remarking wistfully that he had not expected to spend his middle years distributing beads to the natives, but I might as well have my share. Now, pressed into the shape of Felix the Cat after a fight with a steamroller, I looked to him for some sympathy and understanding, but to no avail. His face graven with stern rebuke, he ordered the hordes of Lucifer to outer darkness and slammed the door. In the resulting tohu-bohu I managed to get away from my duck press position without giving up my place in the forefront and soon enough was running through dirty towels and discarded tapes toward that twenty-second quote that is the parsley on a news piece. At the time I decided that some exit must be found from a business in which nice people like Harold are turned by circumstance into the menacing masters of lunatic asylums. At that, I must say for Harold that he was unarmed. At the Kansas City dressing room door in New Orleans in 1970, I was present when a large deputy drove us back with a club, then acting on some odd feeling that a man in a clown suit must be harmless, pulled me through the door and slammed it on the others. I was flattered at his approval, but since he had left the camera crew outside, I was a playwright without actors, a swordsman *sans épée*, a politician without a speechwriter. I made a great deal of ugly noise about the punishment that William S. Paley would loose on anyone who thwarted those who wore his livery, and at last had the door opened again, but by this time the alert crew had got through another door and were, humiliatingly, about to do the interview without me.

Television naturally concerns itself with winners since it is an entire industry that lives for mass approval, a reward rarely won by dwelling on the disagreeable, but I could not help, in those Super Bowl gold rushes, but sigh for the days when, as a newspaperman, I was allowed to spend a quiet moment with the defeated. At the legendary one-hit loss sustained by Bill Bevens in the 1947 World Series, I gratefully escaped the madness of the Brooklyn Dodger locker room where hero Cookie Lavagetto was being treated as small children treat cats, hugging them to the peril of their survival. It seemed to me that nothing sensible was going to be said there for a long time and I crossed the rotunda to the Yankees to find that I, first of the press to arrive, had entered a silent film. Twenty-odd players, several coaches, and a manager were moving about the rather constricted confines of a less than luxurious visitors' quarters without a sound. No one spoke, no one dropped a shoe, no one whistled or murmured or groaned. It seemed a time to talk to a sage, so I went to the stool where DiMaggio, as yet undressed, was unwinding with a cigarette before his shower. I muttered something about shock and Joe said, "Well, these are the first words that have been spoken since the winning run crossed the plate." Then, being a stickler for accuracy, he reflected a moment and added, "No, there was one word. Bevens stood in front of his locker, undid the first button of his shirt, and said 'Fuck.' After that he finished undressing and went into the shower."

I forget what euphemism I used in a 1947 newspaper story, and I am one of those old enough to write the word with discomfort, but f—— sounds like one of the "vile oths" in the novels of Penrod Schofield, so there it is, what Bill Bevens said, and who could blame him.

DiMaggio was rare in being, if laconic, a person sufficiently detached that he could make intelligent comments about a game. Usually the great are so deeply involved that they are unable to tell you how anything happened and are sometimes not even sure exactly what, in fact, did happen.

Usually, as corporals know the state of the army better than generals, and bit players know when a show is going to close, so it is the substitutes, observers rather than participants, who have a clearer notion of what happened than those more directly involved.

A perfect example occurred in the Colts-Jets Super Bowl of 1969 when, as expected, the favored Colts moved confidently downfield in the first quarter until Earl Morral threw a short pass into the end zone which struck the receiver on the shoulder and spun end over end into the air. Randy Beverly, a Jet defender, after a long lateral run, gathered it in and the Jets had the ball on their own twenty. As the Colts offensive team came off the field, halfback Tom Matte said to me with an expression of awe, "I never saw a ball hang in the air so long."

A dispassionate watcher with a knowledge of schoolboy physics would understand that the type of spin had a slowing effect on the rate of fall of the ball, but to the Colts, who had just had happiness dramatically snatched away, it seemed a sign that some malign group like the Furies, the Norns, or the Witches of Macbeth had taken the points with the Jets. The

Colt attitude visibly changed from that moment and their play never regained the arrogant crispness that marked it before the mishap.

Some injured member of the special teams, suited up against the possibility of great gaps in the ranks of the regulars, might have given the best postgame interview about the subsequent frost on Baltimore's fire, but in the competitive world of Big Game coverage, we don't talk to scrubs no matter how knowledgeable.

In our aforementioned coverage of Super Bowl I, the advertising department may have been annoyed at our light-hearted approach to an event they had been selling as the Ultimate Rolled Into One, but Gordon Manning's beef, which he mentioned for two or three years thereafter whenever we strayed too far from the conventional, was that we had not had a shot of Vince Lombardi in the Packer locker room, slamming a ball from hand to hand. Gordon was sure this was the essence of the afternoon and felt it was proved by the fact that ABC and NBC had run the shot.

Now that it's all over I'll say that I still think the high point of a dull day was a couple of poor daredevils with rocket knapsacks who flew fifty feet into the air during the halftime show. In that opinion you may see a reason why I left CBS News at the end of 1975, not to return until 1979.

Sometimes even the dispassionate observer has a hard time figuring out what happened, which is supposed to be the principal reason for instant replay. I have written elsewhere about my feeling that instant replay, however it may improve sporting scholarship, is an interference with the natural flow of a game. It is rather like the first reel of an old-time movie serial which reveals, by sort of repeating the action, that the hero wasn't in any danger after all in the last moment of the previous week's episode. I got the same disappointment in the theater as I do now when the great play is shown to be the result of some missed block. If I'm not careful I will begin to belabor the issue again, however, so I'll just say that because I was closer to the play than anyone save about sixteen of the twenty-two participants, I have never been able to figure out exactly what happened when Duane Thomas fumbled the ball over the goal line in the Dallas-Baltimore game of 1971. I was on the line when the ball bounced out of his arms into the end zone, and it is my distinct impression that thirty people had their hands on it before its last errant bounce took it over the backline and into deadness. The rules of the game obviously make this number unlikely, but as I rerun the play in my head, and I often do, I count the pairs of hands which are inexplicably unable to gather in the leather talisman and I usually end up with thirty, although if I'm sleepy, it is sometimes only twenty-eight or-nine. It was, in any case, an immensely vivid experience and one of those occasions when it seemed to me terribly exciting to be a sports reporter and in the middle of things.

Obviously the young reporter just released from copying scores in the office and sent for the first time to a live event is all aquiver, but one of the problems of the profession is the quickness with which that excitement gives way to the fashionable langor of the veteran observer, a state of mind that is okay for the student of the political scene, perhaps even valuable, since skepticism is a valuable weapon in that arena, but dangerous in sport.

Perhaps because I had seen it happen to me in the long ago of my newspaper career, I tried to bring to the big games the same excitement that I caught from the fans at the Iowa State Girls Basketball Tournament and, looking back, I think I managed it pretty well in my reports. The enemy of the excitement was to me the very type that was supposed to breed it. As the veteran theatergoer grows progressively more detached when the child actress must weep over a dying puppy on the very day that Mummy and Daddy are going to separate, so being battered by the bean-filled bladders of athletic press agents eventually leads some of us to a sullenly mutinous feeling that we won't be hustled into hysteria. It is essential, though, to push this feeling aside when the game begins. As John Drebinger of *The New York Times* used to say, "The fans don't care if the sandwiches are dry in the press box so don't write about it," and a correspondent's resentment of a clumsy attempt at seduction through shrillness and souvenirs must be kept in a separate compartment.

It is, of course, possible for a reporter to care too much about the outcome of a game and be thereby reduced to the incoherence of the involved. Writers and broadcasters who refer to "our boys" often give the kind of reports that one might get from a cheerleader, and they are as informative as the defiant bulletins put out by defeated armies.

I do remember an occasion when I cared too much, but the caring was so divided as to give me an agonized objectivity. The event was the first fight between Joe Frazier and Muhammad Ali at Madison Square Garden. I had been through the whole rise of Frazier and Yank Durham, his manager, in a series of TV pieces which had given me a real affection for this pair of attractive personalities, and I had spent enough time with Ali to fall under his theatrical spell and be amused and amazed at the skill with which he made puppets to his purpose of all his enemies and friends.

Watching them fight I felt like an uncle whose two favorite nephews were engaged in a battle whose every blow was bouncing off the avuncular sensibilities.

On a CBS News special later that night I managed to describe Frazier's victory in the appropriate objective manner but I think that fight involved my personal emotions more than any other major event I covered. Earlier I expressed some scorn about the "our boys" school of sportswriting, but that doesn't mean that the observer is best off without any feeling at all. To be caught up in the excitement but not to be blinded by it is an ideal best realized by Thucydides in *The Peloponnesian War* and the fact that we sports correspondents achieve it only occasionally is no surprise. Historians like Thucydides and Red Smith are not that common.

Sometimes, of course, the emotions aroused by the big event are violent but not actually connected with the normal rooting interest.

Such a one was the famous Pittsburgh-Oakland football game of 1975. As the crew and I paced the sidelines of Three Rivers Stadium in Pittsburgh, word reached us from New York that a Steeler victory would provide us with enough film for next Saturday's speculative advance piece on the ever more feverish struggle to reach the Super Bowl. If, however, the Oakland Raiders won, I would have to be off to California in search of additional footage. We would need to flesh out our rather meager file on this efficient but rather colorless football team which seemed to take its moods either from the somber black of its uniforms or the snarling competitiveness of its managing director, Al Davis. Add to this the fact that Oakland is a city of legendary bleakness, and you will see that my balanced view was twisted out of shape by the alternatives. Oakland seemed to have the game in hand in the closing minute and as the Steelers were already foretasting the acrid tang of defeat, I was foretasting the oddly dusty greasiness of one of those gray slabs of nourishment with which airlines insult the memory of that elegant epigrammatist, François René Chateaubriand. When the famous pass bounced off someone's knee into the arms of Franco Harris and gave the Steelers the victory, Pittsburgh owner Art Rooney was in an elevator on his way to thank his players for their efforts, the Oakland players were in shock, tears running down their faces and streaking the black anti-sunglare smudges under their eyes like the mascara of Mary Astor in the last scene of *The Maltese Falcon,* the fans were in a state of delirium, and I was in that glow of happiness possible only to boys who are told they are not returning to boarding school, or to middle-aged correspondents who will not have to fly to Oakland.

Big events have caused me to fly to such diverse places as Caracas, Venezuela, a city described by Bob Schakne of CBS as "a Los Angeles that doesn't work," and Du Quoin, Illinois, a town not quite big enough to handle a high-school baton twirling contest, yet which somehow manages to survive each year the influx of fans who come to see the Hambletonian.

The one thing these big event towns have, naturally enough, in common is an extreme shortage of accommodations, although I must say that my memories of little Du Quoin are warmer than those of the luxury-misery layer cake that is Caracas. Arriving in the Venezuelan capital to preview the George Foreman-Ken Norton fight we presented ourselves at the Hilton with enough documents and guarantees of accommodation to get a rock band and its groupies into the Ritz in Boston. The documents proved to be so many dead leaves in the view of the suave man whose delicate shrugs beautifully managed to mix regret and indifference, and I was about to consider the possibilities of the airport lounge, when it occurred to me that there was one document I had not shown, the steel-engraved portrait of Andrew Jackson, that magic slip of paper that can build a table in a crowded restaurant or make a hotel clerk remember that one's reservation was, after all, put in the wrong file. Sure enough, there we were, hidden for some reason, in a bunch of dry cleaning receipts. At least, that's where the suave man said he found us.

Caracas was just one of many cities that, aided by television and the tax laws, can provide a setting for sports events that might not normally be considered appropriate to their cultural matrices. After all, neither Foreman nor Norton had any Latin-American ties, and the people who had assembled to see the fight seemed to regret that it was not being held in the place where they were most at home, Las Vegas.

Any place where you can plug in a camera is a sporting site, however, and if the Vegas people and the cameramen can get there, the media will not be far behind.

Du Quoin, on the other hand, represents the older view that as there are, according to *The Golden Bough,* certain sacred groves where rituals have meaning that can be achieved nowhere else, so there are places sacred to sporting events that take their sense of importance from their ambience.

Since the Hambletonian is widely considered to be the ultimate in countrymen's fun, the bucolic answer to such big city games as the World Series or the Super Bowl, rural Sparta versus urban Athens, it seems natural that it should be held as part of a country fair. Du Quoin, a city which you will be able to locate if I tell you it is about midway between Pinckneyville and Benton.

I think the place where we had reservations was a little closer to Pinckneyville, but wherever it was, it was the only spot within a hundred miles of the fair where we were going to be able to lay our heads, so there was some consternation when it appeared that there was room for only half our group. Andrew Jackson proved useless here, and we were told that even U.S. Grant, whose portrait is worth fifty dollars, could not open doors that did not exist. We were about to set out for Darmstadt or Marissa, or any place far enough away to be outside the lines of saturation booking, when an emissary appeared from the governor's suite with an invitation to me to attend a reception. I was explaining that I would be delighted were I not on the point of departure, when, as from a puff of purple smoke, another man appeared beside me, identified himself as the hotel's manager, and said that I could go to the governor's reception since space had been found for us. I realized that the invitation from on high had opened to us the accommodations I think of as the Jaqueline Onassis rooms. I have noticed that when this glamorous personage and others of similar réclame wish to go the theater, there are somehow always available tickets, however hot the hit. I presume that until curtain time or, at hotels, until midnight, space is held for the possible visits of the famous, and now, it becoming clear that Mrs. Onassis wasn't going to make it to the Hambletonian, the Holiday Inn was making her space available to me. There have been few occasions in my life when a sense of my own importance, that glowing self-satisfaction that is so vital a part of the star makeup, has swept over me, but this was one of them, and I subsequently greeted the governor with a touch of genial condescension that he must have found puzzling.

To the fan, of course, his simple presence at the Big Game is prestige enough, and he will lace his conversation for some months with references to his impressions thereof, or date happenings in every day life as "a week or so before I went to the Super Bowl," or "I'm sorry I had to break our date but I had tickets to the World Series." If he has not become blasé through repeated visits to the battlefields of sporting history, he may even show you his ticket stub and explain how superior was the location of the seat.

Those of us who attend the big games not as a privilege but as a duty are, of course, aware that there are the occasions when we must be as strung up as the contestants since we are, after all, contestants, too, against all the other writers and broadcasters in the country, all of whom are as anxious to be remembered for their descriptions of the action as the creators of that action are anxious to be immortalized.

It occurs to me that from the endless voyages of my first major sporting event, the 1946 World Series and its preceding National League playoffs (to St. Louis by train for the first playoff game, to Brooklyn for the second, to St. Louis for the first two games, to Boston for the next three, and back to St. Louis for the last two) to the latter day TV-oriented big ones, the complications of coverage have increased as the complications of travel have decreased. But then, even as I say that, it occurs to me that life itself becomes more complicated as one gets older and that my observations would not march with those of the eager young who, I recognize sadly, look and feel as I did on that recent yesterday, which, on examination, appears to have been in the era of funny clothes in faded college yearbooks, five-cent hamburgers, and a fantastic ability to run up stadium steps while carrying a typewriter.

For those who are stepping on our heels, then, there is still the pleasure of watching millionaires and jet-setters waiting outside gates that are open to the press, the pleasure of wearing elaborate badges that testify to one's In-ness, the joy of the Where-It's-At and the Happening.

I am not so far along that I cannot enjoy some of these things myself, but I guess I have become one of those whose second thought is "How exciting to be here," and whose first is "I hope there's an elevator."

12

"THE GREAT SOURCE
OF PLEASURE
IS VARIETY"

When Dr. Johnson invented his rolling downhill game he was doing something which, in its simplest form, is done by babies who lie in their cribs and rattle their tongues in that bubbling joyous sound that makes us forgive them all the troubles that are adherent to their upbringing.

The phenomenon is scientifically called autokinetic play, which means the simple enjoyment of sending messages to the muscles and getting back entertaining answers. The baby likes the sound he makes and he enjoys his own facility in producing it, just as Dr. Johnson enjoyed the effect of gravity on a tublike body and the occasional tilt by way of steering which kept the tub from damaging itself on some riblike reef of rock.

This is sport in its simplest and in some ways most enjoyable form, but the long history of human endeavor suggests that chaos is anathema to most of us and that we feel more comfortable when we have added a shape, recognizable to all, to our endeavors, and so we go from Dr. Johnson and the baby to games.

At their freshest level, however, games are still, like the bubbling and the barreling, played for the sake of the pleasure they give the participants, and it is these games that I most enjoyed covering in my TV news years.

Consider the case of Weldon Haney, an athlete you probably never heard of, yet who was the pivotal member of a national championship team in a sport probably played by more Americans than any other team game. Mr. Haney, a carpet layer by trade, pitched for the title-winning Clearwater, Florida, Bombers in 1969, and his reward for this titanic achievement was that the city government promised they would get him all the carpet work he needed to keep him happy in Clearwater. When I talked to Mr. Haney it did not occur to either of us to discuss what he could have made by bringing his reflexes and kinetic sophistication to the task of throwing a smaller, harder projectile in organized baseball. Mr. Haney liked softball, liked carpet work, and got a considerable pleasure out of his skills. The "press agent" for the Bombers was a lawyer named Tom Moore, who hoped that his play at second base might attract the attention of someone who needed an attorney with good hands and a nice turn of speed. Moore got to be the publicity man because he had a typewriter and an answering service, and he, like his teammates, seemed to me to have a nice balance between the pride of playing well and the recognition that it was, after all, play and not a lesson in citizenship, training for leadership, or proof to the Communist powers that it would be unwise to go up against a nation that had shown its superiority through the exploits of its softball players. Neither Moore nor Weldon nor any of the others on the team showed any of the truculence that has become so much a part of American sport. This dour quality is instilled by parents at the first level, coaches at the second, and economic competitiveness among the professionals, who are always justifying their egregious nastiness to their opponents on the ground that "They're trying to take the meat off our tables." This cliché is widespread in pregame interviews and seems to no one but me to suggest the ugly image of a bunch of jackals snarling at one another over the remains of a carcass.

If the Bombers live long enough and lose none of their zest for the game, they can eventually join the Kids and Kubs over in St. Petersburg and enjoy the limited, but therefore doubly precious, kinetic activity that arthritis allows. One presumes that by that time Social Security will be putting the meat on their tables, but the only team trying to snatch it off will be the Inflation Corsairs, and the game can continue to be what ideally it is, a flight from reality rather than an extension of it.

When people discuss the odd sports that Lamoreaux and I brought to the CBS Saturday News, the one most often mentioned is the National Marbles Tournament, perhaps because marbles symbolically suggest a kind of Norman Rockwell-cum-Tom Sawyer atmosphere of childhood pleasure.

In fact, the tournament we covered in Wildwood, New Jersey, had all the ills that sport has become heir to, including overorganization and excessive pressure.

Marbles, as I remember the game from my faraway boyhood, was a game in which the losses were largely paid off in worthless clay marbles called, if memory serves, "immies" and there was occasionally a big game in which one wagered "glassies" on one's ability to drive an opponent's spheres out of a dirt-drawn circle. The idea of risking one's genuine agate shooter occurred only to types who would later be found dead outside a casino, having taken "the only way" after losing both fortune and honor.

Once a year the newspapers would feature a picture of a freckled youth smiling as attractively as preadolescent tooth gaps would allow and sporting a gold paper crown won at marbles on the big-time level. Someday a study will be made about the correlation between freckling and digital dexterity, but I leave it to the science-minded.

What I discovered at Wildwood was a tournament that was part of the hype for a summer resort, and what was at stake was the price of a truckload of aggies, a college scholarship fund.

Gone was the camaraderie, the kidding, and the exchange of clay lumps and glass balls. This was serious business under adult supervision, and I could not but admire the kids for the polite surface calm with which they faced the problems of playing a game of delicate touch for high stakes.

Imagine, if you will, a boy holding a round object balanced on his forefinger, about to be propelled fateward by his thumbnail. If its course toward the now impossibly distant circle is true, he will, he imagines, go to college, marry a cheerleader, have a split-level home and two wonderful children, and be, as a result of his superior education, president of General Electric. If, and his thumb, now wet and slippery, seems to be inadequate to the task, he is a shade off line, he will spend the rest of his life carrying heavy bundles from supermarkets to customers' cars. In fact, a boy and a girl from that day in '69 are now on their way to that glorious future through the kindness of the Wildwood Chamber of Commerce, but the shot from that piece that sticks in my memory is the losing girl, walking, tear-stained and inconsolable, by the sea, while the winner and a friend try to tell her what is kind but untrue, that it was just a game.

I was puzzled by the reactions of people who, having seen my interview with the winning boy, affected amusement at the seriousness with which I took his accomplishment. I tried to explain that there was no irony in my momentary reverence. I've always thought that to be the best in the world at what you do, assuming that you're not the public executioner or something of that sort, is, however transitory, inspiriting. All human endeavor is, at last, lost in the cooling of the cosmos, and it is one of the joys of sport that its very artificiality, its basically ritual nature, gives it a wonderful quality of happy fantasy. When you load it with things like putting the meat on the table or money for playing marbles, some of that fantasy is lost. My favorites seem mostly those where the prize is secondary to the pleasure.

Some devotees of sport actually scamp their tables, substituting nourishing noodles for the red meat so prized by the press, in order that they may engage in their games. Fishermen, tennis players, and golfers of the Sunday fun type are obvious examples, but the most remarkable group of spenders for sport that I met in my TV years was a group of contiguously dwelling Illinois farmers who spent the winter months toiling over their tractors in order to compete in the pulling competitions at agricultural fairs. In these tests of power, lineal descendants of those bucolic battles in which pairs of Clydesdales and Percherons heaved at stone boats to the cheers of straw-hatted men called Silas and Hiram, the tractors are hitched to a sled that drives itself into the ground and can, in less than fifty yards, stop that freight train, which was so long the test of motile inexorability. It was for an extra inch or two along the painful path of those fifty yards that the farmer-mechanics in our news show, the Mackinnon family, slaved through their spare time, adjusting and readjusting the iron hearts of their champions. When we started shooting the piece, which was not to be finished till six months later, it occurred to me at once that in the yard, which was the equivalent of Indianapolis Speedway's Gasoline Alley, there were many more tractors than could be possibly necessary to plow or harvest the surrounding county.

It occurred to me also that the house where we were given lunch cost a good deal less than the array of red and yellow dragons ranged around it.

The lunch was a reminder, too, that the homogenizing of America has a way to go. The message of women's liberation seemed to be still some years and miles away as the females of the family, from the oldest to the youngest, bustled about like so many parlor maids handing platters to the camera crew and the senior male members of the clan. In my awkward Eastern liberal way, I asked our hostess if she wasn't going to join us and she looked surprised, pointing out that we were just the first sitting, with the younger men and the boys to be served before she and her fellow cook-waitresses would be permitted to settle down to the scraps.

Lunch over, we filmed the modern Silas-Hirams traveling with wrench and screwdriver through the trackless jungles of their machinery, as sophisticated as NASA engineers in this world, however stuck in the stone-boat days were their social mores.

I asked one of the farmers if the wives and daughters had any role to play at all in this complex and expensive game. Male chauvinism shone out of his smile as he said, "Well, every now and then you ask one of them to bring you a glass of water."

With the whole family assembled on the well-worn furniture of the small living room, I asked the eldest Mackinnon if he had ever calculated what had been spent on the tractor team and if he had ever considered selling any of it off. He was as politely incredulous as an old squire who had squandered his substance on hunters, but from the back of the room came the rebellious murmur of the only young wife who wore lipstick and bell-bottom jeans.

"I'd sell all of them and go to the city," she said defiantly. In the shocked silence that followed this remark we said our au revoirs, and I wondered as we left how many days of dishwashing would be the penalty for such presumptuous plain speaking.

Six months later in Louisville we rejoined our tractor-mad friends, spiffed up for the occasion, not in the straw hats of yesteryear, but in those ghastly caps that proclaim one's allegiance to feed, fertilizer, and farm machinery. There were innumerable classes in these pulls, ranging from little machines hardly bigger than a suburban gardener's toy to be-hemoths that seemed capable of pulling Superman out of his boots. Our friends were represented in every class and showed the depth of tractorial dedication when a young cousin was tossed off his machine as it bucked and tore at its task. As soon as his broken collarbone was first-aided, he climbed back and won the class.

The Louisville pull is one of the big ones, a kind of Diesel Derby, but even here on the big time the trifling prizes hardly paid expenses. The seamed, solid faces of these slow-spoken men in dirty coveralls did not shout "Sensitivity! Imagination! Creativity!" but I saw it there because I knew of the endless hours of delicate and expensive drudgery all directed toward a glorious, rearing, smoke-belching moment when one just might turn out to be riding the most powerful steed in the state. By gum, with a little adjustment of the thingamajig valve we might just break that sled's grip on the ground and pull it out the back door of the hall. Maybe not this year, but next year let's rebore the cylinders. . . .

The amazing thing is that the devotees can bear to ask the machine to mute its fury and become Pegasus at the plow for the serious business of farming. They must pat the iron flanks and promise something special for the gearbox when the last furrow is ready for the sower.

If tractor pulling is a game where the women contribute nothing save the occasional reviving glass, another mid-west sport we covered was the essence of family fun, with husbands and wives cheerily and equally sharing in every phase of a game-cum-social event which can make Duluth, for a few jolly moments, seem reasonably warm in winter.

The sport was curling, a kind of frozen shuffleboard, invented by the Scots long ago. As played by my ancestors it needed only a frozen lake (to be found at any time in Scotland except for a few days in August) and some large flat-bottomed stones, also plentiful in that harshly beautiful country. It made a thrifty change from the other game we invented, golf, which was a real money-burner with its feather-stuffed leather balls and hand-carved clubs.

Nowadays the stones are beautifully shaped and have metal handles, but the idea of sliding them over the ice at a target area, from which opponents try to knock you away with their stones, has remained the same. The big refinement, and half the fun, is the addition of pairs of sweepers who pad down the ice with the slow-moving stone, spanking the gelid surface with corn brooms either in front of or behind the stately projectile to make air currents that will slow or speed it to the proper place near the "button" in the "house."

Teams of four play the game at gatherings called bonspiels and this is where all the socializing comes in. You can be the worst curler on the last-place team but you will not go home without a trophy. By tradition everyone gets a little pin peculiar to the host club, which he or she then hangs on the tam o'shanter that is the curler's helmet. After an active season the tam jangles like a jester's cap.

Primarily, and despite all the fierce concentration which the game on its highest level requires, a bonspiel is a social event, and it is a tradition as old as the game that the two teams, called rinks, shake hands at the end and it is an agreeable custom a good deal of the time that when the last stone stops, everyone sits down to a large meal prepared by members of the club. The separation of sport and sociability is a twentieth-century development, one of the ills of the prevalent fang-and-claw competitive spirit.

Women's lib came early to curling and the mixed bonspiel is the commonest form of competition. About the only curling activity that is largely feminine is the knitting of the tams in appropriate colors, and a bonus for this drudgery was confided in me by a female curler who pointed out that she did enough sweeping on the ice to feel justified in skipping it at home.

Television's endless search for games to fill its sporting hours often turns up a pleasant small-town game that has brightened the doldrums in some out-of-the-way place, and drains it, under lights and hyperbole, of all its fun. I suppose I helped to do this to what used to be a jolly weekend in Petaluma, California, home of the National Wrist-wrestling Championship.

I had been told about this ritualization of the old elbows-on-the-bar test of strength and had been asking for a couple of years to be allowed to attend. Gordon Manning and Paul Greenberg thought it was the kind of undesirable obscurantism to which I was unhappily prone, but they changed their tune when I rushed into the office carrying a "Peanuts" strip in which it appeared that Snoopy was going to try his hand, or to be more precise, his wrist, at the Petaluma games. It didn't matter that Charles Schultz, who lived nearby, was giving a little gentle publicity to a town whose distinction otherwise was that it was the egg capital of Northern California. If Snoopy was going, I could go too, and our piece was enlivened by an interview with Schultz, a gentle, wistful man who is Charlie Brown grown up and unexpectedly successful, a middle-aged boy who built a million-dollar ice rink for the town of Sebastopol, California, with the proviso that he be allowed to play hockey with the town's kids.

Snoopy was disqualified from the competition according to the strip because he had no thumb, but those who possessed this useful appendage got together for a couple of days of competition in the general atmosphere of an interfraternity touch football game, where the anger of physical combat is dissolved in beer.

The next year, ABC's Wide World of Sports bought the rights to the wrist-wrestling championship and when I saw it a couple of years later on the tube it was Horatius on one side of the new elaborate competition table and Lars Porsena on the other, with the fate of Rome at stake. The ten seconds or so of puffing and panting had become of such moment that each competitor who lost would seem to have no option but to join the Foreign Legion and hide his shame among the lost souls of *Beau Geste* and *Beau Sabreur*. For all I know Petaluma has now given up the egg business and spends all year getting ready for this modern version of the Field of Cloth of Gold, and I'm sure they love the eminence. For myself, though, I had a fine time and still treasure a drawing of Snoopy, unsuccessful athlete, and gloriously successful personality. I'm sorry I helped to turn arm games into Armageddon.

As far as I know the three networks have not yet interested themselves in the Paul Bunyan Days festival in St. Maries, Idaho, despite the boost I gave it, and I'm glad because I'm sure no network would let them have their wonderful bandless parade. The festival, which features competitions in all the woodman skills that have been made irrelevant by the chain saw, takes place before the local high school is back in action, so the procession that opens the games shuffles past as silently as some trooping of Trappists. Even the children, who are got up in assorted prize-seeking costumes, seem affected by the curious quiet, and they march along, grinning at the attention of the sidewalk crowd, but keeping their whoops and giggles for later. Assorted civic organizations keep in sort-of-step as they pass in review, and the floats, which concern themselves with St. Maries' glorious past and glowing future, roll to the rustle of inadequately anchored silver foil and polyurethane foam.

The only real noise, in fact, came from the gearboxes of two big trucks that brought up the rear, one full of gravel which would be auctioned off to help pay the expenses of the day, and one full of firewood which was going to be the grand prize for some wood-cutting contest.

When a town of only twenty-five hundred people puts on a whole set of games it becomes clear that some fields will have to be filled by the merely willing, and as assorted good-natured dubs fell off logs into cold water or sawed away as if they were cutting granite while the champion cleaved cream cheese, I realized that here the Olympic ideal of Baron de Coubertin was being realized. He would be surprised to discover that the amateur ideal which he considered a chivalrous aristocracy's example to the proles at play, should flourish in such humble places.

Here it was, the joyous competitive get-together with everybody taking part except the big plastic Paul Bunyan that smiled down impartially on everyone from the skilled winner of the load of wood to the last soft-muscled merchant who broke a few saw teeth while filling a field and losing to a log. Of course, in the eyes of Lord Killanin and his fellow successors to the old Belgian baron, that load of wood spoiled the whole thing and made it a crassly commercial blue-collar fiesta, but to me, the hills of Idaho had, at moments, the air of the Greek mountains in the long-ago days before the Emperor Theodosius had a look at the stadium cost overruns in A.D. 393 and decided to call off the games for good.

While some sports are beribboned with symbolism and high ideals, others just belch a little good-old-boy beer-barrel cheer. This thought and others of greater and lesser profundity ran through my mind during the long, difficult trip from the Derby and the high emotions of "My Old Kentucky Home," to the chaotic jollity of the annual Crayfish Festival in Breaux Bridge, Louisiana.

In order to be there in time for the rites with which the town celebrates the existence of the comestible that supports its citizens, I had to leave Louisville at 4:00 A.M. the day after the Derby and its attendant festivities, and drive to Cincinnati. I kept awake on this trip by listening to a round-table discussion of the financial problems of denominational junior colleges for which I and the ultimate backer of these schools must have been the only audience. I left Cincinnati and the unresolved problems of religious education at 6:00 A.M. on a plane for Atlanta where I changed planes and flew to New Orleans. Here a feeder line took me to Alexandria, Louisiana, where a chartered helicopter took me over some traffic jams to a dock. There a military patrol boat let me hitch a ride to Breaux Bridge where my cameraman met me with a bag of boiled crayfish and the Chamber of Commerce presented me with a prize-winning strawberry shortcake. On my study wall, to remind me of those brave old days, hangs a picture of me, staring grayly across a red-spotted field of swirling whipped cream at the beaming face of the teenaged baker.

Breaux Bridge that day was knee-deep in a richly fragrant detritus of beer cans and gutted crustacean corpses, and we climbed over mounds of this stuff to see crayfish races, crayfish shelling contests, crayfish eating contests, and a bacchanalian parade dominated by King Crayfish, looking suddenly menacing and dragonlike when reproduced in seven feet of papier-mâche.

The abovementioned contests were the excuse for the TV piece being in the Saturday sports spot, but it did not seem to me that we were straining for the connection when you consider how much, in the old days, sport and feasting were associated. There wasn't, in an agricultural society, time for much of anything except the terrible round of plant, tend, harvest, and start planting again, and when, on a holiday, everybody relaxed by kicking a ball around, food and drink were anodynes for bumps and bruises, as in frozen Duluth they had been providers of useful extra calories.

On "wake" Sundays when English churches raised funds by selling beer, Joseph Strutt, the English sports historian, tells us that "Being come from church, the remaining part of the day is spent in eating and drinking and so is a day or two afterwards, together with all sorts of rural pastimes and exercises, such as dancing on the green, wrestling, cudgeling, and the like."

Merrie England, meet Cajun Louisiana, although I doubt that the sports of Crayfish Day and the accompanying jovial gluttony could possibly have been sustained beyond the heartburn-heralded sunset of the day we filmed.

Looking over my list of local festal sports, I am impressed with how often they are linked to the stuffing of the self. Right next to the picture of me looking appalled at the prospect of a whipped cream and strawberry topping is a shot in which I am holding ice to my head with one hand and the words of my script in the other after being run over by a horse at the root festival and rodeo in New Portand, Oregon.

For some weeks before this event, women of the Piute and Wasco tribes roam the soft and beautiful Oregon hills—hills so achingly perfect that when the white man completes his takeover of the country with some gabble about the public good, they will be covered with tacky cottages—in search of roots that burgeon there in spring. Their preparation and consumption are connected with tribal religion and the rolling turn of the years and seasons, which makes a sporting festival, a robust competition of Indian and animal, a natural capstone to the feasting.

I was standing in the arena saying something of an expository nature into a microphone when the horse hit me. I did, fortunately, have a moment of warning. My wife, who has played Lady Macbeth, and has the voice for it, saw the approaching runaway from a perch on the fence and brought a shout of warning from the soles of her feet. Turning toward the drumming sound of hooves, I realized that though horses will avoid you if they can, this one was caught in a tunnel between the wooden wall and an outrider who was grabbing ineffectually at the trailing bridle. It is said that one's whole life passes before one's eyes at such a moment, but only about six seconds of mine was visible to me in the succeeding wink of an eye. I saw and heard Bull Hancock, the master of Claiborne Farm, saying to me a couple of years previously, "Heywood, a horse has about a twenty-one-foot stride."

I remember wishing that Bull didn't speak so slowly and I remember realizing that at the alarm the horse was about twenty-one feet away, so I didn't try to get back to the fence, which would have resulted in a straight and disastrous collision, but simply turned my shoulder outward and took a glancing carom, which bounced me off the ground. Since four other horses then passed over me, and since some blood was visible when Lamoreaux rushed to the rescue and pulled my limp form upright, my wife's agitation at this point was understandable, but, in fact, I had suffered no more than a bloody nose, a black eye, and a certain rattling of the brain that made me wonder for several days whether my skull was big enough to hold it. In the finest traditions of the media we climbed a hillside, stuffed tissues up my nose, and completed the on-camera narration before my eye disappeared behind a purple curtain of engorgement.

From the warmth of an Oregon spring to the formidable chill of a Quebec winter is a quick trip on the typewriter, but the next event in this rambling chronicle has a natural link to the last since the rowboat races across Quebec City harbor were, like the root festival, part of a food-and-drink extravaganza tied to the march of the seasons. Unlike the Indian celebration of the fruitfulness of spring, the rites attendant on the reign of Père Carnaval in Quebec are a defiance of February's iron grip. Perhaps because nothing much is harvested at this season except icicles, the grains of autumn have been transferred into the distilled spirits of winter. Père Carnaval, in his red voyageur cap and sash, is reproduced extensively on the heads of plastic canes, the shafts of which are filled with whiskey. The cane thus serves the dual purpose of livening the fun and keeping the more sloshed revelers from falling down.

After a prolonged party and a torchlight parade it seems natural and laudable to hardy teams of boatmen to try to cross the partially frozen bay. The crews row the heavy boats across the small channels of open water, leap out into ice and slush to drag them over floes and frozen islets, often plunging up to their armpits in the dirty sherbet that lies between solid ice and saltwater. At such times a good grip on the gunwale is essential to survival, and protective clothing must be kept to a minimum lest it drag one under by its water-soaked weight.

What are the sounds one hears as the men are plunged again and again into the frosty filth? Laughter predominates and manic cries of defiance ring over the sterile meadows of mushy crystal. As man may thank the gods on occasion, so he must from time to time defy them, be he Prometheus or a French Canadian sailor.

These are the occasions when one sees the rightness of Huizinga's *Home Ludens* parallels between religion and sport, and when we distort or misuse those sports that are associated with rituals, we do damage to the fast-decaying structure of comfortable custom and Things As They Have Always Been. Sometimes the ritual and the sport are so intertwined that they cannot be separated, that Huizinga saw having broken geometric rules and meeting in a puzzling mixture of the mystic and the muscular. The most obvious example is the series of systems of combat that make up the oriental martial arts. Admittedly some of them, particularly as practiced in drive-in movie bloodbaths and seedy side-street studios, seem to be no more than nasty solutions to the frustrations of the kind of people who get "Born to Lose" tattooed on their arms.

At their best they try to put the uncontrolled violence of anger behind the fire screen of ritual, and some of them essay with icy discipline to put out the fire altogether.

Such an exercise is aikido, a Japanese system of self-defense in which aggression plays no part. At the time that Bud and I did our piece on aikido, I was endeavoring to do my job for CBS while rehearsing a large role in a play en route to Broadway, a dual task that had left me abrim with the petulant aggressions of the weary, and it was therefore a healing pleasure to sit in a viewing room and look at tranquilly beautiful Japanese footage of aikido's founder and master, Professor Morinei Uyeshiba. Watching the professor in meditation, which plays an important part in the system, I felt my nerve ends beginning to surrender their cymbal play, and as they snuggled down for a rest, the professor picked up a fan and began to walk through a garden whose artful disarray had been achieved through centuries of skillful work. As he walked, attackers kept leaping out at him from behind the rocks and bamboo clumps. The professor, eighty-five years old and encumbered with a classic kimono, looked like one of the Sennin, those Eastern sages who are permitted a few thousand years of respite from transmigration, provided they think no carnal thoughts. He had the traditional weedy beard and didn't look much bigger than one of the netsuke figures in which the Sennin are so frequently represented.

However, as each large bully leaped at him with a savage cry, the little old man extended his folded fan and the bully bounced off it as off the bumper of a Mack truck. I was torn between admiration and suspicion. Was the fan electrified? Were the bad guys acrobats who could reverse their trajectories in midair? Or had Uyeshiba got hold of some power I would love to use against the forces that were frazzling me?

From the viewing of pictures we went to the viewing of people, led by a CBS film editor who was laboring in one of the lower classifications of the art, to an aikikai, as the place of study is called. Moichi Thoei, a disciple of the founder, lectured through an interpreter on the positive aspects of tranquility, the class did exercises with varying degrees of aptness, and it all seemed pretty much like another vague effort at health through higher thought.

Suddenly, however, Mr. Thoei put a point on the tranquility talk, the point of his little finger, which he invited six members of the class to lean against. As the students, at increasingly urgent angles, collapsed against the finger, the master smiled gently and gently willed himself not to give way. It was a suddenly invented game, "team finger pushing," but because a palpable spiritual force was at work, it was game and rite combined. It had the spirit lost long ago when the Greeks spoiled what they had found when they started their games at Olympia, a spirit which pops up now and then when play is engendered by joy and controlled by nothing more or less than The Rule.

There are, of course, sports which are not Things as They Have Always Been, but Things as We Wish They Were, those games, often played by the earnestly inept, in which the trappings of glamor are wistfully simulated. The most usual example is two bunches of small children calling themselves the

Yankees and Dodgers, and the most touching, to me, was a bunch of Walter Mitty Manoletes listening in their heads to the brassy trumpet notes of "La Virgen de la Maquerena" as they entered a Mexican practice ring to make cape passes at a determined bull calf. The members of this San Diego club had saturated themselves in the fire-and-syrup prose of bullfight literature, and when they weren't doing their nine-to-five jobs, gathered in assorted backyards to push double-horned bicycle wheels at each other, to shout defiance at the rubber-tired toro, and get themselves ready for Sunday's small moment of truth in Tijuana—or should it be moment of small truth?

We filmed their practice sessions and accompanied the club on the big day. It was interesting to note that those members who were just going to watch retained some degree of reality, but those who were going to be alone with the little bull had withdrawn to the inner caverns of fantasy's world and hardly knew we were there.

The effect of being hit by a bull calf is about like that of a head-on tackle from a pro football lineman, and the weights and temperaments of the two attackers are about the same. One is unlikely to be killed, but big bruises are a likelihood, which made some of our amateurs awkward with apprehension and others foolishly anxious for the honor of a visible mark of valor. There were moments of grace here and there and the whole business was too earnest a striving to escape the big prison yard of ordinariness to elicit mockery. It may be that a club of business and professional people which calls itself Los Muleteros de Aficionados Practicos de Las Californias is flying a little above the airlane reserved for common sense, but common sense has small place in sport and can be saved for use in that world from which the Aficionados were taking a holiday.

There was obviously no sword play on this day of competition between baby bull and Little League matadors, and indeed the bull, assumed to have learned faster than the humans, was barred from further fighting, thereby assuring him a better and longer life than the short active careers ahead for his brothers. We made clear in the narration that the only blood was a subcutaneous effusion on the hips and thighs of the less practiced of the club members. All this did not spare us from the spate of letters that suggested that I do my next piece from the gore-slimed floor of a slaughterhouse, that I had corrupted children or doomed them to bad dreams with my glorification of the world's most brutal sport, and so on ad tedium. It had seemed to me that a bunch of sedentary dreamers seeing themselves in shadowy suits of lights was about as brutal and sanguinary as a war fought between two groups of tin soldiers toppling over to the sound of juvenile voices crying "bang, bang!" Please, however, do not not send me a letter saying that your parents' group is lobbying against military toys. If I may generalize from the particular, however, I'll say that after a childhood in which I must have, at the head of my army of three boxes of Highlanders, decimated the armies of the world several times, I could not, when I finally saw a German in the sights of my rifle, pull the trigger.

I am not a fan of either bullfighting or war, but I would suggest that there is as much brutality in the children's games in which adult supervisors express their fury through the living little soldiers of regimented pygmy contests, as there is in the blood sports which rouse automatic liberal horror.

Having made the liberals mad let me complete the circle by saying that in ten years, and despite the occasional urging, we never did a piece on any form of hunting.

Some sports are so obscure that no one except the handful of devotees has any attitude about them pro or con. Such a one is fives, a kind of arcane handball played at a handful of English schools, including Rugby, Eton, and Winchester, where variations of the game were devised, and in the United States only at Groton and St. Mark's. Some may dismiss the sport as fancy fun for rich kids, but the game is actually a classic example of that earliest and purest form of sport, the game devised to fit existing circumstances. It is one with the children's puddle games described in the first chapter, with the orchard baseball played by James Rodney Richard and his friends, and with all the games that are proof of the desire to play and the ingenuity expended to make it possible. The variations of the game are based on the variations of the architecture of the schools where boys in the time of Queen Elizabeth I discovered that a dull hour could be brightened by bouncing a ball off buttresses and angled walls.

A good deal of ritual language has accreted over the years and the American courts, especially and expensively built, are based on the Rugby model. Through the centuries the game has retained one valuable proof of its origin in the athletic Eden. *There are no officials.* In a game between sensible people it is obvious that cheating takes away the pleasure of play and the joy of winning, so the fives player himself must determine whether he unduly blocked his opponent from the ball in the narrow stone corridor that is the court. Watching and filming the annual match between the two schools I saw all the competitive fire that a grit-and-games headmaster could desire. What I didn't see was any of the modern athlete's rule-bending gamesmanship. Nobody tried to break his opponent's rhythm by stopping to retie a tied shoe, and nobody shouted obscenities, although I must say that although prep school boys know all the obscenities, I cannot imagine an occasion when they would shout them. That sort of thing may be okay for Wimbledon and the West Side Tennis Club, but at Groton and St. Mark's so much as silent mouthing gets a summons to the headmaster's study.

Even grownups, given a stick, a stone, and some natural boundaries have been known to invent games, one of which, the oldest form of tennis, was devised to take advantage of the jogs, knobs, and holes in the wall of a monastery courtyard.

The difference between the children's made-up game and one like court tennis, to give its official name, is that sticks and stones are free but that the construction of a mock monastery yard cost in 1915, when the last one was built, one hundred fifty thousand gold-backed dollars. We visited four of the seven remaining American courts in the course of our collection of odd games, and each time we stepped into one of the hushed caverns where down-stuffed balls roll off the eaves of nonexistent roofs, we were time-machined back into the world of America's Edwardian opulence, that display of wealth which even the materialist English found excessive, and which our immigrants dreamed of achieving. The players, in the faultless whites that clothed Charles Dana Gibson's square-jawed heroes, were always reminding us that this was the game to which the Dauphin challenged Henry V, and I reminded them that this was the game in which millionaire Jay Gould achieved eminence after asking his social adviser, "What game is played by the fewest people in this country? Get me the best teachers. I want to be a champion."

The best teacher at the time of our filming was Pierre Etchebaster, who was probably, in terms of absolute skill, the greatest athlete of his time. Nearly eighty when we met him, he could still hold off the best for a set because he had so calculated the innumerable angles of the sag-netted yard in which the game is played, that all his shots were planned to force his opponent to hit a return which would fall in Etchebaster's reach for a kill. Far past the fierce aggressions of the insecure competitor, he displayed the gentle majesty of absolute mastery. As Pablo Casals found something new every day for half a century in the cello suites of Bach, so Etchebaster was, after a similar stretch, still finding refinements in his game.

Lost with its English inventor is the secret of the special cement of which these courts are made, and as they irrevocably crumble, they will become places to store the excessive mimeography of the society that had no place for their overexpensive elegance.

I had a purely personal trip into the once-was when one of the camera crew, professionally sharp-eyed, pointed out my grandfather at Boston's Tennis and Racquet Club in one of those sepia groups that dot the tobacco-brown walls of venerable institutions. Looking at the little gray eyes on either side of the long nose of this modish middle-aged man whose skill at billiards had been his social sesame, I realized that I was now the same age as he had been when the picture was taken at the opening of the Greentree court in 1915. Looking at Heywood C. Broun— myself in a high collar—I wished that, along with the nose, he had left me some of that serene Thackerayan self-satisfaction that made his life so pleasant. The golden age is always, of course, the one just passed, but the selection of smirks in the group around my grandfather suggests that this bunch felt itself spang in the middle of the best of times. The only frown is on Gould, sitting, dressed for play in the middle of the picture and worrying, since Etchebaster's ultimate virtuosity never was vouchsafed him, that someone was going to beat him in front of all those fashionables.

Pastimes like court tennis fairly breathe the wine-scented air of good living that those wicked but jolly old monasteries kept alive through the grimmer days of the Middle Ages, but at the other end of the sport spectrum are exercises that suggest the hair shirts that were the preferred underwear at the water-drinking monasteries whose courtyards were used not for tennis but for the storage of turnips.

The long-distance runner, we are told, is lonely, but consider the long-distance walker, who is not only a solitary but also, mysteriously, the object of a good deal of active unfriendliness. Mark Spitz achieved universal recognition with his clutch of Olympic medals, but when, in 1970, I interviewed the man who had won more assorted track medals than any other American his name would have taxed even a trivia expert. Ron Laird, practitioner of that odd gait that makes people yell and throw beer cans, was another of the many mighty champions I met who got none of the big money that fortunate athletes can command. On his lunch hour from a job as a draftsman at the Pomona, California, Water Works, he would rip off a few miles, and after work he would settle down to serious walking, his big problem to find places where he would not be jeered, pelted, or bitten by dogs who shared the human suspicion that creatures who moved in that odd manner must be evil. His favorite place, deserted, and, for pictorial purposes, sensational, was a closed amusement park, and our pictures of him, heel-and-toeing past gaudy barker booths framed in the webbing of silent roller coasters, and appearing, for a moment, in front of the telescopic eye of a fun house tunnel, were among the most beautiful, in their outré way, that we ever put on the air. Laird's awkward purposefulness, laminated onto the background of a commercial frivolity frozen into its death grin, was the kind of shot that needed no words, though since I was being paid for them, I provided some.

After the amusement park we moved on to a cemetery, where Laird found that the departed were inclined to let him walk in peace, and there we got one of those shots that are so perfect that no one later believes they were not achieved through cajolery and/or bribery.

Pacing past the gray slabs, our walker was suddenly confronted by a pair of laughing children who leaped from behind a headstone and proceeded to entertain themselves with imitations of him. What strange errand brought them there we never found out, but the malevolent vitality of the tots in this setting of silent stones, the concentration of the walker who may be taken as the symbol of purposeful life, together were as close to the world of Tennessee Williams as sport is likely to get.

More often the world of unpublicized sport is closer to the muscular morality of *Tom Brown's Schooldays,* and it was Tom's own old English game that we found in the unlikely setting of the D.D. Palmer College of Chiropracty in Davenport, Iowa.

On second thought, perhaps a school for chiropractors is the perfect place to play rugby, a game of vigorous bump and run which results in a certain amount of slipped gears and cogs among the participants.

Rugby has never really caught on in this country and I suspect it is because it lacks the war game precision of its American cousin, football. All those men in shorts swarming up and down in a confusion of kicks and carries makes it impossible to have those strategic discussions that American fans love. Like soccer and lacrosse, rugby is exasperatingly fluid, but only soccer has won acceptance in America, more through skillful publicization of stars and their salaries than through comprehension of the game.

What rugby does provide, if my observation of the game is correct, is an immense amount of pleasure to its players. Swarming may be more difficult to understand than the intermittent confrontal crashes of our autumn battles, but it seems to fire up the blood and the air is always filled with fiercely happy cries as the packed scrum into which the ball is dropped dissolves into a thirty-man whirlpool.

For all the talk of American coaches about team effort, it is possible in sports like football and baseball to put the blame for a loss on an individual, the man who struck out with the bases loaded, dropped a flyball in the ninth, couldn't hold a pass, missed a crucial kick. In true team sports like rugby this finger-pointing is a lot more difficult, which may be why I found the players at Palmer, scab-nosed to a man, full of good cheer after bashing about on a cold and muddy day. Many of them expected to join rugby clubs and go on playing after college because they loved the game.

You hear a great deal about love of the game from our college football players, but unless someone goes on paying them, raising the stakes from the scholarships and fake jobs of college, they seem to end up on golf courses and tennis courts.

Of course, the reasons for playing games are so various that the writer who tries to work out a coherent philosophy ends up holding a useless net containing nothing but a few dead generalities while the colorful exceptions wriggle through its gaps. I don't know what general principle joins old Italian bocce players I watched creaking around a silent oasis in lower New York, getting their thrills with tape measures, and the daredevil hang glider enthusiasts I filmed leaping off the hills of Kitty Hawk, one of them rising from a downdraft disaster to tell me, as he smiled through a mask of blood and sand, "I can't wait to get back to the top and try again."

I cannot make a philosophical bond between the fanatical perfectionism of the Chinese Ping-Pong team I saw in Ottawa and the free-form fun of the hot-air balloon men I followed across cornfields while they went where the wind did, waving at envious farmers and barking dogs from a weightless wicker nest in the sky.

Covering sports has taken me from a bridge tournament in a Los Angeles hotel where middle-aged women got master points sauced with a soulful gaze from Omar Sharif, an emir at the card table, to an enclosure in Arizona where a huge pump pushed waves out of a plastic tropical cliff so that surfers might have a moment of Tahiti amid the motels and shopping malls that smother the desert.

I have been to a cheerleading school where girls moaned in affected agony at TV replay of their antics, while mothers rushed at them with needles and thread to correct costume details, and I have watched nuns in full habit joyously leading the yells for a minor league pro football team in Manitowoc, Wisconsin.

I have watched joggers solemnly pumping themselves full of monoxide as they ran the esplanades of traffic-choked Los Angeles boulevards, and I covered a tuna fishing tournament that, after a fishless week, left the trophy with the team that had caught something the year before.

I saw the jolly Kids and Kubs have fun with softball in St.

Petersburg and I marveled at their serious cousins in the same town, carefully assembling their custom-made jewel-tipped shuffleboard shovers for highly competitive tournaments where sly guile substitutes for the open fury of youth.

I am often asked by lecture audiences what was the most memorable or exciting event I covered, or who was the best this, that, or the other that I saw. (Once a schoolboy startled me by asking what was the worst job I had ever done for CBS news. That was easy. It was a piece about a steeplechase jockey whose courage on a horse was not matched in front of a microphone where a series of strangled squeaks was all I got in response to an increasingly labored set of questions.) I give different answers to the first question, depending on my mood, and beg off the second because "best" defined subjectively is meaningless and statistically answered doesn't do much better.

Sitting down to write this book and looking up the six-hundred-odd pieces I had done, I was surprised at how many of the colorful and exciting ones I had forgotten and how many of the routine, straight-arrow jobs had, like a pebble in the shoe, lodged in my memory.

There was more to like than there was to deplore, although I know I've done a good deal of deploring, and the mechanical hospitality of press agents—"Love your work. Just sign my name at the bar. When will this be aired?"—was outshone by the part-time publicists full of town pride, school pride, and general goodwill who helped us get things done in the never-enough time that work against the clock decrees.

Indeed it is the sense of rush that remains as the dominating flavor of the decade of my weekly pieces. Airline travel in America is like train travel in Bulgaria. The trips themselves are never long, but the schedules are totally chaotic, and I remember endless runnings down coldly gleaming airport corridors in a hopeless effort to make the connection which, if it were as off schedule as the plane I just left, might not yet have departed. Usually, unfairly, it had, and we rented a car and drove the last two hundred miles, or slept for hours or tried to sleep, awaiting the next plane in those airport chairs whose function it is to make sure you don't doze through the announcements of further delay.

Once I threw a crutch at an airline gatekeeper in San